prai

Back to t

A fascinating internal journey of a woman determined to go her own way, taking readers along as intimate companions while traveling from misadventure to disaster to illumination. In *Back to the Garden*, Patrice Dickey faces her life with naked frankness and learns from her (many) mistakes to find a way to the light.

—Alex S. Jones, Harvard University, co-author *The Patriarch* and *The Trust*

You have certainly led a most remarkable life. It is quite clear that through your work you hare having a most positive impact in changing the lives of others.

—Condace L. Pressley, host of *Perspectives* on News/Talk 750 WSB, Atlanta

Back to the Garden. . . is a highly readable mix of personal memoir and advice based on her work as a workshop leader and personal coach.

—Cliff Bostock, Ph.D., columnist, *Creative Loafing*

Back to the Garden is a unique and compelling read that is worthy of your time and attention. With this book as your roadmap, you will experience spiritual and emotional growth in every aspect of your life. *USABookNews.com*

Anyone who's experiencing the ups and downs of life or has suffered a loss will find *Back to the Garden* a refreshing, uplifting companion. It helps you pick yourself up, dust your-self off, and start all over again.

—Colin C. Tipping, author, *Radical Forgiveness*

"We've all got deep stuff. It's just a matter of learning to use that as fertilizer rather than becoming buried in it."
—*Atlanta Journal-Constitution*

Patrice Dickey taps into the mysteries of the unseen in a stunning, evocative exploration of her own journeys into the intuitive and the universal mind. *Back to the Garden* beautifully reinforces the power of personal choice and the numerous tools available to manifest and create the lives we love.
—Laurie Monroe, president, The Monroe Institute

You have created a brave and beautiful thing here. I truly admire your courageous commitment to wellbeing, sanity and compassion. I wish you and your lovely book much success.
—John Stephens, founder/artistic director, Theatre Gael & WorldSong Children's Theatre

Gee, where to begin—bold, brave, scholarly; also sincere—tried & true honest, fun, poignant. And it is practical wisdom in small healthy doses; to-the-bone "truth," not "truthiness." Love the design, too. The Haunted Bed—YIKES!!
—Marcia R. Oliver, Earth Mother

Your book inspired me to take some bold steps myself, to move beyond my comfort level and leave the Midwest for New York. It has helped me rise above the shackles of complacency and lack of direction.
—Kent Johnson, businessman

Back to the Garden is a courageous story of grace and wisdom emerging from chaos and trauma—reminding us to let go of outcomes and step out on faith.
—Joyce Kinnard, co-author *The Lemon Book*, cancer survivor

I absolutely love this book. It hits at the heart of what many deal with these days: how do I create a happy life out of the frustrations of my former struggles? The easy flow of the writing gently seduced me. In reading the stories of the author and her friends, the lens she held to their life events and insights led me naturally to my own inner exploration. We may not know the number of our days, but through the profound illustrations in this deeply moving book, the author gently guides us as to how to make the best of them.

—Robert E. Dallas, Ph.D., The Dallas Center

Your wonderful book touched me at the time when I needed it the most. It is such a good read as well as being inspirational, uplifting, evocative and engrossing. I laughed, cried, was transported to the places, and came to know the people you wrote about. I can still smell the fragrance of your magnolia flowers! I'm halfway through it again!

—Kim McLagan, entrepreneur

It got me in touch with my feminine side. More than once while reading it, I had to take to bed with a box of Kleenex and a bottle of Midol.

—Mack Ray, Arkansas farmer & columnist

A beautifully written book; reading it is like visiting with a friend or having a conversation with the author by an open fire on a winter's day.

—Nancy B. Clark, retired teacher

Back to the Garden:

Getting From Shadow to Joy

Patrice Dickey

Dickey, Patrice
     Back to the Garden: Getting From Shadow to Joy

Photo Credits: Patrice Dickey, Houston D. Smith III as indicated,
     and family photos
Photo Retouching: Steiph Zargon, Zargon Designs
Heart Art: Claire Vohman
Cover Design: Garon Hart Graphic Design
Editing Angel: Joyce Kinnard
Layout: J. L. Saloff

10 Digit ISBN: 0-9770865-1-8
13 Digit ISBN: 97809770865-1-1
Library of Congress Control Number: 2005909840
Copyright No: TXu1-248-537

Second Edition, September 2006

Table of Contents

Table of Contents

Table of Contents

Table of Contents

Table of Contents

Back to the Garden

To all those loved ones, here and gone,
who have enriched my life and
the lives of others with your presence.
Thank you, thank you, thank you!

Back to the Garden

Introduction

I am so grateful to my hundreds of teachers and the authors of inspirational books who have helped me open my awareness to new possibilities and happier, more fulfilling ways of living.

As I tell participants in my own classes and workshops, once your consciousness expands into new worlds, you can never stuff it back into that smaller box where it used to dwell. It demands more!

Of course it's always our choice whether or not we'll pay attention to the clarion call of our Higher Self to grow into our full expression, into the joyous lives we're meant to live. Often books serve as guides into those rich realms within us that await our discovery, unlocking and sharing with others.

I offer this book as one potential key to your inner world: a different kind of "self-help" book, non-linear, without checklists and exercises, because the path of life rarely shapes up as a straight line. Great thinkers throughout history, including John Lennon, have shared the wisdom that "Life is what happens when we're busy making other plans." Don't we know that!

The healing heart does not operate by lists and schedules, but by fits and starts, one step forward and two steps back, treading old territory until it suddenly breaks into the clearing of joy. It grows into wholeness through hints, suggestions and the sudden flash of recognition—the Aha! epiphanies that it is not alone in its struggles.

Back to the Garden: Getting from Shadow to Joy is an amble through the sorrows that darken our lives back into the light of full creative expression; of discovering who we really are; of finding ourselves, finally, "at home."

It is a ramble through the lives of many ordinary people whose positive outlooks, inner strength and heartfelt glory in life itself have made them my heroes and sheroes. May their heroic journeys serve as inspiration to you.

This meditative journey through my garden, into nature and through this world and the next with many beloved teachers is meant to help reassure, calm and guide any hurting or fearful souls who are in the healing process themselves, and all those who are seeking to pull themselves up to the next level.

In my studies of the workings of the subconscious mind, which believes whatever we tell it, good or bad, I have discovered that in conveying similar messages in many different ways, resistance begins to melt away and subtle, powerful positive shifts occur. As you read, you too will shift in many wonder-working, powerful ways. Your wellbeing does make a difference to the world. May you enjoy and learn from your life adventures!

The Next Level of Healing

Traffic crawled along the expressway, giving me plenty of time to ogle the latest glittery thing that had caught my attention: A giant male torso with a tanned and well-muscled back. His left arm was fully extended, pointing to the left like some buffed-up, naked version of Captain Ahab questing after Moby Dick.

FOR THE NEXT LEVEL OF HEALING, giant letters spelled on the outdoor board, TAKE THE NEXT LEFT.

It was an ad for an orthopedics clinic, but that day it held much deeper meaning for me. I had to chuckle at the synchronicity and cosmic humor blaring this unmistakable, larger-than-life message.

As Jack Canfield, co-author of the *Chicken Soup for the Soul* series would say, the appearance of this sign was "synchro-mystic."

I'd been here before, plenty of times. Depressed over the latest losses; burned out on work; directionless and despairing of ever having a meaningful long term relationship, since it seemed the people I usually attracted were workaholics, eccentrics, or some captivating combination of the two.

And if "you attract what you are," that bit of self-analysis didn't set too well on my psyche either.

I'd just left the hypnotherapist's office and was feeling some relief over untangling an emotional knot of not-goodenoughness in my stomach. That knot had been roiling around in there for far too long—all through the holidays and into March—and had re-appeared in a dream so profound that I KNEW I needed professional help to unravel its message.

Fear of change had me stuck. I couldn't move for months, and this dream served as just the right dynamite to blast me out of my rut.

Dreams don't lie, although up close they're sometimes hard to decipher. The hypnotherapist's guidance into my subconscious mind had helped me crack its code.

And right there above me on the expressway as I left her office was an unmistakable declaration from the Universe that I was on track.

That giant naked torso on the billboard was a second message from a dead man, whose own well-muscled back had looked remarkably like the one on the board when he was alive. Only *moments earlier* he had appeared to me, as plain as if he were alive, during the hypnotherapy session.

I'd loved my perilous-living, adventuresome friend so deeply, and the way he lived his life, both the positives and the negatives, had spelled out huge lessons to me and to everyone who knew him.

Never one for the beaten path, his life spoke this message: "Go ahead—take the left fork, the road less traveled. For the next level of healing yourself, go left. See what's inside you and bring it out. Explore the darkness and the light. Illuminate some of those shadowy fears—your scary demons will melt into the flickers of illusion that they are. What do you have to lose?"

You too can venture down the uncharted path of mayhem and monsters to the miracles inside you. With God's grace and the ideas and techniques expressed here, you can lift yourself up from the murkiest muck to the mountaintop. Seeing what others have done, you too can convert monsters into allies, transform fear into forward energy, and shape your life into a whirling, waltzing journey to joy. Simply by becoming willing, you have already taken the first step.

Midnight Train

Earlier, in my hypnotherapist's office, her soothing words led me in a guided meditation to unearth what was bursting out of me and demanding that attention must be paid.

Looking down at my shoes I discovered to my surprise that ruby slippers glinted on my feet. Directly beneath them beckoned the Yellow Brick Road. Here I stood on the road to Oz!

The Scarecrow appeared first—looking snappy and happy, cocky and intelligent. He already had quite the brain. In fact he was ready to give me directions, very important directions, and was pointing to the left, his gangly left arm outstretched.

A closer look revealed to my amazement that the scarecrow was actually someone I *knew*—Fred Dresch, the aforementioned dead man, who in life had been an expert at telling people what to do.

In fact he made a career of it, therefore no big surprise that he was giving directions now from beyond the grave. The director and writer of films, Fred had lived a full, rich life. At his memorial service when someone mentioned that we'd been together for four years a friend cracked, "But how many years is that in 'Fred Years?'"

"For the next level of healing, go left."
Fred Dresch at the Tybee Island house.

The crowd of friends laughed knowingly. Being around Fred meant having a tiger by the tail.

However, this rich life of his seemed a dichotomy because of his perpetual state of being out of balance. Either he was slaving away on the latest TV or movie project and the money was rolling in, or he was in a long dry spell between productions and using everything he'd earned on the last project to keep himself afloat.

Being broke in the film business was part of the rough game. But it's important to remember that broke is a temporary condition and poor is the state of mind that will keep you there.

Fred was never poor in any sense of the word. His life brimmed richly to overflowing—a bounteous cornucopia of creativity, love, optimism, hope, laughter and sharing of his many gifts.

And, as the Scarecrow, he directed me to the left.

In my waking vision under hypnosis it didn't seem at all odd that Fred should be directing me to the left. He'd lived that way for years in the film business.

I met him after he took the midnight train back to Georgia from LA at age 43, high-tailin' it from working on B-movies and Neurotic Thrillers (as we joked) where he'd been forced by necessity to earn a living. In Hollywood he always lived hand to mouth at best, but was a trusted friend and confidante of models and stars who appreciated his down-to-earth realness in glitterworld.

Like most people who get into the film business with a dream of expressing their own creative visions, he hated compromising his standards to the almighty buck. But he was always so optimistic that his big breakthrough was just around the corner that he stuck it out in the Hollywood hellhole for years –and during that time he had to eat.

5

A shocking transition—the sudden, unexpected death of a fishing buddy his age from an undiagnosed heart ailment, drew him back to his roots in Georgia.

At home once again, in his rambling pre-Civil War house, which had been spared Sherman's torch because it had served as a Yankee military hospital, he left the dark memories of LA behind. Back to his roots, he focused on "rightness" and lightness and what thrives above—the good, the truth, the light.

And he always attempted to muscle his way to outcomes. With Fred, it was his way or the highway—which made him completely endearing and completely maddening all at once.

Of German and Italian heritage, Fred's swarthy olive skin seemed perpetually tanned. His fine but incredibly thick brown hair either flopped over his glasses into his eyes, or was trimmed up in a stylish cut that inevitably sprouted to shoulder-length within a matter of a few months—growing like kudzu. With Fred, you never knew what persona you'd encounter next; he continually reinvented himself.

Besides being a film writer and director, he had modeled himself after one of his heroes, actor Jimmy Stewart, whom he met at the Presbyterian Church they attended in LA. He said that Jimmy had a stipulation in all of his film contracts that he'd be able to fly out to attend his home church (if humanly possible; if they weren't shooting, for example, in Nepal) and be back on the set for Monday shooting.

So when Fred moved back from Hollywood to Atlanta, he joined Oakhurst Presbyterian Church, where he served as a church elder. During his remarkable ten short years in that welcoming, loving church, he impacted the lives of hundreds of people with his emphasis on two of the finest ways to bring people together: good food and good music.

And he passed into the next realm one summer during the writing of the stories in this book.

That's where I was stuck. I was afraid to peer back into the long journals I'd written about his passing, afraid of reliving the pain, when I knew that in order to get beyond the pain I'd have to walk back through it again.

There's no way out but through. That's partly what this book is about. In getting myself through, I hope to help others as well.

"Those who sow in tears shall reap in joy." It's a quote on a framed watercolor by Stephen Hudson that graces my office wall, just beyond my desk. Sharecroppers weighing in cotton at harvest; few lives are harder. When I forget, it reminds me that salty tears are powerful fertilizer for an actualized life, if we let them be.

And so here was Fred, apparently trying to help me, now appearing from the "other side" in this hypnotherapy session as he had so often in dreams. Even in the waking world he was unexpectedly popping up. Oddly, people who didn't know of our connection randomly mentioned his name in the most unlikely of places: Yoga classes, the YMCA, places he had never stepped into and people whom he had never met.

In this guided meditation of the hypnotherapy session Fred was directing me to "go left"—leading deep into the space of spontaneity, creativity, non-linear thinking, and even chaos. The place where people have visions and dream dreams—the place of deepest soul-sustenance—but only if we're willing to gird ourselves, walk up to our personal demons and shake their hands.

As you read the stories of many here who have journeyed from shadow to joy, my hope is that you'll gain insights about how to release outcomes and stop trying to control every last thing, while learning to live more comfortably in "the place of not knowing."

7

Meet your illusory demons, live through the encounters and come out happier on the other side.

Hmmm, Sinister

What is left? asked the hypnotherapist. Interestingly, *sinister* is the Latin word for left. This ancient word long ago evolved from a simple directional term to something dark, underworldly, perhaps even evil—as the patriarchal church leaders did their utmost to shift peoples' perspective away from the feminine earth religions and toward the masculine "God the Father in the Sky."

Traditionally, feminine energy surges up the left side from the earth, and the feminine aspects guide the left side.

The Latin word for right, *dexter,* evolved into such meanings as dexterous, meaning right-handed or skilled. Or just plain right. According to myth, masculine energy pours down from the sky into the right side.

Over centuries, persecution and witch burnings stamped out most vestiges of the goddess religions (except for the Catholic faith's loving worship of Mother Mary and the female saints even today).

Sinister began to connote dark and evil while *dexter* spelled right.

And back in those days, right meant might—muscling things to their perceived right place, rather than permitting their unfoldment through the divine act of witnessing. Forcing outcomes rather than letting go of them and expecting the highest and best to evolve naturally.

Even if upsetting a bit at first, a journey to the left, off the beaten path, may unfold into the most soul-satisfying pursuit for those willing to cast aside any preconceptions about what it's supposed to look like.

I know this for sure—it's not a straight line from here to there!

No question that I "got it" from the giant naked torso billboard, even though I'd done my best to ignore so many signs throughout my life; choosing to shut down my light under a barrel, creeping back into the safety of the known world, the "golden handcuffs" in a business I hadn't enjoyed in years.

The message: Keep going, keep creating, keep traveling through the darkness and stay faithful to your vision. Your own light—the light of God shining through you—eventually illuminates the way.

"God alone knows the secret plan of the things he will do for the world, using my hand."

This beautiful sentiment by Toyohiko Kagawa from a book of Hazelden meditations has been posted on my refrigerator for nearly twenty years now. The red ink has faded and it's been splashed once or twice, creating streaks on the 3x5 card. Were those tears that splashed it as I meditated on the idea, crying out to God for direction?

"Lead me, Guide me, Dear Lord!"

And always the still small voice replied, "Stop whining! You know what to do! Just do it! "

Has it come down to God sounding like a commercial for athletic shoes? How irreverent—and how absolutely relevant to moving forward on the path of life, one step at a time, hopefully wearing some sturdy shoes.

At times on this journey, the pain is so great that it's all you can do to breathe, one step at a time, one breath at a time.

You've got to believe in the silver lining after the storm—what else is there? For the next level of healing, keep going; keep diving into the creative center. That was the message that the giant naked man on the billboard reinforced. And it appeared in a delightfully juicy visual that I wouldn't want to ignore, even if I could!

In the hypnotherapist's guided meditation after seeing Fred the Scarecrow, I guessed that some others might be showing up.

Two other cherished male friends had also taken leave of this earthly plane and gotten on board early flights out of here. They died far too young in my opinion, but who are we to guess when it's our time to go?

Living through so much loss, including the physical deaths of so many loved ones at "young" ages, I have learned that we just never know when the magical journey with those we love is going to come to an end. Somehow, in the process, we learn to live without the reassurance that they're out there somewhere, cheering us on—often believing in us more than we believe in ourselves.

We learn to tap other sources of strength.

Witnessing their full-out, high intensity lives I've learned the importance of appreciating the moment, right here, right now, because who can tell when a house is going to fall out of the sky and land on your head—or the head of someone you love?

Unbearable as it feels at times moving through pain, as we put one foot in front of the other we discover, looking back, that we have created our own hero's journey. And that meaning exists, after all.

The Heartfelt Tin Man

Next up: The Tin Man, Robin Clark, brilliant writer and

"Write fearlessly, and from the heart." Robin Clark,
20 years old, under the Davie Poplar at UNC-Chapel Hill.

journalist, who had captured hearts (and mine especially) while reporting for the *Daily Tar Heel* at UNC-Chapel Hill. Upon reading Robin's feature story on a raucous frat party featuring Doug Clark and the Hot Nuts, I'd remarked to myself, "Wow, that girl can write!"

Shortly after that I discovered that Robin was quite the delightful opposite of a girl. Although our romantic relationship eventually ended, our friendship stretches forever.

Robin had sent me a postcard only months before his sudden, devastating death in a collision on the Pacific Coast Highway at age forty: "You're an original, Patrice. Write fearlessly, and from the heart."

Upon his loss, editors and journalists all over the country eulogized him—deeply praising his humanity, wit and grace in both his writing and his life. Even Dominick Dunne, who met Robin while covering the O.J. Simpson trial, praised his whip-smart humor in a *Vanity Fair* "Letter from L.A." as the endless source of hilarious one-liners about every colorful character in that drawn-out drama. As the Philadelphia *Inquirer's* west coast correspondent, Robin brought his special zing to the tedium of endless O.J. coverage.

And here he was in my hypnotic trance, beautiful Robin with his big, ice blue eyes, deep, resonant voice and heart filled with ageless compassion after suffering his own father's suicide when he was a boy of sixteen.

As the Tin Man, he conveyed a vision, a knowing, a loving awareness on the yellow brick road.

"Believe! Have faith! Write from the heart—it's the only thing that matters! Let your love show!"

How our hearts broke when he was taken away.

The messages resonate in so many forms, but they're all the same: To live a life full of love. They're just different ways of stating it.

The Courageous Lion

And finally, sheepishly holding his tail, was the Lion—Patrick Hudson, my dear, devoted high school stalwart, the rangy, red-haired and freckled boy who left a dozen yellow roses and a love poem on the front doorstep of a dreamy 15-year-old girl in the Memphis spring.

A boy who loved a girl to distraction as only a teenager can, despite her petty, cruel adolescent behaviors, including dating his brother, the artist Stephen—oh, unforgivable! And yet Pat forgave eventually; he was a bigger spirit than I.

Years later when he was 24 and we were still in close touch despite the hundreds of miles that separated us, he worked as a bargeman on the Mississippi and led a life of adventure, our own personal Tom Sawyer. And like Tom, just one time too many he broke the rules. He'd probably been drinking, and against all the laws of the river he swam from one barge to another in the swirling, dangerous waters of a lock. And there he drowned. And we drowned in our tears at his untimely death.

Looking somewhat shy to see me after all these years, he stood fiddling with that unruly lion's tail. Almost thirty years have passed since his departure from this planet, and yet in dreams he's as fresh and lovely and red-headed wild as he ever was in life. The young man who vowed he'd be my second husband. But that's another story.

His message echoed the Tin Man's—reinforcing COURAGE, of course. And we know that the words courage and encourage both come from the Latin root *cor* into the French *le coeur*, for heart.

Portrait of Pat Hudson as an angel
by his brother, Memphis artist Stephen Hudson.

Does this path have a heart? If so, then follow it. Have courage, step out in faith, believe. Above all, just begin.

And that is the message in our ramble back to the garden, along the path to joy. Won't you join my forever lively guides and me?

Come to the Garden Alone

I didn't come to plants at first; they came to me. Friends would give me flowers and plants long before I was capable of receiving them and their bounty.

I lacked the confidence to believe that I could nurture even something as simple as a plant! After all, it wouldn't wake me in the night squalling for a bottle; it wouldn't need a diaper change or walks in the park or early Mozart training to reinforce the budding nerves and synapses in its growing brain. Nor would it eventually need a college fund. Its knowledge would unfold naturally.

Even so, the notion of keeping a plant alive was daunting. How could it possibly survive in my neglectful presence? Surely it would lose its leaves and eventually its life.

This *death-to-living-things* was a perfect reflection of what was going on inside me: An emotional wasteland—a burned-out, codependent shell, completely drained by the situation in my own family. I wanted nothing in my immediate sphere that depended upon my efforts or ministry.

You could say I was pretty low down on the spectrum of self-esteem.

I was clueless about a lot of things—certainly in the fog about the four pillars of a happier, more fulfilling life: Self-awareness, self-acceptance, self-respect and self-love.

15

My life was definitely lacking in joy.

However, with patience and a willingness to begin being gentle with myself, all this eventually began to shift to self-awareness, self-acceptance, self-respect through the recognition of the God within, and, ultimately, self-love.

The old, hard road was paved with negative labels I'd absorbed along the way. I believed I was poisonous to myself and others.

Now after years of applying the simple principles and techniques that are included here, all the trials, toils and snares that snagged the silken hem of my garment—the tree limbs that snatched at my hair, tangling me in seemingly intractable old patterns, are almost completely gone.

Occasionally I'll still step into a mud puddle, by mistake, or not. But I recognize I don't just have to stand there feeling sorry for myself about my pathetic situation in life. I can step out of it.

At a certain point I did the only thing I could do—shifted my perspective—it was simply a way of looking at things after all! And suddenly life became much, much easier, and old aggravations no longer seemed to hook me. The long road truly led to Happy, Healthy and Whole. Isn't that what you want too?

The Resounding Yes!

Sometimes the most powerful means of launching onto the path is simply the strong affirmative word, "Yes!" The blessed yes. Yes to faith; yes to what is.

The struggle to get to yes can be tremendous, soul-sapping. Often it's a negotiation of the mind—weighing all the options. How long do you continue the struggle?

Or do you cut and run, pack up your vulnerable little self and tear out of there—perhaps even counting on the "geographic cure?" The only problem with that, people discover, is that wherever you go, there you are.

Should you connect with friends who lift you up, whose interest is in your greater good and who don't choose to engage in self-destructive, self-denigrating behaviors? Although the logical answer to this question is Yes, of course, there's the other side.

Occasionally we all experience *"la nostalgie pour la boue"*—the longing to roll in the mud a little bit—or a lot!

How my English literature professor chuckled when he defined that French literary term to college freshmen, who spent entire semesters—even years—engaged in those most self-revealing activities in the mud!

But how many times, really, do you need to wake up over-whelmed with remorse before deciding that this is simply not the way you want to travel any longer?

I recall the July 4th weekend that my car got towed for illegal parking—well past the college years, I was 28 and going nowhere fast. Completely clueless, totally in party mode, all about the next good time. My chief objective in life was to forget my family's pain, but the means I chose to do it often resulted in more pain, not less.

However, it took me several years to see that simple truth.

My pathetic-but-beautiful, congenitally broke friend lived in an empty apartment with only one piece of furniture: her bed. Her clothes were strewn in piles or slung in a closet. For weeks on end she and her child survived on nothing but pota-toes. Yet she still had the time and money to party.

The night my car was towed from her place, we didn't

stagger in from our night of dancing until daybreak, when the bad news greeted me.

Eventually I found my way out of that way of living, but not until my very life was threatened. Sometimes it takes a really strong jolt to wake us up.

The problem is Out There!

In my case it seemed to take many strong jolts. I took forever to get a clue, and I consider myself intelligent. But as we know, intellectual acumen and emotional intelligence are two different things, as Daniel Goleman so brilliantly spelled out in his book *Emotional Intelligence*. And you have to factor in self-love. At that time in my life, self-love was in very short supply. Quite the opposite.

In my twenties, life was out of control. The problems were always with the jobs, the bosses, the boyfriends, the people around me, the world in general, and especially my parents, whose issues made my life look like a cakewalk. I was never the problem.

Somehow I'd hooked up with the wrong man—again. This time it was a married man, because as I told myself, all I wanted was the sex, not any genuine involvement. Then he did the unthinkable—he divorced his wife and deserted his pitiful little daughter in order to be with me.

Horror of horrors! I had no idea that what I viewed as some casual hook-up could nightmarishly and very quickly ramp up into this very real situation. This unbalanced man then proceeded to lose his job, his money and his apartment and somehow ended up living with me!

All because I thought I could use him for a good time.

At that phase of my life I really had a love/hate thing going with the opposite sex, although I wanted to have them in my life. The Deep Bench, I called it: when one is down and out, or simply not playing up to par, bring in the replacement. It was a mechanical, heartless way of looking at the world, as users do.

This strategy of course prevented me from ever having to feel anything because I was always able to medicate with partying—and lots of it. What they don't tell you about "no-strings-attached" fun: Not true!

If this serves only as a cautionary tale to anyone who thinks they can engage in mindless partying without experiencing any consequences, so much the better. However, I fully realize that most people have to live their own experiences to learn their truth.

This love/hate relationship with men stemmed from several causes.

One was observing my own parents' relationship, not an easy path. Another was that I never had a brother so I could learn how the male thinks, loves and functions. I had plenty of friend-boys, but they were still a mystery to me. Cute, dangerous, fun and all part of a grand adventure.

Bad First Impression

My mixed emotions regarding the other gender stemmed, in a large part, from the unfortunate event which was my "coming of age initiation." I'd call it a date rape, except that we weren't on a date, and that term wasn't in vogue during the full flush of Flower Power's "free love" era.

In that crazy, easy time, I'd convinced myself that I was a

19

flower child or at the very least a wild child, full of life; the world was my oyster and perhaps I was sent here to help save it, one poem at a time.

But in order to save myself or anyone else, I had to prove myself; a self dominated by adolescent hormones.

What better means of severing the bond with childhood and childish things than a physical act, "losing my virginity"— a rite of passage that should be sacred and meaningful, and certainly not something involving losers, losing or being lost. And why is it that the female "loses" something, and the male gets patted on the back by his male elders while putting another notch on his belt? Where's the fairness in that?!

Whether or not my subconscious was drawing me to exhibit my power by acting out sexually and crossing some imaginary line between childhood and adulthood, in my case my accomplice assisted me in creating something tawdry, drunken, forced, painful and filled with shame. I was thirteen.

Since the parental *zeitgeist* in that era didn't include such a notion as date rape, it basically came down to the girl being fast, bad, easy. For the boy it was a no-fault experience—just a matter of doing what comes naturally. (That annoying little song that Ado Annie sang in *Oklahoma* runs through my mind!)

Here's what happened: I confessed the experience to my mother because I feared I was pregnant. I felt devastated, scared, heartsick, remorseful, completely ashamed, and totally put down. Upon learning the situation, my older sister joined my mother in shaming me. Who could blame her? The boy was one she'd had a crush on for years. My father, when he eventually found out, said nothing that I recall, but he was obviously not pleased.

Undefended by anyone in the family, my own inner voice

battered me ceaselessly for years as I absorbed the damaging message from them that this one mistake had ruined me.

However, I was the villain who hammered it home far more ceaselessly than they did, with their occasional sniping reminders of my unforgivable blunder.

And what happens when we in-corporate a message, any message?

We take it into our bodies *(in corpus)*. Therefore my body absolutely had to express the message in some way.

It chose a very effective method to manifest.

In my opinion, this psychological and spiritual imbalance resonated my shame on a deep cellular level, developing the seeds of fibroids, or benign tumors of the uterus, which would cause me, more than three decades later, to suffer horrific physical symptoms.

Ultimately the energy blockage in the second chakra (energy center), seat of creativity and creation, made hysterectomy the only viable solution, even after I tried numerous natural alternatives including Reiki, homeopathy and nutrition over the years to clear the problem.

Is it purely happenstance that during that time I handled public relations for Dr. Tom Lyons of the Center for Women's Care and Reproductive Surgery, one of the top GYN surgeons in the world?

When Dr. Lyons performed a laparoscopic procedure using minimally invasive techniques to correct my huge problem, the visiting surgeons were awed. These Korean experts observing the procedure were astounded at the extent of the damage (and his ability to remove it through tiny incisions).

The organ of creation and reproduction was literally eaten up and totally distorted. We called it The Alien.

My shame had destroyed my creative center.

21

Any situation can shape our lifetimes either for bad or good. The glory is that we can reframe them mentally, emotionally and spiritually. If it was a negative, we can reframe it into one that lends us strength rather than weakness. Although it took me years to recognize this and act upon it, thank God I did.

I don't consider it any major coincidence that approximately one-third of young or adolescent girls have been sexually abused or have experienced emotional abuse around their sexuality—and approximately one-third of women have manifested some unexplainable "female problem" such as fibroids or endometriosis.

No doctor can explain definitively the cause of these problems other than suggesting that they are genetic, which was not my case.

Rather, I hypothesize that it is sexual shame passed down from generation to generation. The mother who dubs menstruation "the curse" even if only jokingly; the older siblings who tease their younger siblings when they begin to develop; the parent who oversteps all boundaries and shares with the children the details of his or her sex life. Not to mention actual molestation or incest.

Add to the mix the sexualizing of adolescents before they are emotionally and psychologically ready, through cultural messages, smutty song lyrics and a proliferation of "sex sells" advertising. It is not fair to the children!

My sister told me that her precious eight-year-old daughter Elizabeth and friends at a sleepover were playing "teenage pregnancy" with their Bratz® dolls. What a chilling thought. When we were that age the most risqué behavior Barbie® engaged in with Ken was maybe a little holding hands and kissing in her salmon pink convertible!

All of these seemingly mild behaviors color the psyche of the budding adolescent, whether female or male.

The tone of the times and my own naivete resulted in my very stupid move at that party. Add to that my sister's longtime advertising—the boy was a very cute sixteen-year-old who she'd had a crush on for years. This young heartthrob played keyboards in a local band, and at the time his arm was broken and in a cast. Which of course added to his "lost puppy" allure.

What could be more endearing to a young girl who wants to "save and mother" those who are hurting? What better way to please a boy than doing what he asks? *Come into the other room with me,* whispering and gently pulling on my hand, after some sloppy kisses on a chair in the middle of the living room. Surrounded by older kids who were smoking pot and drinking—and I was pretty high myself.

What I thought would be some innocent enough kissing on the order of Barbie and Ken in the convertible coupe got way out of hand and suddenly there I was, scared, hurting, sniffling a little bit, and definitely no longer a virgin. Even in the hippy era, striving to lose one's virginity was not the goal it seems to be today.

Rather, the social code was quite the opposite. Girls had to be very careful of their reputations or they would be branded. Which of course would mean ostracism by all the other girls except those who were "like that" too. It was a pathetic, emotionally searing social structure, and in some circles it still exists.

Swept along in the tide of the times, my other teenybopper girlfriends all had their first sexual experiences in that rousing rock 'n' roll summer—we just couldn't wait to become hippies!

Regrettably, several of them spiraled into heavy drug abuse, including far too much speed and acid, even heroin.

23

Two of them lost ten years of their lives to addiction. No telling how many friends from that time and place in southwestern Ohio lost their lives completely to drugs. And it gave me no pleasure to learn, years later, that the boy with the broken arm had grown up to become a pathetic addict himself.

The blessing for me was that, at a critical moment, my family was transferred to Memphis, Tennessee—decades and worlds away from fast and loose Ohio. People hardly even smoked cigarettes in Memphis—but I did.

The physical damage had been done—and then I began allowing the feelings of shame, blame and revenge to wreak their havoc—on me. I had no idea how to channel my fury and hatred effectively, so I focused most of it on myself.

Bodhisattva

Enlightened beings or Bodhisattvas choose to appear in the form necessary for the one in need—sometimes male, sometimes female, at times as children. They may be animals, angels, or even the guiding light of a lighthouse that shows sailors at sea how to avoid crashing on the rocky coast.

Mine looked like a friendly troll, this spry, grandfatherly Jewish shrink who specialized in wacko teenagers. The child psychiatrist my parents rushed me to see offered this thought: "It's important for you to develop a healthy degree of self-assertiveness."

Hmmm. Healthy degree of self-assertiveness. The early plank of the Just Say No campaign.

Eventually I got that one down. Just ask the people who request my involvement when I'm feeling overwhelmed—and how quickly I'm able to snap "No!"—often regretting my tone, later.

Another encouraging statement from my adolescent Bodhisattva, so pivotal to lightening up my long darkness of misunderstanding: "You're not the one who's messed up; it's really what's happening with your parents. You're what's called the identified patient."

What joy! Suddenly, from the depths of my agony and self-hatred I had been given license to blame: to point the finger of blame outward at all the bad guys and ignore that three fingers were pointing right back at me.

Insane? Yes, but psychiatrically sanctioned. And very satisfying to my young ego. And that's the way most people spend their lives—blaming outer circumstances for the pathetic mess where they may find themselves.

Granted, the family had plenty of problems to go around, but that's not the point of this story.

The point is how I got off a young girl's Path of Possibility and onto the path of shame, blame and irresponsibility, leading me to a place where I feared for my life—before I began to wake up and see the results of my choices and actions.

I had boys and my parents to blame; so I chose to blame them. Not only was I well trained in the art of blaming "the other," but also it's the essence of our entire culture. Just look at the lawsuits everywhere today. At its most insane and unconscious level, it blossoms as war.

And if I could blame others and turn them into objects of blame, I could turn them into objects, period.

When other people become objects, we easily feel justified in projecting all of our self-hatred, shame, anger and ugly feelings onto them and making them something to be used, or the enemy, or the bad person, or evil, or the perpetrator of the crime. Who doesn't want to punish that?

25

The problem is, since no crime manifests in the outer before it manifests in our own hearts and minds, this makes for a very sorry waste of the heart and mind.

I'd gotten into the negative habit of objectifying men, manipulating them and making them wrong for whatever I didn't like about my own life, just as men so often do with women. Just as we all do with each other, using people for our own ends—not witnessing others as unique, shining, and glorious, but hoping they'll be our favorite station on the radio dial: WIIFM (what's in it for me?)

And that's how I ended up being terrorized by the ex-married guy who was broke, unemployed, and a crazed cocaine addict, crashing in my apartment after he'd been on a $3000 coke binge in Florida –using money he'd cadged from his dirt-poor parents to "tide him over" until he got another job.

A beautiful picture, yes? It gets better.

"Get the knife and just end it for me. Now!" he begged from the bed. Of course I knew who would end up dead if he and I got into a tussle involving a butcher knife.

"Get him out of there!" my mother hissed at me over the phone, and somehow I did while he was still stupefied on one of his main drugs of choice.

For the rest of the summer I secreted my car on a side street whenever I was at home. Every weekend I disappeared to the lake with the new boyfriend I'd latched onto, just to rescue me from the sorry scenario in Atlanta.

I had definitely lost my way.

However, rampant partying kept this rather transparent truth from my own awareness.

Not only did I still believe the problem was all "out there," I honestly didn't realize how much pain I was causing myself with all the rotten choices I was making. But I'd sworn not to get married and repeat the even sorrier history of my parents, so I was enacting my heart's desire: always go for the unacceptable or unavailable man because deep in my soul at the time, I felt I wasn't acceptable or available either, so why even pretend?

Perhaps ex-married-lunatic-with-the-knife was one of my Bodhisattvas too.

Odds are, that critical situation really helped me see that using men was a go-nowhere, backfire situation, and that I was experiencing karma of the most instant kind.

I was beginning to get the message. Finally, at around age 28 I began to shift.

However, not until many years later did I grasp the full gift of some of those early experiences—the years of using others and being used, and thinking that was the way life would always be.

Perhaps my mother's tough love, shaming me into a modicum of "acting right" during high school, kept me from losing ten years or more of my life to the heavy addictions that so many close friends experienced. I too may have sunk into the pit of drugs and all the other poor choices that go along with that life if we'd stayed in that Ohio environment.

I had a good four years of high school for maturation. And even though I was "emotionally arrested" at age thirteen by my poor choices and their consequences, I still excelled academically and in leadership roles and got accepted into Chapel Hill—an excellent university hundreds of miles from the spiraling-out-of-control insanity of my family.

Simple Truths of a Plant

The gift of a plant taught me that no flower blooms until its roots are dug in. Its support system must have fully established strength before it blossoms into what it was meant to become from Day One.

It's no wonder that many children who don't receive the proper nurturance fail to thrive, grow into juvenile delinquents or die far too young.

A lovely succulent in an amply sized glazed pot was evidence enough of the importance of sturdy roots. For some reason I thought it had reached its dynamic zenith with its dark shiny leaves and thick, twisting stalks. My friend hadn't told me what it might become when she gave it to me, so I wasn't aware of its nature.

This mysterious plant continued to grow and spread its curlicued branches, exponentially exploding outward with its dark, shiny greenery. For all I knew it was morphing into Audrey II from *Little Shop of Horrors!* Just when I believed it couldn't possibly become any more graceful and beautiful, this fabulous toss-off kalanchoe burst into tiny, rich-red flowers on its waxy green base, a giant bouquet, completely unexpected.

What a powerful lesson the kalanchoe showed me. We really have no clue of the wonders we may manifest until we've granted ourselves enough nurturance and foundation to exhibit what springs forth from peace and wellbeing—the fruit of the spirit.

Plenty of shadowy springboards into personal power exist, quite true. La Muse eats people alive if they ignore her urgings to grow into what they are meant to be—their personal manifestation of The Creator.

28

La Muse is just as voracious as the Hindu goddess Kali— Creator, and Destroyer—always ready to chomp down the ones who ignore their own creative impulses, their own gifts from God.

Jesus, our Elder Brother and Way-shower, had a disciple nicknamed Doubting Thomas who also questioned life's deeper meanings, and he expressed a similar message: **"If you bring forth what is within you, what you have will save you. If you do not have that within you, what you do not have within you [will] kill you."**

This mysterious Zen-like statement comes from the Gospel of Thomas, one of the Gnostic Gospels unearthed on scrolls discovered in Nag Hammadi, Egypt in 1945, shedding new light on the teachings of Jesus.

We can try like mad to stuff down our natural inclination to grow into ourselves and bring forth what is within us by rushing to stifle the Muse with anti-depressants, food, drugs, sex, alcohol—or "malling" ourselves to death. And then we learn the truth.

Salvation is not at the mall! It's in the inner garden!

The Best of All Possible Worlds

On my twelfth birthday my mother's eyes twinkled, which was unusual for her. That was really my father's bailiwick, his being the handsome Scots-Irishman that he is.

"I think you're old enough for this now," she smiled as I tore into the wrapping of a very special but rather thin book, Voltaire's *Candide, or The Optimist*.

I could tell it was special because it was hard bound with an extra red shell into which the book itself was inserted. And

My mother, Mary Beth, at about the age she presented me
"Candide" and encouraged me to "cultivate your garden."

so I was drawn into this bitingly funny political/philosophical tale from the 18th century.

Naïve Candide travels the world over, is captured on the high seas, is nearly burned at the stake, falls in love with a woman whose left buttock is carved off and eaten by some famished pirates, lives with her through outrageous harrowing escapes and life adventures only to discover that the best of all possible worlds is wherever we are, in whatever circumstances, if only we learn how to shift our perspective and view it that way.

We do that by learning to cultivate our own inner garden.

That Candide was a cockeyed optimist, and plenty would call him a fool. But why not be an optimist, if it's true that what we believe is what we end up seeing?

More than two decades after reading *Candide*, I stood in Washington DC before the Vietnam Memorial wailing wall, emblazoned with the names of thousands of dead soldiers. It was a powerful experience, and I felt slightly nauseated thinking of all those beautiful young men—and women—who lost their lives or struggled to make lives for themselves after being involved in the stupid political gambit of Vietnam.

I remembered our own pool lifeguard going off to fight when I was a kid, and coming back with half his leg missing. It was a devastating wake-up to the harsh realities of war.

I remembered the horror with which my mother viewed news of the young soldiers returning from war paralyzed from the chest down, or the waist down. For some reason the notion of those horrible injuries riveted her attention, and she truly grieved for those shattered lives.

As our group grew older and the draft lottery began, every year was a white-knuckler to see whose birthdays would be drawn among the top numbers, which spelled certain selection by the draft board. Boys devised ingenious ways to flunk

31

their physicals (word on the street was that soap in the armpits raised blood pressure). Many became conscientious objectors, or crossed the border to Canada.

And thousands served, especially those whose politically unconnected fathers couldn't slot them into safer duty. I turned to my friend who had served in Vietnam and asked him whose name he was going to search for on the wall.

"I don't know anybody who died in Vietnam," he replied.

"That's impossible! How could you spend a whole year in Vietnam and not know one soul who died there?"

For him it was one large 18-year-old's adventure. What he believed was what he ended up seeing.

Even in a place of war this latter-day Candide let his eternal optimism bubble up and lead him along his path. More power to him!

Granted, we all have our own paths in life. And yes, death and destruction definitely exist, especially in times of war.

But what if we're asleep to the messages that might lead us along a gentler path, a path of possibility? What if the only path we know is one we've forced ourselves to hack out with a hoe like some hardscrabble pioneer?

It is absolutely not necessary to make life so tough!

Universal law teaches us that we create our reality in order to learn what we need, so as to advance to higher levels of consciousness. It took me a lot of years to discover that I was the one who was making my life hell, nobody else.

Nature and her lessons of the cycles of life are helpful here.

Consider the patience exhibited in nature. Blooms unfold in the fullness of the natural timetable without forcing them. Even though forced blooms are beautiful, they fade faster than those allowed to come to fruition on the proper timetable, with no hurry-up and hustle.

Rooted deeply into the earth, giant trees may sway and toss in the gale, but they weather many storms if they've received the proper sustenance along the way.

Nature does not complain that it is too hot, too cold, or a Monday morning. The storm passes over. The sun peeps through, the birds awaken and begin to chirp; the dew ascends from blades of grass back into the atmosphere.

A dog barks nearby and others bark in response. A slug trails its slimy wake along the flagstones. The air begins to warm. The leaves rustle faintly in the breeze.

No complaints. Just gentle acceptance of what is.

"On the knees of bountiful gods we live in the ease of acceptance, Taking, until we are twenty, God's plenty for granted," stated poet Louis MacNeice, Born in Belfast, Northern Ireland, and sent to an English boarding school at age ten, MacNeice's search for identity and "home" color all his work.

On my nineteenth birthday, Dr. Armitage, my favorite English professor, sent me a hand-penned copy of this poem in his proper Oxfordian calligraphy. In his early forties at the time, he well knew the truth of those lines.

Frivolous, bold and unfazed by life, I could hardly grasp its meaning. I was a wild horse! I would gallop unfettered, forever!

So we live in this magical state, sometimes until we're five, sometimes until we're twenty.

Nature continually reminds us that our attempts to bend the flow to our own egos are futile. These attempts bog us down, literally. We cannot dam it; we cannot contain it. The flow will either float us, or dispassionately drown us in it. So why fight it?

Simply accept what is. The flow is all there is—and it's our choice whether we wish to sprinkle it over our heads in a personal baptism, or whether we choose to dive into its infinite depths, its vast oceans. Whether we will sip it with the daintiest of teacups, or dig a well that taps its endless artesian resources. Or we just may choose to push our canoe from the bank and float merrily downstream upon it.

If I sound for the moment like the voice of Her Royal Flowness, let me include here that I waged a mighty battle against the flow for years, and guess who won?

Consider Ozymandias, a great mythical ruler from ancient times, lionized by poet Percy Bysshe Shelley. In his poem, a desert traveler encounters a gigantic statue crumbled in the dust—this "permanent" monument to posterity now reduced to sand and shards.

> *...And on the pedestal these words appear—*
> *'My name is Ozymandias, king of kings:*
> *Look on my works, ye Mighty, and despair!'*
> *Nothing beside remains. Round the decay*
> *Of that colossal wreck, boundless and bare*
> *The lone and level sands stretch far away.*

When the monument was fashioned, the great Ozymandias was certain that he would be glorified forever in this shape hewn from stone.

Seeing the mummies and their elaborate multiple caskets and sarcophagi in the great museums of the world confirms what none of us really wants to face.

Bottom line: even the Trump Tower will be dust some day. So why slave over monuments to our egos, when they are absolutely not going to fill the inner void?

So what? All is vanity! All but the inner garden, wellspring of the flow.

34

A Chipmunk Morality Tale

Is the chipmunk sad when it yields to the flow by shifting forms into a cat snack? Granted, it struggles to get away, and occasionally does succeed in leaping to safety down a nearby hidey-hole. And yes, it may feel a chipmunk kind of terror as its grip on life is loosened by the ways of the cat.

It doesn't even need to know that it's part of nature's flow—it lives in the only time present to it: Now.

A chipmunk doesn't have much in common with the desperate striver, mired in the debt that's accumulated in order to have more in order to appear to be more, loaded down with fancy gas-guzzling, mammoth cars and faux chateaux; the lake house, the boat and all the trappings. What do all these trappings offer while the financial ax dangles overhead like the sword of Damocles?

Ball and chain, weighty burdens holding us and our families hostage to the slavery that drives the consumer feeding frenzy—continually generating more sprawl, more malls, more, more more of everything—except peace of mind.

I'm not advocating that those out of work and out of a paycheck in our schizophrenic economy simply give up and be eaten like chipmunks—chomped down in the cultural maw.

What I am advocating is a deeper reliance on spiritual solutions—the ever-bubbling fountain within, rather than the linear, "logical" path that has already wrought its own brand of misery.

Our best thinking got us here—what are we going to do, think ourselves in a little deeper?

So, like nature's little chipmunk, ever on the alert for the fortuitous route out of trouble, it's time to cultivate our ability

35

to quickly slide down the hidey-hole into the depths of our own souls.

And what rich rewards greet us there.

Consider J.K. Rowling, so broke she had to scribble her ideas for the Harry Potter series on napkins—and now she's sold more of those books than any author of all time! She did not rely on linear thinking to get herself out of her temporary state when she was being eaten alive. She tapped into her creative wellspring and it's never stopped. And she was rejected numerous times before becoming successful.

An observation: during the recent times of corporate cataclysm and massive layoffs, it seems that men more than women rely on a paycheck to define themselves, rather than looking toward the source of infinite supply as the solution.

A woman will do almost anything to achieve her objective of feeding and protecting her young. Often when the linear path takes a sudden jag to left or right, men seem to have a more difficult time regaining equilibrium. Perhaps their egos are so completely defined by their paycheck persona that when the role shifts they no longer know what to call themselves.

"Don't get thrown off the track by every nutshell or mosquito's wing that falls upon the rails," said 19th century transcendentalist Henry David Thoreau.

I love that pithy statement. And I have to remind myself of what nutshells and mosquitoes' wings really look like when an unexpected bill arrives, or an important deadline is missed or lightning blows out the electricity for a few hours. You can't push the flow.

Learning to breathe into the moment instead of going into a panic is definitely a learned skill for me, one breath at a time.

Although the loss of a certain job or paycheck and its

accompanying "status" may appear overwhelming or tragic at the moment of loss, it is honestly Nature's way of opening new horizons. Now that jobless person is forced to tap the inner resources and discover resiliency and creativity that bring them fully alive!

This marvelous shift occurs for two reasons:

Unless totally out of control with an addiction to spending money, people out of work spend less because they don't have as much to spend, and therefore can't medicate with the usual suspects—drugs, sex and rock 'n' roll or their infinite variations. Or if they do attempt to medicate, eventually these pastimes wear thin and the addict hits bottom. The options: a spiritual shift back into sanity; or, loss of life, which is an even more conclusive spiritual shift (and just as effective in changing behavior—ask the chipmunk).

Job loss is Nature's way of helping egos to crack open, in order to help people open up to new ways of thinking and being.

Job loss compels us to step out on faith, one tiny baby step at a time.

Ruminations on an Unripe Banana

Have you ever tried to peel a banana that isn't ripe? It's virtually impossible! Get out a chisel, because that banana skin is STUCK to the fruit and it's not letting go without a struggle.

My point: eat no banana before its time. Serve no wine before its time. Let your realizations come to fruition in their own time, and don't beat yourself up if you don't "get it" right now.

Perhaps you'll get it later; perhaps not. So what? Accept what is. Stop trying to push the river or hurry up the flow.

(An added bonus: bananas taste ever-so-much-better when they're ripe—even if churned up in your protein shake!)

As we know, we can't simply snap our fingers and the change is so. That's for fairy tales and dictatorships, but even dictators need time to force their subjects to respond to their wishes.

Our inner world operates more subtly than that—needing to be nurtured and guided along, and respected for all its facets, even that aspect of ourselves that condemns our failures.

Guess what: failure is an option! Yes, it is okay to fail, because from our failures we learn, and therefore they become successes.

Did you know that former *Today Show* host, loveable Katy Couric, now anchoring CBS evening news, was told on her first television job that she'd never have a career in TV?

We've all heard the old adage that if you fail to try, you try to fail. The important thing, as the Japanese proverb states: *"Fall down seven times; get up eight."*

Gain the World and Lose Your Soul?

It's not that the world lacks soul—it's that we've forgotten our way back to the Garden. We've learned how to gain the world and are losing our souls in the process.

Along the path we encounter those people who have learned how to retain their souls. Inevitably it's through going within—greeting their own muses, befriending them, receiving their creative gifts and then offering them to the world.

Don't you honestly believe that if everyone knew themselves and their purpose in the world well enough to manifest its unique, creative glory, that no one would have time or inclination to project their negative stuff onto "the others," make them wrong and start wars?

Fred Dresch, my friendly scarecrow pointing the way, was such a man. He had tapped his creative purpose in life and manifested it in an endless, Da Vinci-like flow!

The spring he was "going to Glory," I preferred this euphemism rather than to say that he was dying; the notion of losing him from this world was just too painful for me.

Although he was simply shifting forms, that process can be a frightening transition even for a man of faith, which he was.

Such an earthy man, so attached to the here and now, with his rock collections, his magical talismans and all the things he enjoyed carrying with him on the planet, including vast storehouses of creative equipment. The film making and photography gear, the lights, the cameras, the cords, the batteries, the editing suite, the CD's, the scripts, the proposals, the computers and file cabinets burgeoning with his projects.

The lapidary equipment to slice stone and hone it and shape it and polish it. The jewelry-in-progress—the cabochons and cut stones; the filigree silver, the hooks, pins and clasps, the tweezers, clamps, chains, leather bands, the bottles of glue.

The wax from which he shaped delicate molds for lost-wax silver and gold earrings and "organic" necklaces, brooches and bracelets, rings, buckles, bolos and tie clips that all sprang from the central stone or gem and his imagination!

Acrylics and oil paints, pastels, canvases, easels and works in progress poised throughout the house. Molding clay from which he formed all manner of creatures.

The Blue Duskies that he fashioned, peering down like quizzical gargoyles from the heights of kitchen curtain rods. His sculptural masterpiece, a phantasmagorical chess set of figures, each a gnarly mini-creature more magical than the next.

Decades ago on evenings in Oakhurst, a leafy neighborhood in Decatur near Atlanta, he and a friend got together to fashion clay pieces and watch movies. The friend's career evolved into Claymation and he has now won two Academy awards for his animation work on the *Spiderman* films.

My point is, he and Fred had equal talents in modeling with clay, and if Fred had chosen this route to exhibit his talents, he may have been up on the Academy's stage as well. That was not to be on Fred's path.

Fred expressed great joy through his music as well. Poised in the corners of his apartment rested a guitar and a saxophone, ready to be picked up and played at a moment's notice. His beloved gospel music—call and response in the church choir, with Fred's booming bass exhorting us to "Hold to God's unchanging hand!"

The GospelFest which he founded, bringing together choirs from all over the city to raise funds and send underprivileged children to summer camp—a time of joy and glory!

The fishing gear—seine nets and fishing rods and cast nets and tackle boxes. The fossil-hunting gear, and the gem mining equipment: pans for rubies and garnets and sapphires and gold flakes from the rushing mountain streams; a giant sifting box for shark teeth dug up with shovels-full of sand off the intercoastal waterway near Savannah. Mosquito netting and broad-brimmed cowboy hats to keep the stinging pests from his face while engaging in some of his favorite outdoor pursuits.

Jars and cabinets and cases jammed with his treasures: a Fairy's Cross collection that would rival any in Georgia, consisting of the state mineral, the dark crystal staurolite, his passion for which had earned him the nickname "Staurolite Dresch" as a younger man.

Hundreds of shark teeth ranging from the giant five inch wide gnashers of the 65-foot-long Carcharadon to the tiny black razor pinpricks of baby teeth, and you wouldn't want to feel a bite from them either! The perfect medium-sized specimens in between, many fashioned into bolo ties and later sported by fashion-forward men at black tie balls.

Shelves groaning with books, including many valuable first editions of macho authors like Hemingway and Edgar Rice Burroughs who spawned Tarzan.

A kitchen stacked with spices, ingredients and equipment for concocting his favorites: Tom Kha Kai soup from Thailand; real Italian spaghetti sauce (the recipe straight from his delightful artist mother's Italian clan in the Appenines); all manner of fish dishes featuring his own fresh catch.

And then outside, onto the deck, every railing perked up by individual ceramic dishes of thriving succulent plants, or tiny seedlings marching in row after row in the sprout planters ready for the vegetable garden below. Dangling from hooks overhead, the organic wind chimes he fashioned from slices of multicolored stone looped to graceful driftwood, or bones and shells and shards clanging together on leather strands.

The magic of his life showed everywhere on his land, his enclave in that gigantic acre alive with stately oaks in Oakhurst. Out back, the little stage area, a performance venue he created for himself and his friends as an adjunct to the woodshop and work studio, all fashioned from scrap lumber, doors and windows discarded along the road or bargained for a steal at flea markets; brass fittings, metal trinkets and trappings. An entire clerestory shed perfect artists' light.

A creatives' paradise—a life fashioned just as he wanted it—a lovely Neverland, the memory of which will always be cherished by his legions of friends and loved ones.

Certainly, even though he's now gone to Glory he will never die, as the spirits of all the loved ones live on in our hearts and minds.

"Plenty good room in my Father's kingdom—you just choose your seat and sit down!" There he sits with the Father who he loved so well; it's a beautiful vision.

How did this man who lived into the richness and fullness of life tap into the greatness of his own "acorn" as James Hillman describes in *The Soul's Code*, the Muse ever spilling forth her wonders to him?

Simple, but not always easy: He granted himself time and space to create.

Although many friends, including me, clamored for his valuable time, he kept us at arm's length so he could have his creative space. It was a compulsion for him, a calling, a force driving energy through him that would not be denied. And he did not deny his Muse.

The irony is that perhaps the bad habits he carried along the way were what did him in.

What You Have In You

Apparently Fred's doctor, when questioning him about his lifestyle, discovered his tendency to stay up until all hours—2 or 3 or 5 or 6am—drinking coffee and smoking cigarettes to stay awake, swilling down sugary drinks while he ground away at his latest creations: the loveable old curmudgeon in *Kudzu Christmas*, or the shrimpers in *Seven Bridges to Heaven* or any of the other characters who popped out of Fred's cosmos to delight us.

In late spring he was visibly downshifting from a desperate grasp on life after more than three hellish weeks in the hospital, craving to get home…. Home.

"Tomorrow," he'd say; every day he'd say it. "I'm going home tomorrow aren't I Eddie?" he'd query his best friend.

Toward the end I wondered if God ever would show up for him. Over two months of denial, as his innards were removed one by one and his systems began to shut down, we all held out the slim hope that he really would beat this thing, this pancreatic cancer. An insane hope, but one can always hope for miracles.

After all, Jesus did make the blind man see, the lame walk and Lazarus rise from the dead, so why not take a man of faith, half of whose intestines and colon had been removed—tubes and ports and ostomy bags dangling from his torso like some awkward bag piper "galumphing" down the hall, and let him live?

Why couldn't he enact his grand plan of healing the cancer, and then have his colon reconnected in a delicate procedure that very likely would have been performed by one of the amazing surgeons for whom we'd produced videos together, ten years earlier?

Except there was one problem. It was too late. Such a lovely euphemism, sugaring, for what had already happened inside him as the cancer leapt from his giant colon tumor (wrapped around the colon, not in it, so it wasn't even detectable by a colonoscopy)—to his pancreas, to "sugaring" on the other organs in his abdomen.

Just a spoonful of sugaring helps the organs come out.

"It's a very aggressive cancer, Pat," sister Susan, a registered nurse and professor of nursing, had told me when we all heard Fred's diagnosis.

"I don't deserve to live, but if God lets me live...." Fred had said, perhaps tasting the smoke of a zillion cigarettes.

Both his mother and I were astounded at the words coming from his mouth en route back from the holistic cancer specialist, two months earlier.

Shocked at his negative self-talk, I shot back at him, "Well if you feel you don't deserve to live, you won't. Of course you deserve to live! What have you done so especially awful that elevates you to the status of the undeserving?"

So that was it. He knew he didn't deserve to live. What horrible thoughts and self-denigration had gnawed away at him for years in a life overflowing with the bounty of God's many gifts manifest through him: writer, director, artist, sculptor, jewelry maker, musician, stonecutter, gem crafter, carpenter, gardener, woodsman, and most of all, good friend. In every direction dangled or glinted or showed out the glory of God that shone from him, and yet he had stated that he didn't deserve to live. And God would surely honor his wishes, spoken so plainly.

Careful what you wish for; careful what you think about. Thoughts held in mind produce outwardly after their kind—

one of the foundational ideas of Unity teachings, and one in which I fully believe. Jesus taught us, *"As you think, so you shall be."*

The body is a temple, they tell us in Sunday school, but what young person treats it that way? Fred simply carried his level of self-abuse far beyond the time when his body could still absorb the input of lifelong habits.

Did you know that cigarette smoking increases by two to three times the risk of pancreatic cancer—especially in men over 50? Fred, bless his heart, was a caricature of that particular type: the middle-aged chain smoker, always with a butt dangling from his lips, even while doing physical labor, hauling equipment or digging in his garden.

The smoking worked extremely well to put people off too, with that little black cloud of smoke always surrounding him. How could anyone get close to that?

If he'd established a more regular schedule with better sleeping patterns, his doctor said, the immune system might have been able to overcome the destruction from the cigarettes and other negative health habits.

Damn it, Fred! Why didn't you take better care of yourself?!!!

This beautiful earthy man, with all his great gifts, was so obsessed with producing his art that he literally tortured his body in order to get it to crank, to bring into being what flowed from his mind.

Balance is everything. The doctor said that Fred's erratic sleep patterns were probably what "got" him, just as much as the smoking and all the red meat over the years, and all the white flour pasta, and sugar.

When we don't sleep in a dark room for six to eight hours a night on a regular basis, the immune system doesn't have the

*Fred tapped his creative wellspring
in life and manifested it in an endless Da Vinci-like
flow. One of his messages to us: "Write with Joy!"*

proper amount of time to send in its janitors and scour down and flush out the free radicals. Like mold, they wreak havoc.

And what of the stress? Stress is such a huge factor in generating free radicals. All the stress of wondering whether one's work stacks up; whether one is creative enough, talented enough, good enough, in the most competitive industry in the entire world.

Certainly all are good enough in God's eyes—far more than good enough. We are glorious manifestations of God; God's thoughts put into action, in the flesh. And when we choose to keep our brilliance under a barrel, or abuse our physical health, the spirit and body rebel and it's "so long" to this go-round.

Louise Hay states in *You Can Heal Your Life* that cancer of the pancreas means the sweetness in life has disappeared. And the metaphor for colon cancer is not having been able to eliminate the waste from one's life. How perfectly appropriate!

How many times did I urge Fred to express! Express his emotions! While instead I watched him physically pack the anger and defeat down into his body after yet one more humiliating blow in that hard, hard business.

What of the sweetness of life? What if it all becomes too much of a struggle? What if, like Fred, one is continually banging his head against the brick wall of rejection and it's simply no longer a pleasure to be "in the business?" A business that he hoped would sustain him—and even bring fame.

All ego and vanity. It's far too easy in our outwardly focused world to believe that the glitz and glam has anything at all to do with one's real meaning.

What is the point of being dead 20 or more years before your time, stuffed with shame and rage over the opinions and acceptance of others, ultimately meaningless.

It's so critical that we embark upon our personal paths

back to the garden—just to experience the unadulterated, full-strength, God-Almighty version of the way life is supposed to be lived—as a series of unfolding miracles unencumbered by the old beliefs that life consists of sin and death.

What is sin, after all, but a disconnect from God's great love and compassion and a turning of our heads in unconsciousness?

But oh, what wonders we create when we are in the Flow!

Our lives are the expression of God, expressing his messages here and now. The Glory we've inherited is here on earth—the Kingdom of Heaven is within. Jesus said it—why do we continue to misinterpret it, or not believe it at all?

Write with Joy!

"Do you think Fred will communicate with us?" asked Maureen O'Leary, renowned for her skills as a costumer in the film and advertising business. This beautiful redhead is Ed Myers' delightful, loving wife; the two of them Fred's best friends since college. It worked so perfectly—Ed, the consummate cameraman, who partnered with Fred in so many film projects; and Maureen who dressed everyone for success.

"Surely he'll appear in our dreams."

"But I mean in other ways," she said.

This multifaceted man was so indescribable that people created adjectives and adverbs from his name.

If a place or a thing or a person held magic, mystery, charm and a dash of·derring-do, it was Fredlike. If an action involved dogged determination and "Never say die" gumption and focus like that of South Pole explorer Ernest Shackleton, it was Fredlike. Communicating with us from beyond death would be Fredlike too.

Invariably this puckish, passionate, enthusiastic, delightful Pied Piper would be leading his motley troops, often including Ed and Maureen's children, Laura and Devin, along with kids from church, off on a woodland adventure or a cool-down fishing trip in the sweet lazy of an afternoon.

Far too often his old VW hippy van would break down miles from nowhere and that would be Fredlike too.

Huck Finn, Davy Crockett, My Samurai, the Gelato Man, Peter Pan, the church elder, the consummate contrarian, aficionado of Native American lore, woodcrafter, survivalist.

As a musician in his earlier years in the Uptown Soul Revue he blasted the saxophone in a soul strut on the Chitlin' Circuit, fronting Bobby Blue Bland. He was the blackest white man I've ever met, whether running a nightclub or a church supper—and irrepressibly Fredlike.

People who met him knew he was one in a zillion—full of zest, always prepared to give things another try, the next chance, the next pitch. A heart filled with hope.

All this, combined with his contrary way of fighting even harder when the situation appeared hopeless. How many friends in the film business spoke of seeing his office wall literally papered with rejection letters when they first met him?

By placing those rejections in his vision he was bucking one of the core principles of life: What we think about is what we attract.

By papering his mind's eye with refusals, he perpetuated that for himself.

If only he'd plastered the walls with visions of victory—even if there were only slim hopes for a better future.

But even with rejections staring him in the face, still he remained optimistic.

49

He'd show them! Thirty years in a business that never nurtured him and rarely supported him financially in a decent lifestyle, yet he always persevered. Always certain that the breakthrough was just over the horizon.

Mentor to many, loved by many. More of a man's man than a ladies' man, but the mama in all of us tripped over ourselves to get to him in our feeble attempts to tame his Huck Finn ways; to bottle some of his Peter Pan magic so we could take a surreptitious swig now and then.

How could he have left us in the midst of the most lush, vibrant spring to grace the South after five years of drought? The day he died, I sensed it down to the hour and said to friends, "He's going to glory even as we speak."

The dismal rain, torrents and buckets of rain, days upon days of it, exacerbated the dreary mood. But after the rains, and after he'd gone, the humidity dropped, the air cooled, even enough to tolerate the un-air-conditioned memorial service at Oakhurst Presbyterian Church on the first official day of summer, his favorite season.

In death, as in life, it was as though he'd stage-managed the weather to give us some respite on the day of his Home Going ceremonies.

As if in response to Maureen's question about whether he'd communicate, Fred had already touched me in two ways.

The day after his transition I high-tailed it to the mountains—my place of healing and solace—a place to lie down on the earth and absorb its good energy—a blessed rejuvenation.

The weather in Sapphire Valley, a gem in the western North Carolina mountains, was beyond perfect—the sky endlessly deep blue, the color of a blueberry popsicle and tasting nearly as rich from my vantage point on the grassy lakeshore. After an overnight and some healing tears, I had absorbed what I needed from Bald Rock's soothing Gaia energy and packed up to head back to Atlanta that evening.

While I streamed along the two-lane highway just before reaching Walhalla (no kidding!), several hundred yards ahead a car pulled out in front of me.

It was an extremely eccentric, demanding-to-be-noticed fluorescent lime green VW bug with large black polka dots painted all over it. I've never seen a thing like it before or since—the car was literally so ugly it was cute. Volkswagens happened to be Fred's favorite form of transportation throughout his life—whether Beetles or Vans, he was a VW man.

Neat white calligraphy stenciled the back window, and I assumed it probably said "Just Married" but I wasn't close enough to see it clearly.

Bald Rock's soothing Gaia energy in Sapphire Valley, NC.

In a rush to get back to Atlanta, I was anxious for my chance to pass. A straight stretch opened up before me and I floored it—reading, to my surprise as I passed the Volkswagen–the stenciled words "WRITE WITH JOY!"

I was dumbfounded. Surely this was a big bold message from my dear friend beyond, who was so diligent with his daily writing and constant pitching of his works.

Although I sometimes resented the amount of time he spent with his creative process and away from me, years after we parted ways I would look at his zeal and determination and find them admirable, and traits to be emulated as well.

The message was loud and clear. Stop Struggling! Write With Joy! The message was loud and clear and meant for me to notice, and the VW connection cinched it to Fred. Especially since the new Beetles are very Fredlike—spunky, cute, never-say-die.

Earlier at the lake I'd hesitated to sit down and write when I had a heavy heart, weighed down by so many of my friends who were in the thick of suffering over some problem or another—financial, emotional, major illness, family upheaval—and here was Fred's unmistakable message from just beyond the grave to lighten up!

Thank you Fred! I got that message!

Had some of the old favorite gospel songs provided solace while he was slipping away? What kind of musical accompaniment does anyone want while concentrating on the realm between life and death, and what lies beyond?

Perhaps it all played in his head as he tried to calm and reconcile himself that he wouldn't be here in physical form to enjoy another gorgeous Atlanta spring—or ever again to experience the comforts of his beloved Pharr House in Oakhurst or his hobbit-like camping cabin at Cherokee Whisper in Mineral Bluff, up near Blue Ridge.

This being who had just suffered every physical indignity that the disease process can inflict was now urging me from the beyond to joyously express myself, to write with joy!

Living Licorice

Another message came from Fred that I shared with Maureen. Earlier that spring I'd bought a licorice plant for my deck. It had been six years since Fred and I had parted ways as a couple, and in the interim I'd forgotten about his insatiable licorice cravings. During his numerous attempts to quit cigarettes, he'd slurp up endless strings of red or black licorice, which he bought cheap at Big Lots.

As a festive touch after installing the licorice plant into its pot, I'd placed a big green translucent rock on display—a specimen Fred had given me nearly ten years earlier when we were deeply in love—a big shining chunk that looked like kryptonite or a bilious-colored emerald.

Funny, I didn't notice that the green stone was heart-shaped until after he died.

Why did it go unnoticed for so many years? How is it that a beautiful message can be right up in our faces and we don't see it until everything is topsy-turvy, forcing us to look at life in a new way?

Those two lumpy protuberances were the top of a heart! Suddenly I got the message loud and clear, and my own heart sank as I realized that I'd missed yet another one of Fred's subtle gestures of love.

So often we passed each other like the walking wounded in our frenetic lives. Rarely pausing long enough to make the crucial heart space for each other, and yet here he had handed it to me in stone. I wondered why I'd been unable to appreciate this message during the full flower of our love. It just seemed like another opportunity for connection had passed us by, which made me sad.

Compounding my guilt and melancholy, somehow I'd ignored the "directions for care" tag on the licorice plant and didn't notice that this plant must be kept well watered at all times. Then one day when I checked on it, bad news—it had completely withered in hot sun on the deck.

As Fred trudged slowly to meet his maker, the plant with his green rock in it died right in pace with him. How I cried over my thoughtless neglect!

Did it have to be a total loss? I still held out hope and didn't want to toss it. Instead I moved it into a shadier spot and became much more attentive to its water needs.

Who can explain how this straggly, dead plant completely resuscitated itself after Fred went to the other side? Eventually it fully leafed out again, as beautiful as before.

His licorice plant had been transfused with a Force far stronger than water, sunshine and plant food. I honestly believe he chose to share part of his soul with that plant as a living reminder to me—to Write with Joy!

The Nature of the Path

The Path does not need to be hard. It can be gentle.

God did not put us all here on earth to have hard, difficult lives, although we certainly have the option for a harder path if those are the lessons our soul has chosen for this lifetime.

Some people deliberately choose a harder path—a choice to live outside of the Flow, ignore it or struggle with it. If we choose that path through ignorance or ignoring the truth, we can correct that.

But what if we choose it for other reasons: The glorious martyrdom. A sense of self-importance. The admiration from colleagues over one's "intestinal fortitude."

It all boils down to Ego. What if all that fortitude stored in the intestines yields a result like colon cancer—instead of the public acclaim for which so many people strive?

The secret is not to give a damn about the outcome or the way it will be perceived by others, but to do it (whatever it is, your creative outpouring) for your-own-self.

"For us there is only the trying. The rest is not our business," said brilliant poet T.S. Eliot.

"You can't please everyone, so please yourself," we've learned from more than one source.

"Ask, and it will be given to you; Seek and you shall find; Knock and it shall be opened to you," said Jesus, and that's gospel!

We don't know what's on the other side of that door, but unless we step up to it and knock, forget it. It's up to each of us to step up to our door, which is just an illusion separating us from our inner resources, and knock.

And how does one do this?

There are so many ways we can manifest our inner beauty outwardly. Just pick something and do it!

Play chess, plant a garden, bake a pie, play with a child, run a race—or perhaps stroll through a park. Finger paint, toe paint, enjoy the kaleidoscopic colors as you twist the cardboard tube. Roller blade, write a haiku, swim some laps, dribble a basketball. Bounce a baby on your knee, knit a sweater, cut a friend's hair or apply make-up. Play hopscotch, jump rope, sing a song—write a song! Read a poem. Birth

Planted pansies manifest inner beauty outwardly.

your book. Take up archery. Sew some doll clothes—or a flag—or a dress for yourself.

Remember how good it felt to sew your own clothes, even if you didn't like that pasty-faced home-economics teacher with the sour expression who obviously hated her job?

Take a course—expand your horizons! Learn Spanish, or yoga, or how to tango. Learn Front Page so you can update your own website. Tap dance. Take up harmonica or guitar. Go shark tooth hunting. Go to culinary school. Do leather-work or get a lapidary lesson. Explore the woods, wade in the water, splash in the waves. Dance, sing, laugh, twirl, fly! And don't stop 'til you're beyond the sky!

Notice the key to all these things: all are active, requiring input, engagement, intensity and enthusiasm. What does enthusiasm have to do with it?

Look at the Greek root of the word: *En Theos* means God within.

Notice also that watching TV or playing video games on a monitor are nowhere among life-affirming activities, because that's what they are—nowhere near life-affirming. In fact those spoon-fed entertainments are, in my opinion, among the chief causes of our detachment and disaffection from the world, and dislike of our own selves and others today.

If I compare myself to the people on "Friends" or any similar lifestyle sitcom, there's no way my income could support the lives they lead, seemingly on the same modest level as mine. It's a joke! The result: sometimes it's self-hatred for not being able to keep up with an illusion.

However, when we support our baby steps into new terri-tory with enthusiasm, even at times "faking it 'til we make it,' we are living the life that God has manifested for us—God within.

Some might find the notion of "faking it" a repugnant idea.

How can we do that, we may whisper to ourselves. That's charlatanism; that's being a huckster or a con—conning ourselves! That means we're becoming that despised creature, the imposter.

But just imagine. Did Lewis and Clark have any idea of what they faced on their heroic trek across the vast wilds of the new world? They were clueless! But wisely, they had employed a very capable guide—Sacajawea—who snatched their supplies out of danger and saved the expedition, before they slipped into the roaring torrent.

They chose the right guide. We can choose the right guide.

The song says, "With God as our Guide, we will never fail."

These explorers, like all the others who traversed territory unknown to themselves, had to fake it until they made it. What if people counted faking as failure, and quit after just a few shaky attempts?

Learning any new skill or acquiring any new habit requires tolerating the wobble factor for awhile—often quite awhile.

Perfectionism

Some people are shocked—shocked—when I tell them that a psychiatrist states that perfectionism is one of the chief forms of self-hatred. How would any of us even know how to walk, if as babies we had believed we must put one foot in front of the other perfectly the first time we tried it? Imagine how many times we had to plunk down on our baby bottoms before we succeeded!

Consider that Lauryn Hill was booed off the stage in her first performance, and then years later she won thirteen

Grammy awards! Did you know that Walt Disney filed for bankruptcy seven times before striking gold with his Disney formula for Mickey Mouse and the Magic Kingdom?

And yet so many people cut themselves off before they've even started—often because they make odious comparisons between themselves and the superstars who have practiced for years to become a so-called "overnight success."

Imagine Olympic skaters at practice wearing the sky-rig harnesses that permit them the opportunity to make mistakes without busting their behinds on the cold ice one more time. That's the kind of mental and emotional support we need to provide for ourselves, even with others outside cheering us on. And if we have no "cheerleaders" in our lives, it's so much more important to build our own reserve power and saturate ourselves in our own vision of success in order to carry on, despite any failures along the path.

There's a big difference between striving for excellence and insisting on perfection. The first is healthy and inspiring; the second is a formula for self-defeat.

Remember the phenomenon of training wheels on your bike? That's a great exercise in learning to tolerate the wobble factor—and a metaphor for how we experience growing into our true selves.

Becoming Competent

Here's how we absorb a new skill or habit until we are well beyond the wobble factor and it becomes part of us.

First, like the little child on her three-wheeler, we are happily tooling about in a very narrow, proscribed portion of the world—our own driveway or sidewalk. At this stage we know we're capable of going in circles. In addition, we won't tump over unless we make a real effort at it.

It's hard to mess up when your world is so small and all the tools that make it function are so easy to use. At this stage, as a little child, we are *unconsciously incompetent*. We're unaware of the many ways that we might be enjoying this place called earth in a much larger way—and it doesn't really matter to us, because things look pretty good from where we sit. In awhile though, the little child begins looking at the older kids on their two-wheeled bikes, and, naturally, envy sets in. The little one wants to go faster, go further, to expand her horizons.

At this stage we become *consciously incompetent*—aware of the areas in which we lack skills that will take us where we want to go.

It now becomes our challenge to ramp up and meet the next step head-on, which requires a very high tolerance of wobbling for a while.

So, ready for the next wobbly ride, we're hoisted onto the seats of our little training wheel bikes, and Dad or Sis or Mom or some older neighborhood kid is often running alongside, yelling and distracting us with all kinds of good intentions. We strain to remember all those things we must do to keep it moving—

Keep peddling! Stay balanced! Hold the handlebars straight! Look in the direction of where we want to go! It takes huge concentration, and we may be scared—we might fall off and scrape a knee, oh my!

Even worse, we might have to endure the jeers of the older kids who experienced this rite of passage, and may have not yet developed the grace to want to see others succeed.

At this stage we're *consciously competent*, paying close

attention to all the details and skills necessary to make a bike move forward. Once again, we fake it 'til we make it.

Finally, and it may take years, we reach that happy place where we can glide along on the bike, perfectly balanced, no hands, steering with our hips and perhaps enjoying an ice cream from the Good Humor man as we soar freely through our vastly expanded world. We are no longer aware of all the mechanisms we must employ to make this marvelous thing happen—this freedom to be ourselves.

We've become *unconsciously competent*. We don't even have to think about doing it any longer; we're just being it, whatever it is.

The Wobble Factor

Remember how you felt riding a bike to your friend's house, no longer having to rely on Mom to walk or drive you there?

Aren't you willing to experience the wobble factor in other areas of you life? Then you'll receive the self-satisfaction of knowing that you've tried something new and let yourself expand into it.

If the notion of wobbling 'til you make it still leaves you cold, consider it as a form of self-coaching. Your inner angel or inner guide who enjoys a nice perch on your shoulder most of the time whispers in your ear, "You can do it! You're doing good! You're doing great!"

Far too often our self-talk runs the complete opposite, as self-torture. The internal diatribe can be endless! "You're dumb; you're too fat; you're a failure; you're incompetent;

you're a slob; you'll never get there; don't be too big for your britches."

Just recounting this type of negativity makes me cringe, and this is mild compared to what goes on in our monkey minds at times.

We are all too good for that! We are all blessed beings on the Path of Possibility, striving to get back to our inner Eden; opening ourselves to joy, which never comes in the form of externals.

It comes only from self-awareness, self-acceptance, self-respect, self-love. And acceptance of what is. We can't fix or change anything or anyone but ourselves, so we might as well get used to that idea right now.

How many times have I stamped my bratty foot over that last one and just wanted to have everything MY WAY?

What if our negative self-talk prevents us from bringing forth the specific blessing that is uniquely ours to offer?

What if Thomas Edison had stopped after testing the 9000th filament for the electric light bulb—if he hadn't continued to that 10,000[th] filament, tungsten, and lighted up our world? He never considered his trial and error to be failure—in fact he told himself that he'd just discovered one more way not to conduct electricity!

What if Julia Child had some notion at age 49 that she was too long in the tooth to begin anything new, and had never brought us the joy and delight of *The French Chef?*

What if, what if, what if we all stayed in our little lives and never tried anything new for fear of looking ridiculous? As if the whole world is focusing solely on us in our 15 seconds of fame?

What would the neighbors think? What would my parents think? Lions and tigers and bears, oh my!

It's chilling to imagine the self-limitations we allow to

weigh ourselves down, out of some ludicrous form of "self-protection" which prevents us from expanding into our birthright of glory.

Marianne Williamson's interpretation of *A Course in Miracles* stresses the teaching that we are far more frightened by our own power than by our perceived inadequacies. We mistakenly believe that we should keep our light under a barrel, when really we're called to let our light shine.

The first time I heard that, I was floored. One of my colleagues had delivered it in a speech, and it resonated so deeply with me, with permission that seemed directed specifically at me to remove the barrel that was covering my light—in fact encouraging me to do so. Now!

Who are we not to let our lights shine? Who are we to tell ourselves that we "don't deserve to live" as Fred convinced himself? Who are we not to manifest all the glory of God that's within us—within every single one of us?

We're trained so well to put ourselves down, to despise our little foibles and failures, that it's remarkable any of us ever give ourselves a chance to step out of the house in the morning!

What a fear-based society we live in! How much time we waste pointing the finger of blame in the form of lawsuits or false expectations. It's not up to someone else or something else, something external, to make our lives as rich and abundant and joy-filled as our Creator created them to be—it's up to us!

In the Image of the Creator

As manifestations of the Creator, what are we supposed to do to manifest our glory? Create, of course!

When we do not allow the flow of creative energy to manifest through us, whether in the form of our children, an architectural drawing we design, a puppy we train, a fresh-baked batch of cookies made from scratch, or some other outpouring of this intense creative energy which we have been granted as our birthright, we are blocking our own good.

My friend, artist Janet Smith, is the daughter of Justine and Dayton Smith, two delightful restaurateurs in Memphis and Atlanta, now deceased. A few years ago Janet wrote a beautiful tribute to her parents: *Justine's Memories and Recipes.*

Although they'd already experienced full lives before they met in their forties, and each had children from previous marriages, Justine and Dayton were a pair of dynamos who built Justine's into the number one dining establishment in the mid-South. Elvis was a frequent late-night patron, along with the upper social strata of Memphis, politicos, entertainers and the entire New York Metropolitan Opera once a year during Opera Week.

Their one Memphis location didn't satisfy their entrepreneurial spirit, however, and they eventually expanded their operation into Atlanta with a move that everyone called ridiculous.

Brick by brick, Dayton Smith relocated the old Pope plantation home from Washington, Georgia, to a swanky address on Piedmont Road in Buckhead. They built it and Justine's son Dan Taylor, famous for his Loch Ness expeditions in a yellow submarine that he constructed, ran it for years. (The restaurant is now called Anthony's—very popular for special occasions and conventioneers because of its old South charm).

At the Memphis location on Coward Place, all day they'd be running the kitchen after mornings working the gigantic, luscious vegetable and rose garden at their acreage on Rich Road. There they cultivated an impressive yield of fresh produce and dainty rosebuds for each table.

After hosting their clientele until all hours, when the last guest finally left for the evening, Justine and Dayton would go out dancing. What an energetic, debonair couple they were, and what fantastic lives they lived!

What truly amazed me about this dynamic couple was that they didn't even learn to ski until they were in their fifties!

Do you remember a time when one's sixth decade seemed ancient?

At the very least, time to slump down in the Barcalounger and turn into a sloth?

No longer. Some of us are really just beginning to get a clue about life by that age. You've heard the expression: "Get over your bad self!" Your bad self consists of every self-limitation you've ever taken on as the truth.

What powerful encouragement, to get rid of all that! Just let go of all the old murky stuff, using every means necessary: counseling, hypnotherapy, yoga, the discipline of shaping yourself in a new way to let the Divine spirit shine out—whatever it takes!

What good is the old dreck doing now, and quite frankly, what good has it ever done you?

All those old tapes from the parents, the bullies, the older siblings, the school system, the college advisor who encouraged you to apply to Drudge College in West Dungheap as your "ace in the hole"—and you wished you had a cream pie to smash in her face right then! (At least I did).

Those old, useless voices—out with them! It's time to get a new mantra (a phrase repeated inwardly to yourself) and it's got to be one you can make your own.

Two fantastic books I can recommend for this purpose are *Creative Visualization* by Shakti Gawain, and *You Can Heal Your Life* by Louise Hay. So many books have been my powerful, healing friends along the way I simply thank God that I believed in the wisdom they offered. I'm doubly grateful that I was willing to take action and follow their advice!

Sometimes it's necessary for us to hit a bottom before we realize that it's our responsibility and no one else's to wrench ourselves out of our torpor, our rut, our slough of despond. Wherever it came from, however it was created, it is something in the past that is not our present reality—and has nothing to do with the true manifestation of I AM!

Powerful words, those. Words used to describe God. I AM! I am happy, healthy, whole and free.

And if you think you're not, right at this moment, here's a great opportunity to fake it 'til you make it!

Life is a Joy Ride

Picture Justine and Dayton Smith out in Vail, learning how to ski in their fifties, and launching their bold new enterprise in their late forties, when neither Memphis nor the entire mid-South had much of a notion about fine dining.

It's not that these two delightful people started out so upper crust, either. Justine was a country girl from a large family in middle Tennessee. Dayton was a Chicago businessman. But they had the guts to work hard in actualizing their vision, and the restaurants blossomed into beautiful places of culture.

I remember Mr. Smith driving Janet and me in winter with the top down in his Continental. The heat blasted right along with his opera tapes. I thought, "This man really knows how to live!"

He just exuded joy—both he and Justine did, because they were living the life they loved. Through their own creativity they set a fabulous example for Janet, who is an accomplished and in-demand artist today.... And whose memoir about the restaurant was out-selling John Grisham's latest novel at a recent book signing where they appeared at the same time. Now I call that living into one's capabilities!

There was a question mark though, whether that would happen for Janet or not, as there is in the lives of many people.

When we were sophomores in high school, Janet was out riding without a helmet on her big, rangy horse Red.

Somehow she fell off and was dragged by the stirrup back along some rocky ground to the house, where she was found in a coma. For days, no one knew what would happen with Janet, who was in extreme pain, having to endure spinal taps and other indignities of the medical establishment while hospitalized.

Triumph, ten days later, when she regained consciousness! Her silky brown hair had formed such a rat's nest from lying on it in the hospital bed that it took days to untangle the knots and smooth it out again.

It's my belief that this fall helped galvanize Janet even more into her intuitive artist's brain where she was more in touch with the flow. There she felt less inhibited and she could let her creativity spill out in a torrent. She was one who managed to escape the educational system with her creativity still intact!

(An aside: Another friend once told me her own architect father designs schools and prisons. He once told her with a knowing sigh, "They're not that different, you know." Sad but true!)

I cite Janet as an example because of the way she lived after the accident—always drawing in class, never really paying attention, creating fabulous cartoons and doodles which were so delicate and intricate there was no question that was her gift, and I saved them in my "book of scraps," knowing that some day she may be famous for her art and I could proudly point and say, "Look where she started!"

Somehow it seemed slightly lucky, despite or perhaps because of her injury, that she was a bit more open to the Source. She began her artistic career right after college while still working part time in the restaurant. Immediately she began to put her stuff out there for public scrutiny, sink or swim—tolerating the wobble factor very well and growing into her gift.

Unlike Janet and many artistically inclined children, I was one of the lucky ones who loved and excelled at school. Regrettably this isn't the case for a vast percentage of children who find their souls completely crushed by the time they manage to slouch free of the brain-numbing factory.

Escape! Escape! Keep your creativity alive and intact!

When we free ourselves from perceived limitations of our childhood in seeking our higher creative selves, something wonderful happens.

How do we manage to keep this channel open to the Source, especially since not everyone is destined, as Janet was, to experience a life-changing "accident" that opened her mind?

Fertile Soil

Staying connected with Source requires fertile soil.

At birth we begin as perfect manifestations of Source, little seeds ready to spring forth into our destined might.

This growth depends a great deal upon whether the soil in which we're planted has been tilled and fertilized and amended along the way, fed and watered and lovingly turned to expose some of the darker aspects to the light, allowing worms and burrowing critters to truly work their cultivating magic.

Conversely, if our soil has been stomped down, never tilled, never fertilized, exposed or watered, and left there to bake in the hot sun and be compacted into clumps of hard clay, we'll have one tough row to hoe, as my parents used to quip about life's hard spots.

Jesus spoke of a farmer who sowed his seed, some of which fell on fertile soil and grew; some of which fell on hard ground and nothing came of it. Scorched by the sun, it withered and blew away.

The same principle applies to our minds, and whether or not they are fertile soil for the ideas and techniques which guide us to live the way the Creator wants us to live—in a bountiful garden, not parched in a bleak desert.

Stroll into the metaphorical interior of your own Eden and examine the soil. Has it been amended, fertilized, and made ready to support your creative flow? Or has it been compacted into hard little clods by years of being stomped by others, perhaps your parents, siblings, school or church teachings, with you fully believing and absorbing all the negativity they dispensed?

Then you may have obligingly taken on their voices and continued to rail at yourself in their place, poisoning your mind with negative self-talk.

At a certain stage, what else is there to believe? You don't know any other way than what you're taught—until you choose to open your mind and learn a new way, the Truth. At this point you may still be unconsciously incompetent, not knowing your options, but by taking this little stroll into your garden, you become aware of some area that could use the fertilization of self-love.

Not too many years ago my soil was pretty stomped down. Quite honestly, it felt like barren ground, a nuclear wasteland to me after surviving repeated emotional trouncings in my family (and from myself). Remember, I took on their voices and became my own worst enemy, and I was really good at judging myself!

I never quite knew which direction the zinger was going to come from, and so I was constantly flinging out my own with the nasty attitude that the best defense is a good offense. Among my mother, my sister and me the house was a battle zone.

During that era, my journal was my best friend—my creative lifeline to sanity. I'm grateful that I clung to it with such tenacity.

Although I felt like I was about to go over the edge, strong survival instincts clued me that there was more to life than name-calling and throwing nasty looks at each other.

I just hadn't seen that there is a better way, as you may not have seen it yet. My all-knowing mother sneered at self-help books, so I picked up on her cynicism and did not expect to find help there.

Regarding one of the greatest "self-help" books of the all time, I admit I've had a love/hate relationship with the Bible because of the manner it's been used to beat ideology into the masses for the political purposes of its authors.

Contrary to the opinions of many, it was not written by God, but by people with very specific political agendas!

Jesus was a man of action, and encouraged us to be so. *"Ask, and it will be given you; search and you will find; knock, and the door will be opened for you. For everyone who asks receives, and everyone who searches finds, and for everyone who knocks, the door will be opened."* Matthew7:7-8

We're going back to the basics here. Amending the soil of our life begins to reconnect us with the basics of our entire being. Asking, seeking, knocking, all reconnect us with our birthright.

First and foremost, we must DESIRE to reconnect with our inherent greatness—who we really are as children of God. Otherwise we can remain enslaved to old notions and wrong ideas and stay cramped in little lives for our entire existence.

Since we all consist of the same elements as the earth, and back to the earth we go after transition to begin another cycle, learning how to amend our own soil is the perfect beginning.

We must have the right tools for the job: a spade, a heavy rake and a hoe to chop up clods. A mechanized tiller is not really the best option for this heavy work because if we move too noisily and quickly through the process we may not be able to comprehend the extent of the work, much less be able to believe how much we've accomplished.

It's worthwhile for us to dig in and experience the rough stuff so we can look back and say to ourselves, "See how far I've come! All the hard work I've done! I'm so proud of myself!"

Another absolute necessity in the amendment process: Plenty of manure. It's God's way of making the soil fertile—he spreads it all around.

And who among us hasn't had plenty of it in our lives? What use have you made of yours? Is it still lying there like a big stinking pile of blame?

Humorist/philosopher Swami Beyondananda states it another way: *"Life is like photography; we use the negative to develop."*

Spreading It Around

A few years ago, within my own small circle of friends and family, three were dealing with breast cancer; one had experienced two rounds of ovarian cancer surgery and three job losses within two years. Another had dealt with prostate cancer. My father and sister were in the process of divorces. And Fred had just "gone to Glory" after his two-and-a-half month knockdown fight with pancreatic cancer.

What about all the health challenges, the family changes and the job losses? What are they trying to tell us? The earth is shifting so rapidly beneath our feet that it's a matter of Adapt or Die. Use this as fertilizer or be buried in it, like the German elephant trainer who gave his constipated pachyderm an enema and then literally suffocated in the result—this is the truth!

We simply must stay focused on our vision of what we want life to be, rather than getting mired in the muck of whatever negative may be happening around us. Regrettably, focusing on what we don't want only draws it to us, especially if we attach a lot of fear or heavy emotion to our projection of the worst possible outcome.

Probably any of us would express that focusing on what we *do* want is somewhat of a challenge when standing atop that mountain of manure. And of course that's when a positive focus and faith in positive outcomes is the most absolutely necessary.

What if life were always peaches? We'd have no basis for comparison—no true awareness of how far we've been able to bring ourselves. No sense of victory. Every triumph is hollow when it appears as a hand-off, especially if it hasn't involved your own hard work with shovel, hoe and rake.

So get in there and start chopping the clods. Georgia clay is my metaphor because I've been dealing with it for more than a quarter century. Stubborn, rain-resistant, intractable red clay that bakes into bricks every summer. The color is pretty and vivid, streaking out to the horizon in the flat cotton and soybean fields south of the gnat line, where the rolling piedmont ends and the coastal plain begins. But it's a deceptive beauty because of the hardness beneath the art of it.

What would life be like with absolutely nothing to overcome? Rather dull, in my opinion. But that doesn't mean we have to continually create more negative *schtuff* just because that's all we're accustomed to seeing.

As one of my rather unruly artist friends used to laugh, "I'm always making something, even if it's only a mess!" We are not condemned to repeat the past continually. We can make a conscious decision to let it go, and to move on up a little higher.

Part of the secret is to learn to appreciate what the lessons offer—maturity, perspective, stimulus—while learning that we don't have to stay in the same lessons forever. The amount of time we need to work on them is strictly our choice.

So hack and hoe and shovel and sift those clods and clay together with plenty of manure—and toss in a little sand of contemplation for a more even soil consistency.

Raking Rhythm

All this hard work is helped along ever so much by lightening up with the most ancient mood alteration of all. It's not some primitive version of fermented grapes or even hemp or peyote. Rather, the secret mood drug is music!

In the garden, either inner or outer, music surrounds us all the time.

It doesn't even matter if it's a city garden. There we experience the rhythm of mass transit trains and trucks rumbling past, the cacophony of car horns, the whoosh of tires and engines in a constant running stream.

But in a more secluded garden it begins with the rustling of the leaves in the trees.

I remember the quote my dear high school friend, a true nature lover, chose for her senior high school photo: *"The leaves rustled faintly over my head. From the sound of them alone I could tell what time of year it was."*

That quote was so evocative to me—of a wily woodswoman or a Thoreau enjoying a lazy dream beneath a friendly tree.

The leaves, the breeze, the happy splashing sound of water on rocks in a fountain or rushing down a hillside to a pool below; the bird songs; the call of a whippoorwill all happy and perky; the chirps of wrens in full social banter; the lonesome call of the mourning dove—all lift us up in the garden.

Dirty  Trees

More than once I have been rescued from depression by the debris and crunchy, crusty leaves that fall from the giant magnolia that dominates my back yard.

During times when I felt that I could barely put one foot in front of the other because of the latest loss, that tree has actually demanded that I get out there and rake it.

Dirty trees, a friend once called them. I didn't appreciate such a magnificent entity being disrespected like that, even if it's true that they shed a mess o' stuff.

I imagine it's rather like being depressed, and having a baby or a little child who requires attention. Diapers and feedings are part of the program, forcing you into the routine of life. Routine can offer healing stability when we need it most.

The fact is, magnolia trees do require a lot of maintenance with their twice yearly shedding of dry brown leaves, broken twigs and seedpods, May and November, steady as clockwork. And the raking, by switching arms, stimulates our brains in a positive way, thus sending endorphins cascading into our bodies and making us actually feel better physically.

So your parents were right when they said, "Get out there and rake some leaves. It's good for you!"

The double reward: In May and June we can count on the white out-burst of those luscious, sweet-smelling flowers, the giant blossoms with their heady perfume, making all the raking worthwhile. Add to that the excellent waist-trimming exercise, and my magnolia deserves to be called magnificent.

How many times while raking I've been inspired by the birds, the breeze, the rhythm of raking itself, to burst into song! Since no one but other songbirds are around to hear, I launch into my best Mahalia Jackson imitation, sweet and low.

"You know I promised (rake!) the Lord (rake!) that I would hold (rake!) out, that I would hold (rake!) out, that I would hold (rake!) out, until He meet me (rake!) in Galilee!" (rake, rake!)

Get a nice syncopation going, and the outer work goes faster while the inner work goes deeper. What's happening on the outer is simply a manifestation of what has already occurred on the inner, generating more of the same. It's a form of self-hypnosis, raking rhythmically and singing an old gospel song about waiting for the Lord to reveal our true path (i.e. "meet me in Galilee.")

By that I mean that if one's inner thoughts are directed toward the highest and best, all of that begins to manifest more easily, readily and rapidly on the outer. Concentrate on what you do want, not on what you don't want.

How do I know this? Since becoming more conscious on an adult level, beginning around age 30, which, according to Native Americans is the age of reason, my entire life has been an experiment in seeing whether all these theories expounded by the great thinkers and leaders, saints and saviors from the beginning of time are true. The way my life is evolving, I'm a believer.

Of course every now and then the universe throws out a lasso, jerks me up into the air by my ankle and lands me on my butt, and I have the opportunity to pick myself up, dust myself off and start all over again.

It takes time and energy to turn an ocean liner or to culti-vate a garden and experience the fruits of those efforts. So I might as well do it with a song in my heart and on my lips. (rake rake!)

Too depressed to sing, you think? *Au contraire!* A song

with a smile on your face will actually trick your physiology into a more elevated state. Fake it 'til you make it; there it is again.

I'm not advocating stuffing or denying one's true and actual strong feelings; not at all. I'm merely stating that by giving ourselves a little friendly prodding, we can begin to alter our depression or down feelings one cracked smile at a time. Maybe by tasting some tears in the process.

If you're physically able, it's much more sane to tackle this work with a rake or with tools that make very little noise.

What could be more soul-destroying than one of those horrific, ear-splitting leaf blowers that deafen the ears and deaden the spirit?

Recently California passed a law, which permits the use of leaf blowers only at certain hours of the day. That way the whole neighborhood can get out and blast each other deaf all at once, and have a blast doing it!

With a rake, you get good exercise and experience the satisfaction of witnessing leaves disappear bit by bit from the areas you've covered, which quenches the soul because you can see what has been accomplished by your own diligent efforts. Thomas Moore would consider this a very effective method of caring for the soul, because the soul craves details.

Raking is a means of beautifying the world, one leaf at a time. And then of course adding them to the compost pile to actualize into the next generation of beauty, all in seasonal rhythm.

At the same time, try singing to yourself. When I sing, it lifts up my spirit. I smile at the birdcalls and breathe deeply of the incredible perfume from magnolias, honeysuckle, gardenias, abelia hedge and the incredible profusion of flowers in the Enchanted Forest of Avondale, where I live.

And who knows? In that space of syncopated silence and

LadyBanks Rose cascades over my pergola next to the giant magnolia tree that towers above it.

contemplative movement, you may release the stress of the week, let go of some outcome, relax. This is how the healing garden soothes our souls. Some beautiful idea may spring into mind—a new song, or the answer to a question that's been plaguing you—simply by allowing yourself the space, the silence, the solitude, the rhythm and the satisfaction of taking a small manual task from beginning to completion.

The evidence in the garden reminds me that I'm capable of doing this in other areas of my life—writing, for example.

Occasionally I beat myself up because I want to go back and re-rake the same leaf until it's all shreds and tatters. Haven't you done that with instant replays of your life?

Why torture ourselves, really, when by tapping the flow of consciousness which is ours for the asking, we can engage in a natural process which is so much like the clean sweep of the yard, only with the opposite effect.

Instead of sweeping leaves and sticks from the lawn in a lulling steady movement, writers sweep words onto the page in a dream state. The result of either effort is a thing of beauty.

Either activity renders a result. The important thing is to keep creating, "even if it's only a mess."

The Really Deep Stuff

Let's examine what may happen with amended soil when the manure has been mixed in really well.

I know a young man who was molested when he was five years old by a trusted male neighbor, his baby-sitter.

This is deep, any way it's viewed. Exacerbating the problem, it was not properly handled by the adults around him, his only source of protection at that tender age. Everyone did their utmost to "ignore the elephant in the living room" and brush off the effect of the experience on the young boy.

When I met him he was in his mid-twenties and had just experienced the crisis of a break-up with his girlfriend, a very material girl who appeared to value mainly his potential as a big earner and future provider, rather than his gentle soul and loving spirit.

This handsome, charming and very bright young man, Doug, was in despair because of his complete lack of boundaries with his girlfriend. He felt that she'd subsumed him with her sexuality, and then when he didn't "act right" and meet her expectations, they split up.

The crisis had brought him to a good place to get some perspective on the deep pile of manure (the obstacles and challenges from both past and present) where he was still standing.

He had two choices: he could continue to pack down the resentment and anger he felt, or he could mix them up with some sand (consciousness) and red clay (the basic material of daily life) to create a more solid but very fertile foundation.

This was his place from which to grow and come to full flower and fruition, as he is beginning to do now that he's taken the steps to go into some of the darker places and release some of the old demons.

I referred him to Colin Tipping's very powerful *Radical Forgiveness* workshop, which without using psychiatry helps people blast through the past, accept the lesson so they don't have to repeat it again, reframe it all as part of their invaluable life experience, and move forward as more mature, conscious adults.

What seemed like hell to him at the time of crisis was simply his wake-up call.

Did he really want to go through life as a lockstep drone,

simply as a money machine for this ambitious woman who saw him as a meal ticket, then found his weak spot and exploited it?

This was really his invitation to delve into his own soul journey, work through issues that would plague him for life if he kept them smothered, choking for air and the light of day as he had when he was molested.

How is it fair to some children when the manure is piled so thickly around them? They feel that they're responsible for their circumstances—in effect, that they caused the problem. They're not equipped with the tools to dig themselves free of it—nor do they have enough advocates to make sure they learn how to cultivate their little gardens successfully.

Imagine the vast numbers of children who are numbed, souls completely destroyed by emotional or physical violations, who spend the remainder of their lives trying to squelch and forget it with drugs, alcohol, sex, food, shopping, and workaholic behavior, the most socially-acceptable outlet of all.

They simply suffocate under piles of it, whatever it is, living lives of quiet, (or not so quiet) desperation as Thoreau described.

But Doug didn't want to suffocate—nor did he want to be subsumed into a codependent relationship, completely lacking boundaries, where a woman could manipulate him to her idea of a man—simply a good provider.

What a gigantic rip-off of men today—so many are suckered into that myth and never get to experience the wonder of their own soul growth after they willingly jump aboard as slaves on the financial treadmill—grinding away at jobs they hate simply because they've bought the society-sanctioned vision.

After a series of coaching discussions on my porch overlooking the giant magnolia in the back yard, Doug's perspective shifted from one of despair to one of hope.

I fully believe a great deal of that shift stemmed from his experience of the *Radical Forgiveness* workshop where he released the vitriol and resentment. When he released blame and was no longer burdened with the shame, he no longer resented the "unfairness" of life.

When you really think about it, how many people have really gotten a fair shake in life? We could all find a bone to pick with life if we try hard enough. I've even known more than one "poor little rich kid" who has wrecked cars and vandalized houses (or worse, cut himself) to get his money-machine parents' attention. When the price is large enough, the parents wake up and take notice. It's ridiculous!

After shifting his perspective, Doug was ready to take responsibility for what he'd created in his adult life. He put himself through graduate school and eventually emerged into the real world again.

"During my search for a job, I was confronted with several corporate jobs that paid well but were, well, corporate," he told me a couple years later. "Before talking with you, I would have taken the first one.

"Remembering our talks, I held out for months and was jobless. I even lived in my car for a few months (I think this may have been the happiest time in my life actually). Now I have the job of my dreams and EVERYONE I know from school tells me the same old story... 'My job sucks but I'm making good money.' They're still looking outside.

"You put me in touch with the part of myself that says, 'I know I'm better than what I've created unconsciously in the past.' To change the outside, I have to change the inside."

He got the message. Thankfully, he got it a lot younger than most people do, if at all.

The Platform
of Self-Examination

My sister, whom I love dearly and who has a very quirky sense of humor like the rest of our family, reminded me that toilets on some German trains have a little platform where the doo-doo drops so it may be carefully scrutinized before being flushed. As a very accomplished professor of nursing, she tends to view certain things rather clinically.

Benjamin Franklin assessed every interaction he'd had every day to see where he could improve his social skills. We too must be willing to examine ourselves and our motivations every day, often on a moment-to-moment basis.

These observations reveal what needs to be released. Then we can live harmoniously in the moment and stop torturing ourselves with bad memories and future fears, none of which exist right now.

Self-observation is a vital habit. On a physical level it may reveal some disease that we need to have checked immediately. On an emotional and spiritual level, our allowing ourselves to take a look may bring into focus the far deeper concerns that caused the physical disease in the first place.

If recognition of the problem is fifty percent of its solution, just by seeing it we're halfway to solving it. When recognized and analyzed, problems dissolve into manageable situations that we can handle one breath at a time.

Charles Fillmore, co-founder of the Unity School of Christianity with his wife Myrtle, said that if everyone engaged in self-examination daily and forgave everyone, including themselves, of whatever perceived infraction that needed forgiveness, then all illness would be healed and all poverty would disappear.

The Fillmores and so many other great metaphysicians profess, "Thoughts held in mind produce after their kind," so doesn't it make perfect sense that if our hearts and minds harbor negativity that negativity will manifest in some form around us?

For example, if we place energy and focus on what we don't want, such as extra weight or lack of a meaningful relationship, based on universal law we'll keep the weight and stay lonely because we're focusing on these things.

To reverse the situations in our lives, we need to focus on being healthy and happy and attracting the right person into our life now.

The same goes for our interactions with others, and especially with ourselves.

When we're unable to forgive, it's like drinking a small dose of poison every day and expecting the other person to die.

Let me state that again: *When we're unable to forgive, it's as though we're drinking a small dose of poison every day and expecting the other person to die.*

This is a ludicrous notion, and yet many people let their lives get sucked into the insanity of vengeance and revenge. It simply perpetuates more of the same.

Many people who have experienced the tragedy of having a loved one murdered expect their pain to end when the murderer is executed by the state. Unfortunately, most find that their hopes for relief are dashed. Their pain lives on.

A very dear and translucently beautiful woman, white of hair, tea-colored skin, with cataracts in her kindly eyes, is one of the pillars of Oakhurst Presbyterian Church and in fact was key in attracting the attention of TIME Magazine to what the church was accomplishing during "the most segregated hour of the week." Our very diverse congregation—white, black, gay, straight, ex-convicts, businesspeople, politicians, retired missionaries, young and old—belied the stereotype that churches had to be homogeneous to survive.

She, along with several others in the church, had lost a loved one to murder. In fact her only daughter was killed decades ago by the daughter's boyfriend.

Despite the horrible pain of this situation, not an ounce of vengeance exists in her soul.

"How can you live with that knowledge without feeling murder in your own heart?" I asked her.

"Patrice, forgiveness is the only way. The *only* way. If I carried that in my heart, I'd only be killing myself."

I believe she speaks the truth.

Attention, Please!

When I was fresh out of college, I was hired as a program administrator for a business education organization. I was twenty-one years old, bounding off the Frisbee™-throwing fields in cut-offs and halter tops—and even had to be coached on how to dress for an interview!

Suddenly I was now telling business consultants where to go—to their classrooms, that is.

The experience woke me up to the world in many ways. First of all, no one had ever told me that people could have so much fun and get paid for it—the consultants leading the classes.

On the whole they were extremely pleasant and bright. One of the consultants, a delightful, worldly Belgian in his thirties, recommended a book called *The Nature of Personal Reality* by Jane Roberts. Along with the dozens of other books I intended to read at any given time, I wrote it on a 3x5 card in tiny print and tucked it back in my wallet.

Possibly five years after I'd written that title on my intended books list, I was strolling through fabulous Brentano's Books at the Omni (long before it became the CNN Center) in downtown Atlanta for their going out of business sale. As I walked down the aisle a book fell off the shelf in front of me. Perhaps someone had knocked it from behind; perhaps it moved of its own volition.

Whatever, it was in my hands. *The Nature of Personal Reality.*

I bought the book and began reading—it was my first exposure to "channeled" material. Although I'd heard of séances and even used Ouija boards in childhood games, I had no idea that people actually wrote books that were dictated from the beyond—lapsing into their other selves, or allowing their physical bodies to be used by beings in the spirit world to convey important material.

Despite my good intentions, in my mid-twenties I was not ready for the message this book held. I wasn't able to pick it up again and finish it until I was 28 years old.

The essence of the book is this: we create our own reality.

How could this possibly be? This is a very tough pill to swallow for someone whose life is in the dumpster. At the time I was basically broke all the time, dating men I didn't really care about, and wasted on weekends after too much partying—only to face a supreme motivational deficit on Monday in dragging myself back to whatever job I was enduring at the time. In fact I flitted through eight different jobs within ten years. Boyfriends rolled through the same revolving door.

In *The Nature of Personal Reality*, something about Jane Roberts' (and Seth's) message clicked for me, eventually. I began to wonder if it might be true—that it really wasn't the entire world that was completely screwed up and out to get me; maybe it had something to do with me. I wasn't willing to acknowledge that I might have a hand in my own misery.

The supreme irony about my life at the time was that my upbringing had consisted of every privilege that an upper middle class family can provide. I'd excelled in schoolwork and had all the extracurriculars. I had even been the president of my high school student body, but yet I still didn't get it that I was responsible for what happened in my life—and refused to pay attention to the clues along the way.

That is until things began to reach crisis mode.

All this was because I'd not been raised to understand one of the very basic precepts of the Bible: As you think, so you shall be. Thoughts held in mind produce after their kind. People become what they think about. Thoughts are things.

My parents didn't understand the power of thought. They taught something quite the opposite: *"Sticks and stones will break my bones but names will never hurt me."*

Let's dissect this idea.

Sticks and stones (the material world) will break my bones (evidencing a certain kind of pain in the physical realm) but names (thoughts) will never hurt me.

On the contrary, psychologists have documented that emotional abuse (the power of the word) can have farther-reaching negative effects than actual physical abuse.

I was taught that it was okay to think something (even if they were vengeful, hateful thoughts) because thinking was not the same as doing. But that's only half the story. When we have murderous thoughts, the mind is poisoned with the residue of cause and effect. Only when we engage in the struggle to release that bile and venom, do we end up not poisoning ourselves.

Lack of forgiveness is a recipe for insanity!

This is why the Jews observe Yom Kippur, the Day of Repentance, which includes forgiveness of anyone with whom they are angry.

The whole notion that our projections of anger, vengeance and hatred are not hurtful if we don't take action on them is wrong. We are slowly destroying ourselves.

On the other hand, Mary-Alice and Richard JaFolla, co-authors of *The Quest* series through Unity Church, offer a different view of the phenomenon of "sticks and stones"...above the physical, beyond the emotional, they take the spiritual view.

"In truth, we have no enemies, no matter how others have treated us. There are two reasons for this: First of all, the other person, like you, is a spiritual being. He or she can act cruelly, but that person's spiritual nature is always intact. Just as the sun can be hidden behind monsoon rain clouds, a person's divinity can be hidden behind hideous acts. But one day the clouds will disperse and the sun will shine again. It always does.

"The second truth is that because we are spiritual beings, we cannot be harmed by the words, opinions or actions of another. We can be cut and bruised physically; we can be hurt on a human level by verbal abuse from another. But who we really are is untouched and can never be influenced by another person. Knowing who and what we really are frees us from the belief that the real essence of us has been injured. *Sticks and stones can break my bones but names can never define my spiritual nature.*"

Even if, at our spiritual essence, we cannot harm or be harmed by aggressive behavior because spirit remains unshaken, it is important for us to be aware that thoughts are things and they carry energy with them.

What kind of energy do your thoughts carry? If your thoughts are poisonous, who is getting sick?

Stuffing it Down Doesn't Work Either

How's this for a crazy-making scenario? Even if you're really talented, really creative, really dedicated and really, really good, odds are against your ever being quite good enough, because you've thrown your lot in with millions of people who believe that they must be appreciated by others in order to be good enough, or to be okay, or even to be real.

That search for external validation snags us every time, for two reasons. One: if we don't know and value ourselves as children of God who have the right to be here, no amount of anything will ever fill the spiritual void that we try to cram full of outside things or experiences. In *The Handbook to Higher Consciousness*, Ken Keyes, Jr., calls these Security, Sensation and Power addictions—based in our lower instincts.

Two: everyone caught in that trap is just as much a status seeker as we are; their attention and focus is directed on themselves, and it's hard to see beyond the glare of your own spotlight to the higher path beyond it.

It's somewhat of a Catch-22 when everyone is saying, "Look at me! Aren't I great?" and no one can tear their eyes from their own mirrors!

For more than thirty years in the film business, dear Fred caught himself up in that ego adrenaline, hanging onto the last car of the roller coaster as it cracked the whip around the track.

Slaving in the brutal hours—20-hour days; first call at 4am and not off the set until midnight. Lugging heavy equipment in the freezing rain or baking heat; stressing over the five million details on the director's or first assistant director's watch. Scratching and clawing to get his scripts read; once they were optioned, struggling to get the money he was owed.

Shafted time after time; getting his hopes up high only to be crushed, dashed, once again. Relentlessly beating his brains out on the concrete wall of commercial success; perpetually broke no matter how much he was getting paid on a project because of the lulls between paying gigs and the necessity of the financial catch-up when money was flowing. Or with cash in hand, spending it immediately on more equipment and then not knowing where the mortgage payment would come from next month.

Never enough sleep; always too much stress. Even when gainfully and steadily employed as in his last few years, the stress over details and his nattering not-enoughness never held at bay.

Always grinding away on the next project; the one that would surely be the one to validate his years of backbreaking work in the eyes of the public—the one that would *make him something*.

It is not a forgiving business.

Yet here's the real dichotomy. Throughout his life, as broke as he may have been at times, he was always prosperous in the true definition of that word, because he was always moving forward with hope, which is the Latin root of the word, *prosper*.

Prosperity is not a condition; it is a state of mind, and Fred lived it.

Even within that workaholic insanity that never truly validated his gentleness and kindness, his sensitivity and wonderful quirky eye on life, he prospered, always moving forward with hope. He simply was too sweet and kind for that brutal business that rewards so few of its budding stars, whether in front of the camera or behind it.

Although I don't dare to guess all of his soul issues, my guess is this: He never took the time to do the inner work and find forgiveness for himself. Thus he found the ideal business to invalidate himself for a lifetime.

Subconsciously, he knew what was happening to him, although consciously he was not aware of the cancer that was eating him up until it was too late. After returning from a documentary assignment in Afghanistan months before he died, he painted a very portentous artwork.

In acrylics he depicted a dark man with a long scythe—the moment he showed it to me I witnessed the Grim Reaper! Why, of all the images he captured in photos, would he choose to paint that one, unless he knew, deep down, that Death would be visiting soon enough?

Art reveals so much, flowing directly from our subconscious. Fred's Afghan version of the Grim Reaper revealed to me what he was unable to acknowledge to himself consciously—that he knew deep down he wasn't going to make it; that his date with Death was near.

The Truth Will Out

In one of my classes, Yogativity™, or Yoga to Tap Your Creativity, we do an hour of gentle yoga followed by an hour of meditation, journaling, dreamwork or art. Already in a deeply relaxed state from the yoga, the subconscious mind expresses more easily through these various creative forms.

A man in the class, Christopher (name is changed), was a professed atheist, scientist, researcher and rather linear thinker. He had recently been thrust into the very non-linear realm of joblessness after a lifelong career as a professor and researcher. Suddenly the world was topsy-turvy, and his best linear thinking could not really sort things out.

Now, instead of relying on a regular paycheck, he had to begin to rely on something inside, some innate spiritual gyroscope to maintain balance and equilibrium on the no-longer-glassy-smooth surface of life.

As he stated in the class, this entire notion of relying on some inner resource seemed crazy! Especially for one who believed that if you studied the right subjects (and excelled in them, as he always had) and if you earned the right degrees, that the world will be neat and orderly and predictable or at the very least manageable.

During the shift to a global economy, millions of people are being forced to rethink their situations as life becomes less predictable and manageable.

We live in a time that demands of us to learn flexibility, bending with the breeze, going with the flow. Adapt or be crushed, as with so many other times of rapid evolution and/or revolution on our planet.

During the Chinese communist revolution, such incredible upheavals occurred—the starvation, deprivation, extreme compromises, the strugglings, the debasement, torture and executions of the spiritual leaders and intellectual elite—such madness!

My own dear Chinese friend's father, a world-renowned scientist, was blinded in one eye during "the struggles" when intellectuals were jeered, chastised, and beaten in the streets until they publicly renounced and denounced the "old ways," and then they were carted off to work the rice paddies for re-education (i.e. brainwashing about the glories of communism and Chairman Mao).

But years later he and so many others were resurrected and lifted up in the scientific community. Chinese politicos now recognize these intellectuals as national treasures, leading the vast country into the forefront of change in the present. Ironically, many of these globally renowned scientists told their children who were educated in the U.S. not to come back to China in the '90s. At the time, the instruments to perform their experiments were not available. Now China is once again becoming a global power.

In such a time as we're experiencing today, a spiritual inner compass is essential.

This is exactly what was revealed through Christopher's very reluctant art.

He confessed that it was difficult for him to exercise his creative brain, having been so analytical during his lifetime of 55 years.

However, hearkening back to childhood he recalled his ramblings through the forest, becoming one with nature—a total right brain immersion, surrounded almost 360 degrees (not exactly like being underwater, but in a forest or in the desert it is certainly a three-dimensional sensory experience).

Beyond that lie the multiple dimensions of what we can't see or hear, but what we simply know. It is from this deep place that our creativity wells up, manifests and speaks.

The art assignment was simple enough. Class participants could draw a picture of the dream that had been inspired by the previous week's guided meditation, or else they could create an artwork showing the path of their life so far. Various milestones such as births or deaths, marriages, graduations or other achievements could be expressed as symbols.

Christopher drew a pudgy baby crawling along a wide path that split into several options, all quite open and smooth, leading up four different mountain peaks. At the top of each peak was a stylized eyeball with long lashes, the universal symbol of inner truth or insight. Eyes wide open.

The way he described it was that as a baby he had sought the truth and now he discovered that there were many truths.

I nodded and let it go, although the image stayed with me because I'd been thinking a lot about Christopher's inner turmoil as he lost his source of income and faced the scary demons of financial shipwreck, loss of face or even the possibility of losing his home.

A deeper sense of the art's meaning didn't bubble up as immediately as Fred's portrait of the Grim Reaper had struck me, but this artwork was shouting out something completely different from what Christopher described consciously in the class.

Although he'd described it as "many truths," in reality all the Truths looked exactly the same—this big, wide-open "Hairy Eyeball" as I jokingly described it. Rather, what he had depicted were the many paths that lead to the One Truth.

His art was expressing what he knew: He was on the path to the Truth within—well on the way toward the wonders of his inner life, simply through following the many paths of conscious awareness that would take him to his higher places—to the mountain peaks, where he would know the One Truth—that Being, the Christ spirit or God, is within all of us.

Even if we don't believe in God, that's irrelevant, because God believes in us. And how can we not believe in Being? We are its manifestation!

God, Universal Intelligence, the All-Seeing Eye, is within

us whether or not we are willing first to crawl, then toddle, then stand and walk or move along that path. The path is a lot smoother when we release the death-grip on the steering wheel and just let Divine Order be our guide.

Although it may appear daunting at first, with the peaks so high and our little baby-selves so pudgy and vulnerable, that is all an illusion. Aren't we told, "Ask and it shall be granted to you, that your joy may be full?"

The paths in his artwork were open, without an obstacle in sight. The grade wasn't even that steep. Even for a vulnerable little tyke, the grade was manageable.

Didn't Jesus choose to appear on earth as a vulnerable baby? Not in the form of a conquering hero, but as a poor child, a vulnerable newborn, showing his ultimate strength through his vulnerability, ready to lead others on his particular path to enlightenment. Follow me! Jesus said.

As we analyzed his artwork, it was truly a revelation to Christopher that the path he depicted was not what his life had been so far. He drew not a single milestone, like the births of his beloved children.

Rather, it was the path ahead—the inner journey, whether he chooses to acknowledge it consciously or not. Nowhere on this path did he depict dollar signs, mansions, fast cars, opulent living or any of its trappings—only the journey to the mountaintop, symbolic of higher insights.

It's true that we can see what's happening with others more easily than with ourselves. That old "forest for the trees" thing.

He did not recognize that the pudgy little vulnerable baby was himself, right then, as he embarked on this next great adventure in his life, unsure of which trail to take. The inner journey is challenging, but one that must be taken in order for spiritual growth.

95

Many paths, one Truth. The Truth is that we hold all the strength within to complete our particular purpose in this life. It is a fabulous awareness when we discover that all we need shines inside ourselves. Our job is to get it released!

How many of us keep it trapped inside by allowing ourselves to be subsumed in our own self-doubt, our own self-hatred and our self-thwarting mechanisms?

From birth we are trained and attuned, most of us, to live in a manner that continuously chips away at our confidence, unless we really work to reverse those self-defeating patterns. If we're not properly raised and bolstered along the way by voices of encouragement, the negative voices of the chatterbox and monkey mind will do their utmost to take us down. The key is learning to lift ourselves up!

A full eighty percent of our thoughts are negative, according to one study. So we must be continually weeding out those negative thoughts, sometimes moment-by-moment, breath-by-breath.

This may include letting go of acquaintances, friends or family who focus solely on the negative. It simply is not good science to immerse oneself in poison if one wants to emerge and grow strong, healthy and whole.

In one of the many forms of group therapy I've benefited from over the years, I recall my amazement over the "Father Figure" therapist's advice to one young woman in our codependency group: "You should have no contact with your mother at all, for at least one year. She's simply too toxic."

It astounded me that taking good care of yourself sometimes involves such extreme measures! Ultimately, the separation did strengthen the young woman's boundaries, and eventually she was able to heal her childhood issues with her mother and re-establish a loving connection.

That's what getting back to the garden is all about—the

power of personal choice. We all have urges to slip back into the muck, however we define it. Remember, there's plenty around to fertilize the soil.

More Nostalgia for the Mud

Life may get going so well for us that we have to create some chaos to disrupt the beautiful flow that's bubbling up.

And we have such a marvelous variety of options from which to choose! Partying to excess and getting sick is popular with the younger set. One friend fell into bed with someone who not only didn't respect her in the morning, he stole her favorite coffee mug on the way out.

Many choose to create some kind of financial shipwreck by spending way beyond their means. Some martyrs may send themselves into a state of overwhelm and snippiness by taking on too many activities or charitable ventures, becoming a "human doing" instead of a "human being." Insanity then springs from being out of balance.

Pick a fight with a close friend or spouse. Get distracted (i.e. go unconscious) and have a fender bender. Fall off a ladder and get injured. Overdo in any number of ways.

Do what we know we shouldn't simply because, even though we have hoped for the best, dreamed of the best and maybe even prayed for the best, when The Best comes we don't know if we're good enough for it. We simply haven't learned to expect the best and then (the most important step) accept the bounty. Expect it, then accept it. Simple, but not always easy.

Acceptance: Why is that simple concept so difficult for people to enjoy and experience? It really hearkens back to the "not good enough" feelings, the imposter syndrome—not feeling as though we've earned the right to accept the good that is pouring down all around us.

And why not? Those negative voices and the negative self-talk. Whose voice does it sound like? Your mother's or father's? A sibling's? A teacher's? Your parole officer's? Your own?

Get The Life You Love

For fifteen years I helped salespeople sharpen their skills as an instructor of Dale Carnegie® Sales Training. I was one of only a handful of female sales course instructors in the world, and for years I won awards for excellent instruction and leadership, as the plaques on my office wall attest.

Although I loved the course, the class members, the group leaders and everything about it, during that entire time I stuffed a folder full of ideas to create my own class. I didn't know where I'd teach it, but that didn't matter. As my roots grew deeper in helping others expand into more successful lives, I knew it would come to fruition some day. The working title on the folder jammed with ideas was *Whole Life Expressions of the Real You.*

Its objective was to help people evolve into their fullest, most joyful expression, and to have rich, full, balanced lives.

Two years after I taught sales for the last time, my hankering to get back in the classroom could no longer be stuffed down and I contacted Emory University's Center for Lifelong Learning, known for its great variety of high caliber enrichment classes open to the public. The director said my timing couldn't have been better—after an 18 month moratorium, they'd just begun to accept proposals for new classes.

I launched the class and taught it for several years with the title *The Art of Positive Change*, but discovered that although most people really don't want to change, they most definitely want to get the life they love. We changed the title to *Get the Life You Love* and enrollment increased immediately.

Everybody wants to get to heaven, but nobody wants to die. Everybody wants bliss, but few want to work at it.

This is an interesting comment on human nature and how much we fear change, when really change is the only thing we can count on in life!

Getting to Know You

At the beginning of each class we have self-introductions, which focus on the positive: What kind of animal we'd be; one thing we like about our lives right now; and why we joined the class.

One young mother, a puppy, said she needed to begin cultivating a life for herself because she'd been doing what others expected her to do her entire life.

One woman, an independent cat, stated that she was happily single. Based on the lives of her married friends the single status was looking rather attractive, but she wanted to discover her passion because she didn't want to miss out on life's magic.

One described herself as a hummingbird because she wanted to live like they do: Have great sex and travel a lot.

We laughed about how many times we'd all done the same things and expected different outcomes.

At a certain point some illusions began to melt away and people recognized, "Hey guess what, it's not the entire world that's at fault for not delivering what I want; it's my view of it!"

We all seek to experience some passion in life, some form of connection, some sense of giving back when much has been given us. A legacy, in a sense.

A recent experiment shows that giving back may be absolutely critical for life itself.

One reason for failure to thrive among orphaned babies is not so much that they aren't being touched and held. Rather, it is that they are bursting with so much love to give—but when there's no one to receive their love, their little hearts begin to contract and they eventually die.

In other words, it is the opposite of what the studies initially sought to prove—that children deprived of love do not thrive.

Instead, any of us deprived of the opportunity to share our love or express our passion—in short, to live in the image of the Creator by creating and sharing our gifts—will not thrive.

In class, we allot ourselves the time to think and write the answers to important questions. We observe what we would change about our lives right now if we could, and what are some of our gifts we can share with the world.

Some acknowledge that by thinking, writing and discussing the answers to these questions about our most important endeavor in this world, the shape of our life, they are better able to get a grip on what they want and what they have to give.

Have you ever thought that you may spend more time planning your vacation than charting the course of your life?

Dear Kitty

When I ask the class how many people keep journals, invariably just one or two hands go up. I see journals as an important tool in charting first the direction that one wants to take, and secondly, a means of keeping a finger on the pulse: are you adhering to that direction? What trials and tribulations have you been able to overcome on your own hero's journey?

Comments and complaints fly around the room.

"I've always thought that unless I wrote the perfect journal, it wouldn't be worth it."

"I have a stack of pretty little journal books that I've never been able to bring myself to crack."

"When I write in my journal I'm afraid someone will read it later and think I'm really stupid."

"For me, I find it easier not to admit to myself what's really happening in my life cause I just get so worked up I just want to shout What the F***!"

"Yeah, sometimes I get so riled when I'm writing that I have to stay up for hours just to get it all out!"

Of course the alternative is going to bed mad, and we've all heard the wisdom against going to bed mad, even if it's only with yourself.

Cheap Shrink

A journal is the most marvelous cheap psychiatrist I've found, and it gives me a chance to sort through my feelings and reach some place of hope that tomorrow is another day. (Thank you, Scarlett O'Hara!)

However, many women in my class vehemently insisted that a journal must be some work of art in order to have any validity whatsoever. This amazed me! To me, this is an extraordinary degree of self-hatred and denigration, when we can't even express our most private thoughts without censuring ourselves.

Why not use it as a dumping ground? The whole objective is to learn how to accept ourselves; how to be gentle with ourselves; how to love ourselves. Eventually the love we're able to feel for ourselves will emanate outward, and every tiny ounce of love makes the world a better place.

A journal can be a handy companion along the way as we begin to steadily shift our perceptions and our consciousness, ever so slightly, day by day.

The shifts occur partially through releasing the old, angry, stagnant thoughts, the negativity into which we pour fear-filled energy, which ends up attracting more negative outcomes.

And that's not what we want! What better way to witness that than through a reflection of our soul-journey, the journal. The book of the day (*le jour*, in French) accompanies us on our journey—in fact it is meant to be our companion on the path.

As with everything, moderation is advised. A recent study by James Pennebaker, a great advocate of journaling, indicates that endless obsessing over the same topic can add to depression. So just write it down and release it, and move on.

A journal is like writing a letter to your best friend—and part of the purpose of the class is to get to know yourself as the best friend you'll ever have. Dear Diary. Dear Kitty, as Anne Frank called hers. Such a powerful and sensitive document,

The Diary of Anne Frank revealed one of history's beautiful souls.

Embarking upon this lifelong path, happily girded with a journal, lessens the need to arm oneself with bandolier and pith helmet (or our far-more-obnoxious contemporary versions of these—handguns and Humvees).

When we learn how to hold the internal demons at bay with a well-honed pen stroke, we have a much lesser need to project our fears outward, on THEM—those people out there.

Embarking on a journey with a journal is beginning the adventure of a lifetime. If the strict "journal" doesn't work for you, use the blank book as a doodle pad, for scrapbooking, creating a document of your life and observing your own hero's journey. It's amazing to look back and see how far you've come.

Nattering Nabobs of Negativism

One young woman in class had a negative inner voice, which sounded, she said, chillingly like her father's. They were raised in a middle class home, but her parents wanted her to appreciate what they had instead of always grasping for more, and so they conveyed the impression that there might be fewer presents that Christmas because of a lack of money. This thought process spiraled in her young mind into an overriding fear that they may lose everything.

Her limiting beliefs steered her away from her love of English, writing and speech to a completely practical field—accounting—in which she's dreadfully unhappy.

Everyone in that particular class had chosen a practical employment instead of following their heart, and in a lot of cases it was making them sick. One secretary awoke with a whole novel ready to "write itself" but she didn't capture the details so it slipped away. A nurse. An information systems specialist.

In my own case my father's cautionary words ring in my mind: "English is a fine avocation, honey, but how are you going to earn a living?"

This guided me into my early choice of professions—sales, always selling ideas, usually for other people. But now, thankfully, after years of promoting ideas for others with my PR consulting firm, I am directed toward a higher purpose, that of helping people progress to their highest and best lives.

We're so trained to put aside what we love that the accountant who was ingrained with "poverty thinking" barely dares to look at the field of speech therapy (something she loves) as an employment option, even though speech therapists certainly earn a living too.

It's time to banish these limiting, negative voices from our heads. They simply are not real! They're what we choose in order to justify and perpetuate our lifetime ruts.

It's time to sift through the dreck that keeps drawing us back to our ruts because it's the only place familiar—and therefore comfortable to us.

But it's not as though we need to chuck everything and suddenly make a radical shift—in fact that's not necessarily advisable.

Simply pay attention to the voice of the observer. Recognize that the only moment is the present moment. Right now we have the power to shape our series of moments into a joyful existence, beyond the ephemeral realms of pain and pleasure. Within each moment, we make the choice.

As one very accomplished woman, a successful accountant, wife and mother, stated at the end of the course,

"I've been working on myself for years and always thought I could snap my fingers and the desired change would result. I've learned that I need to set my sights higher when making a goal to change, and be very specific, and do the work. The work includes the blame stage and taking responsibility."

With each breath, we choose whether to focus on the moment or let ourselves be distracted by woes that may never happen.

At one point in my life when I was gripped by fear of crashing and burning in my new venture, I posted this pithy poem by another famous transcendentalist, Ralph Waldo Emerson, next to my bed so it was the first thing I saw every morning:

> *Some of your hurts you have cured,*
> *And the sharpest you still have survived,*
> *But what torments of grief you've endured*
> *From evils which never arrived.*

He certainly knew how to put things into perspective!

The negative outcomes we imagine usually stem from fear and deservability issues. Shift the picture of the outcome to positive and see what unfolds!

An artist in my class had let her art lie fallow after a painful breakup. As though to punish herself, this extremely talented woman had somehow let beauty lapse from her living situation and surroundings. To make things even more challenging, she earned her living in a high-stress law office as a paralegal in a job she really didn't like. Life was not easy street.

She'd shoved all of her photography and art materials into the back of a closet during her time in the emotional wasteland. One day in class she mentioned that she'd bought a basket of flowers to hang outside her window. This simple gesture signaled a rebirth of being loving to herself and nurturing her creative instincts.

A few years later, now honoring the importance of balance and expression in her life, she supports herself with work at the law firm, and she's launched an outstanding career as an artist. She shows her extremely powerful art at private galleries—her works are selling and winning awards!

We don't have to thwart ourselves by insisting on being the best right from the start, or making a career of it. The important thing is to pick up what you love and start incorporating it into your schedule. Who knows what could blossom—perhaps your bliss.

My parents named me after Patrice Munsel, the opera singer. I do love singing, and also opera. One of my childhood fantasies was to become an opera singer. Although I know now I don't have the voice or the training to do so, that doesn't prohibit me from singing in choral groups that I love, nor does it prohibit me from enjoying opera.

Why deprive ourselves of the activities we love, simply because we don't excel in them?

How do we grow into excellence, anyway? Not by watching it on TV. By doing it. Set a date to begin on your calendar—do it now!

Beware the Pile

We have so many ways to short-circuit our bounty as it begins to roll in: Poor sleeping habits can disrupt our customary rhythm of life; we start slacking off on exercise and our energy level drops; we eat or drink too much of the wrong things; we grant ourselves no time to get back in touch with us.

We deny ourselves time and space to be creative. Disorganization and the inability to find anything whittles away our time and energy. The needs of others, or the bills to be paid, or the cleaning, cooking and carpooling begin to take precedence over the lifeline of our own creative outlets.

It's time to honor our creativity! Whether woodworking or wand-waving, there is always some magic found in the act of creation. And as the "spittin' image" of the Creator, that's what we're here on earth to do.

Remember, "When Mama's happy, everybody's happy." Keep that in mind when planning your day and week. Try to maintain a balance between your needs and everyone else's. Schedule time for yourself to enjoy, and honor that time.

Once we create time and space—giving ourselves a little place in which to be creative, whether it's setting up an easel next to the window with good light, or rearranging the furniture to accommodate a laptop and some notebooks, or even getting "a room of one's own," we must capture our ideas.

A Spanish proverb states, "The shortest pencil is better than the longest memory." We demonstrate that we value our ideas by writing them down or recording them.

Respect Yourself

Years ago I received an unsolicited business card from a literary agent and thought, "Surely there must be some mistake!"

I never contacted that person. It was as though I didn't want to be a member of a club that would invite me. One can only guess how he found my name, but my self-esteem and self-love weren't equal to the challenge of replying to his query, even though "being a writer" had been a lifelong goal of mine.

As I look back on that episode, I think how pathetic was that! But my roots of self-esteem weren't firmly established yet and I wasn't ready to blossom to the next level. I couldn't force the bloom.

Look at movie stars and music moguls who crash and burn on drugs or inappropriate behavior when they hit the upper limit of what they believe they deserve. Where's the self-love there?

On the surface, we may look like we have it all. Underneath the façade we may be quivering and shivering with fears that if anyone really knew who we were, they'd run screaming in the opposite direction.

Usually the people who feel this way about themselves conduct rather decent lives. In fact, out of paranoia that they'll be "found out," they may be pillars of the community in their quietly desperate way. Imagine how much sweeter their lives would be with self-love. We all deserve to live in glory.

Look at the messages in country music—a lot of busted up relationships and go-nowhere situations. People suck up those negative messages and choose to continue to wallow in their misery. Those pitiful lyrics about jail, broke-down trucks, busted lives and runaway brides are enough to make you want to go out and get smashed!

They hearken back to "the beautiful sorrow" stemming from Celtic lore—those baleful Irish who love to live and relive their sad heritage through heartrending plays and poetry and song. Don't get me wrong; the Celtic background is my own. And I love their stories and wailing weeping hearts, but only to a certain point!

If sorrow is what we concentrate on, that's where our paths will lead.

Beware of that big pile of manure ready at the back edge of the garden. Use it to amend the soil, but while you're at it, don't jump back into it. When I'm upset or venting about something to my father, he often jokes, "You stepped in what?"

What is Fear, Really?

Bounty so often appears in the form of the beautiful spirits I meet in the classes. One delightful woman, Karen (name is changed), was a single parent and successful doctor who loved her profession completely, but had issues regarding other aspects of her life.

We were discussing the topic of fear, and what fear really is. Serendipitously, in stumbling over my own explanation of fear, I probably imparted a bigger lesson than if I'd glided through it perfectly.

By mistake I reversed the explanation of fear with what to do about it. I laughed with them that in the past I might have feared their scorn or ridicule, but now I didn't mind in the least and simply righted my course in the turbulence and kept on paddling.

This is the acronym I learned from a friend in Al Anon (which is the organization for friends or family members of alcoholics; its purpose is to offer experience, strength and hope).

FEAR is simply . . .

False
Evidence
Appearing
Real

Although love is real, fear is an illusion, something we make up to prohibit ourselves from living happily and productively in the moment.

A couple of acronymic alternatives spell out some choices in dealing with fear.

We can . . .

Flee
Everything
And
Retire

Or we can . . .

Face
Everything
And
Recover, Regroup, Rise.

Karen stated her great wake-up call.

"My whole life was fear. I found that it began to constrict me into a box that became narrower and smaller until it was all squeezed down into a pinhole of *the one possible negative outcome.*"

And yet she decided to take the second alternative. During her 48th year, after watching several siblings fly their own planes and sail their own boats on long ocean junkets she grew tired of letting her world be circumscribed by her fear-fulness.

Time to truly begin living—she dared herself to plunge into life in a bold new way. In a contract with a pair of friends, they pledged to conduct their lives as though they'd been told they had only one year left to live. The results were incredible.

She began actively taking on the areas that formerly consumed her with dread. Her fear of the water led her to learn kayaking—and to use the paddle to roll herself success-fully when the craft flipped upside-down. Righting oneself in turbulent waters is a most necessary survival skill!

Next, Karen took on surfing—in California waves! Even though they were nothing like the giant breakers in *Riding Giants* or *Step Into Liquid*, she was able to step onto the board, pull herself up and catch the wave! What a victory for a woman in midlife, who had spent years in a self-created tunnel envisioning certain disaster.

"I was able to deal with the water turbulence seated, and then I was able to deal with turbulence standing," she said modestly. "I was able to envision it all as energy—the moun-tain whitewater as energy and the breakers rolling toward me. And then I was able to capture that energy and use it to my advantage." What a rush!

It's a process of letting go of the trapeze that's in your hands, flinging yourself out over the void and catching another big bright trapeze that swings your way.

Granted, it's much easier to let go of that illusory trapeze when we don't have to do it on our own. When it's wrenched out of our hands in downsizing, termination, plant closing, or when other external forces make us move along.

One friend frames it this way: Losing a job or experi-encing other turbulence in life gives people the opportunity to go new places, meet new people and do new things.

The Relationship Conundrum

Most of the people in my classes are single women—always looking to fix themselves—so, naturally, we get onto the topic of men, and whether one exists out there for them.

A very lovely, sweet and attractive nurse said she just didn't know whether a relationship would ever happen for her. I suggested she open her eyes and look around. Couples are everywhere; it's all a matter of what people are willing to compromise in order to be in a partnership. Are we willing to sacrifice our freedom? Our control issues? Our vulnerability? Our peace of mind? The myth that one person can be every-thing, like the love songs tell us? Always having everything our own way?

It's not about looks. It's about personal choices, like every-thing in life.

I shared the story of my cousin Deana, one of my "sheroes" who has been willing to pursue her vision throughout her lifetime.

As a young woman in her early thirties, divorced with three little children, she decided to do something radical to escape the bleak New Jersey winters: She applied to teach English in Jamaica. She and the kids trekked down there and lived a totally different life for a dynamic year.

Later, living in Boulder and still teaching, she set her sights on creating a stained glass art business. In order to support her children, she worked as a commercial cleaner at night and launched the glass business during the day. Eventually she married the co-creator of the stunning glass and metal art pieces they produce, a lovely man with a braid all the way down his back, sixteen years younger than she is.

112

Chuck Young and Deana Blanchard
bask in the glow of Selena Glass and Metal in Burnsville, NC.
www.selenaglassandmetal.com

Now they're living in paradise—an artist's colony in Burnsville, western North Carolina, near Asheville. They are beautifully compatible.

I mentioned in class that at that very moment I could have on my arm a delightful, brilliant, kind and loving man, who happened to be the best dancer I'd ever known, IF I were willing to pay for everything.

By the time I learned about his financial situation I'd "been there and done that" enough times in my life to know that an insolvent man is simply a deal breaker for me. However, if I really wanted this man, he'd be there. Someone chimed in, "And no one but you two would know who's paying." Yup. Just he and I would know our little secret.

Later, the nurse revealed why she just didn't know whether love could ever happen for her—a very strained relationship with her father, "a nasty old alcoholic" as she described him.

However as class continued over the weeks, her perspective on him began slowly to shift. One weekend she took the initiative and drove 400 miles on a Sunday just to have lunch with him and his wife. She'd planned it so she wouldn't have much time with him; the mere thought of spending more than fifteen minutes alone with him made her flesh crawl.

Divinity had a hand in things though, and she forgot about the change in time zones between Georgia and Alabama. When she arrived, his wife was still at church, so she and her father had a full hour and a half alone together. Looking around their sparsely furnished home she noticed that the sole decorative items were photos of herself and her sister throughout the years.

Suddenly she recognized an unconditional love from him that she believed had never existed.

On a soul level, she finally began to see herself as acceptable, as lovable—as someone who deserved a relationship and deserved to be happy! While she expressed this miracle of self-acceptance, my entire body resonated with chills. After years of hard, stony separation, she began to realize that neither her father's humanity nor her own vulnerability would annihilate her.

"Seeing the way his wife loved him helped me see him with a whole new set of eyes," she said.

Those new eyes also permitted her to see herself as worthy of love too. Within a matter of a year after that she was in a deeply committed relationship.

The Easy Subterfuge

There are reciprocal relationships where both partners bloom and flourish, and there are codependent relationships. Entering into a relationship in a totally needy state is a set-up for codependency, which is another reason why it's so important to know yourself.

The truly perfect self-sabotage is a bad relationship. In a very sick codependent relationship, we can direct all of our energy into bitching at our partner, or, even more juicy, bitching *about* our partner and letting the sympathy roll in from our loyal troop of friends, which of course solves nothing and entrenches us deeper into martyrdom.

Let's be honest. How many times have you siphoned your time and energy into some go-nowhere relationship, draining you of the life force necessary to conduct your own creative life?

No excuses. If the partner is lame (and hobbling you in the process), it's obvious.

You know the type. The ones who are never quite on the same level as you, emotionally or spiritually, and so you have to drag them kicking and screaming to a certain point. They may be a chronic liar or a cheat. They may be a slacker. The issue may be something health-related like quitting cigarettes or cutting back on the alcohol, or something as damaging as an addiction to Internet pornography.

If you're involved with someone like this, the questions loom: What for? What's in it for you? What dubious rewards are you receiving from carrying this load?

Does the mantle of the martyr sit well on your shoulders?

It's easy to wallow in the sympathy of friends as you spill out the never-ending tale of woe about ole what's-their-name, but don't you know your cronies are getting tired of hearing the same *schtuff*, different day. Even if they seem to sympathize, or empathize, on the other end of that phone line their eyes are rolling back in their heads as they wonder, "If he's such a jerk, why doesn't she get rid of him? If he hates his life so much, why doesn't he change it?"

Believe me, there are worse things in life than being alone—and sometimes the enforced solitude is the only way we permit ourselves to get to know the best friend we'll ever have—that would be our own selves!

One Year's Celibacy

I was personally challenged to stop medicating with relationships for a year by one former longtime boyfriend. He also happened to be my former therapist. Obviously I've earned the right to expound on all these self-defeating behaviors because I've lived them myself!

Spring pansies and snapdragons lift the heart.

It sounded like a death sentence. As we parted ways he told me, "You need to be celibate for a year; you need to learn to be on your own."

I decided to meet the challenge. It was one of the most painful, and ultimately one of the most rewarding experiences I've ever had. I found that through taking the path that didn't seem so easy, I learned to be by myself; to quench my thirsty, lonely soul with the flowers in my garden or with the wet snuffle of the neighbor dog's nose in my face; to sing myself into solace as a mother would soothe her crying baby with gentle songs; to force myself to take my camera and do the shooting assignments for photography class by myself; to sit alone at my table, reading magazines endlessly over meals and almost catching up on my stack (magazine-a-holics recognize this as quite a feat); to host special dinners on the porch and not feel as though I weren't whole because I didn't have a date of my own.

All of these emotional stretches were opportunities for true inner strength to blossom. I learned to travel by myself—and drove to visit friends or relatives whom I'd previously only visited as half of a couple. Of course they welcomed me just the same.

Perhaps the biggest hurdle of all was spending numerous weekends alone in the mountains, where I knew no one. In town where I live alone and work on my own, I have a solid social life with plenty of friends and group activities.

My solitary ventures to Sapphire Valley and Bald Rock, the power spot at the pristine, silent mountain lake served me with salvation.

For seven years I'd bitched about my man and his many shortcomings, and finally I put the focus on me. Amazing how much less I had to bitch about!

And what an incredible blessing that was! I was so

depressed I was barely able to put one foot in front of the other as I trudged around the glistening, sparkling, divinely deserted lake. But the solitude and the journey within healed me. From that long trek through the Void, creativity began tumbling out.

How does anyone get back to the rich fullness of life from some blasted wasteland in only a handful of years? I have to remind myself of Nature's gestational cycles, and that a baby is born after only nine months in the womb.

First, I treated myself very gently. One false move and I might crumble, or so I believed.

My heart was so broken. Finally I'd gotten the message that only I could heal it this time. No more grabbing for externals like the next new man, or the next new thing to afford me some miraculous diversion or conversion.

My own lyrics to the tune of "This is my Father's World"—the old Methodist hymn—became my Balm of Gilead.

It was, and is, a love song to myself, and to my valiant little heart, shattered as everyone's heart is over and over in life. That is, until we learn that in the present moment nothing can harm us; it is all grasping memories from the past or fearful worries of the future that cause the pain. But my song helped me get through it.

The effects of this powerful little ditty on my heart were an amazing experience. My heart eventually began to pop out again, like a tiny chipmunk peering from its hidey-hole when the feline danger has slunk past. After having been stomped flat, truly crushed, it did begin plumping itself back out, and beating steadily once again. What a resilient muscle the heart is!

My heart filled with hope, just as the art on my office wall attests: Hearts Filled With Hope. Never give up.

How do you get back there when you're crushed—

My Little Heart Song

I love my little heart; I make room for it to grow...
When it peeps out, I want to shout, 'My heart, I love
*   you so!'*
My little purple heart—it expands as it grows
*   whole—*
And all God's love flowing from above fills up my
*   hopeful soul!*

Heart filled with hope. Color it in!
Beautiful heart art by Claire Vohman.
Thanks, Claire de Lune! www.ClaireWasHere.com

stomped flat? First, a nap. Especially if sleep was elusive the previous night. Or a deep meditation to release and recharge.

Sleep, healing sleep. Ask God to relieve the pain. "Take it off my heart!" is the statement I've heard my choir conductor use, and that says it all. "Take it off my heart, please God! I don't want my heart to close in fear, so take this burden, please!"

From that time alone sprang a new person, one who recognized that being in a relationship was not critical for my life; not mandatory for my happiness. Although I would prefer to have a partner, the idea is no longer an addiction for me.

I discovered that I was quite capable of cultivating happiness within myself—that I was my best resource.

Considering my previous mindset that only the externals would fill the void, and that I must have a man on my arm to feel complete, this was a huge breakthrough. As it turned out, the void was filled by God within.

The Lessons of Rocks

Rocks are a key element of consciousness in any garden. They serve as power centers, holders of the forces from deep within earth's core. Rocks not only hold energy, they also symbolize it. In the Japanese garden, stones and boulders are used to connote miniature mountain peaks and the hills where hope resides.

"I will lift up my eyes to the hills, where I find hope."

Even more than their energetic properties, the beauty of rocks reminds me of their endurance in the face of the onslaught of elements—their hardiness, and in a sense, their heartiness.

Elements like fear, doubt and worry may take eons to wear away the rock that is our foundation, our innermost self. Or they may never wear it down at all.

Perhaps that's why Fred always carried rocks in his pockets—touchstones, reminders of the "rational radiance of stone" as expressed so beautifully by Nobel Laureate poet Derek Walcott.

Imagine the endurance of these crystallized formations, these stones—their mystery and magic; the secrets that they've witnessed through the centuries, worn just by fractions as they washed down the eons through turbulent times.

Ancient Sanskrit says, *"God sleeps in the minerals; awakens in the plants; walks in the animals; and thinks in you."*

Stones focus us and remind us all that we are the stronger stuff of stone, as well as the easeful grace of plants, the jungle awareness of animals and the spiritual connection to God—all comprising a graceful and joyous human life.

Have you ever seen a little flower peeking through a crack in a rock—the flower that shattered the stone? It demonstrates the great secret of life: vulnerability and strength at the same time.

Shattered by the vulnerable flower's force, the boulder is broken into smaller rocks, eventually dissolving to sand.

The great healer and psychic Edgar Cayce often recommended that the ill travel to Virginia Beach with its strong energetic properties, and bury themselves in the sand as part of their cure. He prescribed coming back to the elements for a healing on the elemental level. One man who had "incurable" parasites and had given up all hope, healed himself by lying on the earth every day.

Fairy's Cross

"Staurolite Dresch," aka The Fred, introduced me to Staurolites, the state mineral of Georgia. These magical dark crystals are only found in certain rare places; a steep bank near his land in Mineral Bluff, up near Blue Ridge, Georgia, is one of them.

Numerous times we walked at a ninety-degree angle, bent over the surface dirt, our hawk eyes seeking the telltale gleam of one of the dark crystal's facets lying in the wash. Fred demonstrated the ideal posture—lying on our bellies on the crusty clay incline for the best vantage point to scratch with twigs at every square inch of dirt. Seeking out the yield just after a heavy rainfall before others on the quest were drawn to the treasure bluff, we snatched our prizes freshly revealed by the rains.

This enriched my soul as I stretched supine on the steep gravel incline and appreciated the colors and glints and false starts that the earth revealed only when she was ready, accompanied by the steady scratch, scratch of a twig and the focus of the seeker.

Usually only shards appeared. They came as tiny pinpricks of the dark crystal, or little shafts, or fragments of an angle. When a staurolite evolves into its perfection it may become a square cross, like a Roman icon, or a St. Andrew's cross in the form of an X.

Crosses or X's are rare finds and evoke great excitement. Fred would get so jazzed over specimens that he'd pop them into his mouth and suck the Georgia clay from them to reveal their angles and form. His irrepressible enthusiasm over these mineral crystals was yet another of his endearing quirks, even though I viewed his clay-sucking technique with a somewhat morbid fascination. Although I challenged him on a number of issues, I never questioned that.

The quest for a staurolite is usually about uncovering the perfect talisman. On this particular quest, which was a full solitary day in nature as part of yoga teacher training, I sought a symbol of my own steady evolution on the yogic path. I wanted a star!

By the time I'd been scratching away at the bank for four hours—from first mountain sunlight until 11am, only shards or tiny specimens had rendered themselves forth for collection. I was becoming slightly discouraged. Plus, I'd just about run out of unexamined earth on that staurolite vein.

So I began to sing.

"Oh Star!" The lilting soprano line from this Robert Frost poem set to music in *Frostiana* is a clarion call to the highest and best. It reminds us of the importance of staying focused on uplifting thoughts and not allowing ourselves to be swept down the gully with the heedless crowds of mindless followers.

Within moments after I sang out to the star, what appeared but the best staurolite I've ever found—a five-pointed star shape. Apparently, the universe was encouraging me with its corroboration.

And what copious gratitude I felt over this simple find!

Silly, because what is a staurolite, really, but an organization of mineral crystals into an interesting shape. It certainly doesn't hold much monetary value—besides, who would even think of selling their magic rocks?

But to me, this serendipitous find flooded me with a simple joy. To me it was a signal that for my journey on the path of yoga, all systems were go!

With a happy heart, a full Zip-loc of shards and a plastic

film can jammed with the prime specimens, I returned home later that evening with my prize, the staurolite Star.

The shards—one might think they were completely worthless—but really they're fairy dust, the prismatic fragments of Fairy's Cross. They're to be sprinkled throughout the garden at the earliest opportunity, because where fairy dust is scattered, fairies love to gather and dance unseen by the skeptic's eye.

In the myth of Jason's quest for the Golden Fleece, one labor he had to accomplish to win the fleece was to sow a field with dragon's teeth, in effect, sowing the seeds that would grow into his own tormentors, his own demons. The dragon's teeth then sprang up into fierce soldiers who had to be conquered. Taking the magical advice of Medea, Jason threw a rock into the center of the warriors and instead of coming after him, they turned upon themselves and killed each other to the very last one.

On the other hand, a good sprinkling of staurolite shards will tempt the fairies and devas to tiptoe forth; all will enjoy a good twinkling romp, and magic will pop out near every boulder, every perfectly placed stone—fairy perches, deva altars, and all the garden places of rest, rejuvenation and eternal repair.

Like Jason, the hero of his own story, at times I put far too much effort into cultivating my demons. Then I remember that I can cultivate my devas as well.

Sleeping Garden

At night the garden sleeps, although animals may stealthily skulk through on a hunt for tasty morsels.

Many flowers like Four O'Clocks and Morning Glories close up shop for the night. Even the fragrant mimosa tree folds its delicate lime green fronds and slips into the dream consciousness of a plant. Lovely life rhythm thrums as the qi (pronounced chee) or life force, moves throughout its branches and leaves. Mimosa musk perfumes the air; it intoxicates.

The depth of rest is so critically important—key to the rhythm of life. Activity, then relaxation, rejuvenation and repair. How some of us seem to forget that important down time, often much to our regret when our driven habits catch up to us and slap us in the face!

Nature demands rest. If we were looking at an EKG or an EEG that zoomed straight out in one direction, it could only mean one thing—that the person was already dead. Therefore it's unnatural to push push push all the time and think that your body should perform like a machine. Even machines need regular maintenance and down time in order to run well.

HALT!

Shedding stress. Living in the moment instead of chafing to get there. "There" never becomes "here," so striving to get there is the perfect setup for failure. One way to stay connected with the here and now is continually assessing how you feel in the moment. Try the classic formula espoused by 12-step programs: HALT!

Are you Hungry? Angry? Lonely? Tired?

Several times a day, ask your body and check in with your emotions to determine what you need. Keep your finger on the pulse, and respond as graciously and generously to your own body's needs as you would respond to a helpless baby, your own precious child. That's all it is, really—your own precious self, calling out to your thinking mind, "Take care of me!"

Are you Hungry? Hear your body call, "Feed me!" If you're not a compulsive eater, it's best to respond in moderation to what your body needs, eating several small meals a day. If you use food to stuff down emotions, pay attention to your feelings!

Are you Angry? Let the anger flow through and release it. Don't store it in your guts only to have them ripped out later in surgery, as the pain that was never released corrupts the sweetness there.

Far too many people suffer from the delusion that anger is BAD and shouldn't be expressed, or even felt.

Wrong! No emotion is bad, it simply is. Just as we have to acknowledge that the water flowing in a creek through the garden sometimes needs to be channeled, we must accept anger for what it is—pure energy—and channel it through our bodies and out again—not store it up in some ancient locker full of insults, indignities, resentment over lack of appreciation and all sorts of other dank and squirmy feelings that will eventually wreak their twisted havoc on us.

All emotions can be fleeting. As various manifestations of energy, they exist to be observed, felt, perhaps evoking a raised eyebrow (yes, even the darkest emotions!) and released—always, just as we allow water to flow through our fingers. In fact, it's impossible to prevent water from slipping through our hands that way.

Whatever becomes stagnant or blocked may develop into a breeding ground for all sorts of pestilence—mosquitoes, disease, pollution, murk, mayhem. So just….let….it….go.

On to the L in HALT. What's your solution for loneliness?

Right off, so many of us tend to reach for some addictive crutch. But where has that gotten us up until now? Seriously consider those consequences. Are they worth it?

If so, go for it. Everyone's lowest point is personal. And how! That is, you may need to sink lower before you're ready to rise. There's something to be said for finding your nadir and deciding that you never, ever want to go there again. It's a powerful motivator, being in the depths.

When you're truly ready to take care of yourself and you're feeling Lonely, reach for a friend. Make outreach calls over the phone. Expressing feelings about a situation often makes it feel far less dire. Our friend serves as a mirror, reflecting the situation back to us and lighting it up in the process.

One coaching client had slipped into a dark place of deep depression. She was fooling around with sleeping pills to shut out the agony of being unemployed. Mired in debt, she was depending on her mother, who was also enduring hard times financially and could no longer bail her out with a loan.

Forcing Ellen (name is changed) to step up to her own reality was part of the solution. By being cut off from the many-strings-attached family money, Ellen began to recreate her life. From this she began experiencing renewed self-esteem.

As dark as everything appeared at the time, for her it was simply a life lesson in learning to trust herself—and her Higher Power—to lead her through this perilous time. What appear to be terrifying circumstances of change are often

God's way of nudging us out of the nest so we'll learn to fly on our own.

One aspect of Ellen that I truly admired is that she'd already grasped the secret of universal happiness—the joy of serving others. When she was lonely or feeling really down on herself, she drove over to Open Door Community on Ponce de Leon in Atlanta, an urban ministry for the homeless and imprisoned. There she served soup or made sandwiches. In mingling with the residents, volunteers and people who lived, literally, in the yard, she felt a spiritual connection that lifted her up.

Here she experienced the living awareness that all we really need is our daily bread, and the faith that it will be provided today.

Alternatively, if she felt used up, tapped out, worthless and no good to anyone, she would honor her spirit by volunteering at a hospice, sitting in the rooms of those closest to God (other than newborns and saints)—those shedding their earthly load. People in their transitional time.

The body and spirit become boundary-less, and the essence of spirit penetrates the entire environment. In that holy hush, Ellen was able to commune with her own truth.

Two years after this dark night of the soul, Ellen and I reconnected and she had come out stronger on the other side. She is director of business development for a non-profit organization, and is contemplating starting her own business to help non-profits.

"It helps me to remember how far I've come in my journey," she said. "It's amazing how self-confident I am now, compared to how insecure I was at that time in my life. However, I know that I am self-confident now BECAUSE of the lessons I learned at that insecure time of my life."

What if volunteering in a soup kitchen or hospice is not

your cup of tea? What if you're simply lonely and need some friendly faces? That is, more than just the friendly faces of pansies blooming and bobbing in your garden?

A good place for the soul is any number of 12-step meetings like Al-Anon, Codependents Anonymous, Debtors Anonymous (for people who financially self-sabotage), all of which are available at almost any hour in various locations throughout a metropolitan area. They can be found through the Internet and in the phone book, usually. If you have a problem, you can usually find its "Anonymous" solution out there, however odd it may seem.

What can be expected upon entering these often tacky but always compassionate rooms?

Friendly people, ready to render service. Struggling souls who know that if they could rise up from the dark place they sank, that anyone can rise up and overcome.

Often it's a question of disentangling the emotions from situations at hand. Sometimes this is a moment-by-moment challenge—questing to find enough love inside for your own bad self, and making a pact of forgiveness with your inner demon.

Tapping gentleness, mercy and peace, all within your own soul.

That happens in a 12-Step group through the sharing of stories. The result: Experience, strength and hope that blossom from having lived them. Through sharing we experience connection, and connection banishes loneliness.

And when we are tired, at the 'T' in HALT, it's time to rest.

The Observer and Humpty Dumpty

One way to accept the emotions and honor their cleansing is to imagine an observer, a guide or a mini-me perched upon your shoulder.

As anger, fear or any other emotion arises, the observer simply and calmly states, "Here comes some anger again. I will let it pass smoothly and completely. I know my person is not the anger, and that it's simply an emotion, like a wave coming up on the beach. Soon in its place will come the next wave, and that may be a wave of joy. Whatever it is, all is perfect and unfolding in Divine Order."

Allow the observer to be your guide, perhaps not so much a conscience as a pal who wishes only the best for you. A pal is going to do his utmost to cajole you back to your true self, the essence of which is only love.

You might imagine this pal as the angel on your shoulder, reminding you of what it means to "re-member yourself"—or put yourself back together again.

> *Humpty Dumpty sat on a wall*
> *Humpty Dumpty had a great fall.*
> *All the king's horses and all the king's men*
> *Couldn't put Humpty together again!*

Humpty's great fall came from believing what his ego told him rather than believing his observer, his pal. All the ego constructs he could muster (the king's horses and men) were powerless to patch him up, once he cracked up on the hard ground of ego.

Humpty required a spiritual solution, which was not readily available through the linear thinking so popular among those who believe in walls. Walling off yourself from your emotions—or from others who might assist in dealing with emotions—is counter-intuitive. Humpty was not an intuitive, open kind of guy!

So rather than getting all puffed up in our egos and anger, let us honor the emotional cleansing that will bring us into the path of the open heart.

How might Humpty have gotten out of his fix?

First, he'd have been better off if he'd not had to falsely elevate himself to a place where he appeared to be "higher than" everyone else. Sure, the view may be fine from those heights for a while, but they truly are false ego constructs— very shaky construction! "Pride goes before a fall" and he learned that the hard way.

There is a major difference between an elevated consciousness and an elevated ego state, of course. Placing yourself on the wall between you and others, the wall of judgmentalism and pride is a precarious position.

"Judge not, lest ye be judged." About age thirty I caught on that this Bible passage did not mean, "Lest ye be judged by others"—but lest ye be judged by yourself, which is in most cases the harshest judge of all.

Illusory thinking may cause us to place ourselves above the rest, but our own harsh and false judgments eventually bring us down.

On the other hand the path with heart easily and naturally elevates us, without ego creating a barrier (the wall) between ourselves and the one true reality. We are all parts of the whole; we all spring from the same source. As such, we are all one.

Deservability

So much self-sabotage comes back to deservability.

It's the sabotage we wreak upon ourselves when we choose not to HALT and take our pulse and take care of what we need *now*.

This well of undeservability springs from so many ancient messages. Our families, schools and churches, the media triggering our own inner voices of "not good enough-ness" if we're not wearing the right brand, or even the kids in the schoolyard who laughed and pointed if we were different in the slightest. If we couldn't run as fast, or kick the ball the correct way; even if we just looked funny.

Deservability. Why are we not able to demonstrate some generosity of spirit to ourselves, and project it outward to others as well? Why this continuous whipping, beating, prodding and flagellating ourselves with insane psychological torture? Why the madness?

Whatever self-hatred we harbor within eventually spills out onto the earth as blame, pollution, war, even annihilation if we don't shift to self-awareness, self-acceptance, self-respect and self-love. First one by one and then by the millions.

In the past, my non-deservability attacks often occurred on vacations with my significant other. Can you envision a better place for self-sabotage?

Did I really deserve to be in such a lovely environment with someone who loved me, and cared very much for my health and happiness?

Apparently not, because before too long I'd pick a fight, make him wrong, manage to wreck the vacation and sometimes even the relationship.

Invariably, each deservability blip would drive another nail into the coffin of that romance. I hated myself while I was engaged in this destructive mode. However, because I had "gone unconscious" I had lost contact with my true self, and lost control. Eventually I became more conscious and stopped that relationship sabotage. But it was only the process of learning to love myself that permitted me to demonstrate love and acceptance to others.

Laura, (name is changed) a very accomplished holistic healthcare professional, has perfection issues stemming from the notion that if she is even slightly off, if she is somewhere less than 100%, then she is irredeemably tainted. Unless she's 100% perfect, she's impure! Certainly that would make her not good enough for whatever good might be coming her way.

Her desire for at least some sweetness in her life added to her cravings for sugar, which caused her to go into an endless cycle of sugar-spike-then-drop, followed by intense rounds of self-flagellation for not being able to control her eating habits.

What is the classic chocoholic's pattern after eating a piece? "Well, if I'm not perfect, I might as well be perfectly awful and eat the rest of the box! So there!"

I suggested she give herself permission to eat just one or two pieces of chocolate, and don't keep more than that in the house.

One key on the path to self-love: Lead thyself not into temptation.

And by all means give yourself some slack if you fall off the chocolate cart. The objective is not to drive yourself deeper into guilt and misery, which of course will be assuaged by more chocolate!

Your guardian angel wants you to be happy! She's shouting encouragement in your ear if you'll only listen! Her self-talk is this: "You're doing good! You're doing good! You're doing good!" (See, she even forgives herself when not using proper grammar, which would be to say very primly, "You're doing well!" Somehow that sounds too formal for a little cheer-leading angel guarding your ear).

Just like *The Little Engine that Could*, she wants you to succeed.

When Laura's new boyfriend treated her to some tokens of his affection and admiration for her, all hell broke loose.

The occasion was a black tie affair. The articles: an evening gown, some new shoes, pearl earrings and a necklace.

The response: "Oh I look so awful in this dress! Look how lumpy and fat I am!"

I suggested that she'd reached the upper limit of the good she was willing to accept into her life, and that when she learned how to receive more, more good would flow to her.

Being adored is a wonderful opportunity. At some point, anyone may begin to believe that the way they are viewed (as an absolutely wonderful, precious human being to be cherished) may begin to rub off. Eventually they may even become convinced that their adorer's interest is quite valid.

How much good can you accept?

Not so long ago I would exclaim "Unbelievable" when a check appeared unexpectedly, or when some other great good would come my way.

In recent years, I've learned to watch the way I think and talk much more. When that check appears out of the blue I say aloud, "I believe it! And more where that came from! Thank you God!"

In the past my attitude was far more accountant-like and scrutinizing... analyzing how, where, when and why such good fortune had befallen me, instead of simply accepting it and expecting more good to flow to me, and expressing my gratitude verbally or in song. God loves music, don't you think?

Hummingbird Hill

Buying a second home condo in the stunningly beautiful Blue Ridge Mountains of western North Carolina almost brought me to a deservability crisis. Luckily my partner was very astute and intuitive, and understood what was happening when I began to act out and project my unholy-bitchiness onto him!

My place at Hilltop, in Sapphire Valley, NC, was situated right over Highway 64—which happens to be the same occasionally noisy road fronting the multi-million dollar mansions in Highlands. The highway noises don't reverberate only for condo dwellers; even the wealthy get this truly egalitarian experience!

Up in the mountains on our first weekend visit after my purchase, it suddenly seemed the entire traffic flow of western North Carolina was conspiring to drive me bonkers with the burp-burp-burp of downshifting trucks, the full throttle overwhelm of leather-clad Harley dudes and their over-processed motorcycle mamas, and an endless whoosh of Cadillacs, pickups and SUVs streaming past, shattering the silence.

As they say in the country, it like to drove me nuts!

Not only that, I suddenly HATED the color of the wall-to-wall carpet because it reminded me of my parents' formal living room. Beyond the color, the place didn't have the remotest resemblance to anything in my parents' home—in fact it had been professionally decorated, tastefully done.

(Theirs was tasteful, but not decorator). I'd bought the place with every furnished accoutrement, down to tennis rackets and balls, board games, fishing poles; even some Roy Orbison and James Taylor tapes for the boom box.

Suddenly the place was awful. I couldn't bear it. I hated it, in fact. It was all wrong. I threw a mini-tantrum in my despair over having made such a horrible mistake. Things could have gotten really ugly, but luckily my partner was wise enough not to take this outburst personally. He could have chosen to count himself among all those things that suddenly weren't good enough.

Somehow he managed to help me see that I had hit an upper limit of what I believed I deserved in life—and was projecting many of my own feelings of lack of self-worth onto my surroundings— making them as bad, ugly, ill-fitting and unseemly, and certainly as unpeaceful as I felt inside.

Now, years later, and during the ensuing years between then and the present, "Hummingbird Hill" became my haven— a place where I retreated to shut out the world, sweetly and completely.

Imagine this: After awhile I no longer even heard the sounds of Harleys and big downshifting dump trucks as they roared down Highway 64. It was my private little paradise.

But oh, the agonies, before I came to believe that I deserved such a lovely retreat!

Doing some time travel and sleuthing, as Julia Cameron encourages in *The Artist's Way*, I determined that my strong reaction might have stemmed from my mother's desire for a second home.

She was always clamoring to my father, "Let's get a condo in Vail while they're still cheap!" (She was a smart one). Or "Let's get a cottage on the Outer Banks!" It never happened.

If it couldn't happen for her, why should I be good enough

to make it happen in my life? Why should I have a better life than hers?

While sleuthing around in my dim past, I stumbled over the family vacation memory of my parents in the front seat of the car; she screaming at him over some perceived infraction and he passively shrugging it off and ignoring her, which, retrospectively, was probably the best response.

All of a sudden she jumped out of the car at a stoplight in Marietta, Ohio, and stalked in a fit alongside us on the side-walk!

Dad inched along beside her, pleading with her to get back in the car, while my sister and I, completely humiliated by this bizarre public display, sat in the back seat, no doubt screaming at her, my father and each other as well.

My mother would have none of it. I don't recall how he eventually got her back into the car and how the four of us made it home alive from that one, even though it was only another few hundred miles.

At that point in my early teens I vowed I'd never take another family vacation.

From this my model of vacation was set: it was obviously a time to act out and wreck the experience for all involved. This is the leisure-time corollary to the axiom that, "If Mama ain't happy, nobody's happy." My mother made sure we knew it.

What I didn't realize then: vacations tend to take us more quickly to the upper limit of good we can accept into our lives. They also slam us right up against expectations, which are a set-up for resentment.

In my case with the new getaway condo, amazed and rather overwhelmed by my good fortune, I had to do something quickly and completely to drag myself back down to my customary lower level. Regrettably, in younger years this level was often quite low and self-defeating.

Since then I've learned to be far gentler with myself, and to be able to recognize the symptoms if I begin to thwart my own happiness. Paying attention to the steps in the HALT acronym helps me divert many negative behaviors. Many others have changed their lives using that simple acronym.

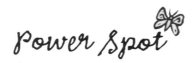

Power Spot

The energy flow in my garden evolved into the creation of a new power spot, prime for prayer circles, full moon midnight bacchanals and other shenanigans under the stars. A magical experience in itself, the evolution of this outdoor haven came from living in the Flow.

Two giant dying silver maples dominated the rear of the yard; it was a question mark when one or both would blow down and destroy the magnolia tree, which blocked them from porch view. Stunning magnolia, magnificent dirty tree, how I love its flawed perfection!

The maples shed giant limbs onto the phone and electric lines way out back, stealing my power and linkage to the world from time to time—a true annoyance in ice storms. So they had to come out.

This involved the "nekkid tree men"—in reality a half-naked, shorts-wearing, shirtless crew, three seasons of the year. All look like escapees from *Braveheart*—big shaggy Scottish men with hair on their heads, faces, chests, backs, arms and legs.

These skillful tree anglers somehow maneuvered around wires and the magnolia. Before I knew it I had three big ugly piles of mud after the stump grinder completed the job, gnashing up the roots, which extended in every direction like octopi tentacles under and atop the Georgia clay. (The third old stump was all that was left of a giant dead pecan way out back).

Three big ugly mud piles and a torn-up back yard. Suddenly the sky loomed huge and starry overhead, as though I'd moved to Montana. People from the Southeast with all its mighty trees and closed-in feeling know the difference in perspective.

Looking at an expanse of sky so suddenly large tends to open your mind too.

In their helpfulness, friends suggested vegetable gardens, water effects and various other solutions that they'd like to impose on the land. However, I had something more graceful than vegetables in mind. Besides, growing vegetables is so fraught with actual work—inspecting, picking off the bugs, weeding, constant tending—and the beautiful Eden in my mind needed relatively little tending—it would manifest out of pure joy for entertainment and appreciation. Plug in the annuals twice a year and watch them bloom, that was my idea.

(All gardeners will now be laughing up their sleeves: a garden with no work—yeah, right!)

However, I didn't quite have the vision of how it should look yet, and I asked a neighbor to whom I am eternally grateful for her artistic opinion. She'd just paid a landscape architect hundreds of dollars for perfect plans for her back-yard space, and was more than willing to share some creative ideas.

This degree of planning is fine if you feel that you must know in advance how everything is going to turn out.

We who live a bit more organically and enjoy experimentation, observing evolution and sprouts in directions that we

A new power spot, prime for prayer circles, full moon midnight bacchanals and other shenanigans under the stars.

may never have dreamed, leave plans to the birds. At least paid-for plans on paper.

But a "vision" is another thing. In fact, it's key.

Hearkening back to the sublime experience of our church's visit to Japan when I was 13 years old, my vision veered toward an eclectic Japanese garden. Revisiting fond memories of those two weeks which expanded my little world immeasurably, I checked a few books out of the library and absorbed as much as I could, remembering that these graceful places derive much of their charm from garden amblers' never quite knowing what's around the next bend, which is, of course, a perfect metaphor for life.

The Asian garden does not include big, sweeping greenswards where one stands with hands on hips, surveying the expanse as would some lord of the manor. Rather, one enters the mystery slowly, meticulously, as a kimono is opened tiny bit by bit to reveal the next beautiful secret.

Although in life we never really know what's next, a beautiful vision held in our minds brings about a stronger possibility of beauty projected outwardly.

Regarding the means of creating this eclectic Asian vision, my observant neighbor pointed out the obvious, which, because I was right there looking at it, I wasn't able to see.

The way the driveway curled around behind the house, she suggested that I create a path as a natural extension of the curve. It gracefully and sinuously wound behind the giant magnolia into the deep back yard and eventually swirled inward on itself like the inward curl of a G-clef.

Only when it was complete a couple months later did I realize that a giant yin/yang symbol had manifested in my yard!

Just as the curve of a chambered Nautilus shell grows into its fluted majesty, my stepping out in faith let the path grow into its own naturally occurring wave, perpetually curling in on itself, the endless universal spiral.

Not only did I step out on faith, I explored my vision and took action upon it.

Surely we're all mature enough to realize that our vision does not simply roll completed to our doorstep without the necessary spadework! There are those who engage in a bit too much magical thinking and not enough reality-based preparation and action—who believe that by wishing, all will come true.

All the wishing, hoping and magical thinking in the world is no substitute for just doing it—whatever it is. Action—taking that first step or making that first call—is key. What we're doing here is planting the seeds of our own paradise—the path into our own hearts.

As Goethe said, *"Whatever you can do, or dream you can, begin it. Boldness has genius, power and magic in it!"*

Cats in the Garden

Cats have their favorite spots, and these shift and change in a most mysterious manner. What makes one square foot on the sunny pathway the absolute cat zenith for weeks on end—and then suddenly it's to be avoided at all costs?

Any perch will do. Often the high ones are the best. Kitty can get the Big Picture from there, strategically gauging her plan to slip down into the hurly-burly and join in a chipmunk chase.

The catbird seat—gazing upon life from the high places.

With absolute contentment the neighbor cat, Feisty, perches in her new spot—a narrow railing on my deck

Hillary Rodham Kitten views the world from the catbird seat—
gazing on life from all the high places.

accented by pots full of brilliant blooms—orange and yellow marigolds; purple, red, white, pink, cerise and lavender petunia blossoms; fire-engine red salvia with its tall outbursts of blossoms. This tiny black "Bonsai cat" contrasts beautifully against the silvery, lacy Dusty Miller like a ghost presence against the vivid colors.

Tumbling out of its basket, the deep maroon Wandering Jew grows strong and healthy in the hot summer sun. This from a pot resurrected in a Garden Club neighbor's trash pile because she said it was dying from the top. Oh, ye of little faith!

After over-wintering in my sunny Samaritan front room, it's ready for the journey once again.

A garden cherub lounges among the pots of begonias, pale licorice, spiky Mother-in-law's tongue—and even some kalanchoe, also tossed onto the curb and resurrected by the scavenger along the path, ever alert for treasure.

A bullfrog on the railing is disguised as a watering sprayer, to be hooked up to the hose for spewing endless streams of expectorant on the flowers.

Haven't needed to hook him up lately, with all the drenching rain. Regrettably, three of my pristine new little Japanese maples drowned in the clay pools that imprisoned their roots during months of deluge.

Silly me, during the five-year drought I planted them in a drainage swale, and then Georgia began living up to one of its namesake songs, the farthest thing from drought, the steady drumbeat of another rainy night in Georgia.

In the past, the deaths of such dainty living things as my Japanese maples would have made me infinitely sad. Now, I work on accepting what is, and knowing that something better is on the way. Bless their delicate, lacy, graceful little souls.

They have slipped away, buffeted by extremes, just as we humans do when not tended properly.

The cats observe everything with a cold eye. It all matters, and yet none of it matters to them—not that they'd ever admit to either. They simply breathe in and breathe out, then jump up with a silent start when they spot the next target for playtime.

In *The Power of Now*, Eckhart Tolle mentions that he has lived with several Zen Masters, and all of them are cats!

My big orange-and-gray cat with the raccoon striped tail, aptly nicknamed Hillary Rodham Kitten by a friend, darts furtively down the wooden stairway, bounding over a high berm of liriope. The tiny black neighbor cat disappears behind it, as though surfing a big wave.

At times Hillary with her exotic Cleopatra eyes chooses the bench beneath the giant magnolia for pause.

Facing the bamboo Torii pergola, itself draped and tumbling yellow with extravagant Lady Banks rose, sweet-smelling Carolina Jessamine and purple clematis, Hillary Rodham Kitten observes the passing of the spirits beneath the spirit gate which honors their continuous shifting between this world and the next.

This is one of Hillary's favorite spots, and it makes sense because cats like to be where the action is. As we know, cats easily peer into the next dimension.

Haven't you ever noticed a cat staring beyond you at something it absolutely *knows* is there? You quickly dart your head around and nothing is visible.

Don't be deceived! We can learn many things from cats!

No doubt the royal cat observes a parading trail of garden devas and fairies who have found a hospitable environment since some of the old dead trees were removed and new energy flows in.

146

*Cherubs, devas and fairies all play
different roles in the garden.*

147

Cherubs are so laid back—they exist to make the garden mellow. Garden devas' tasks are quite specifically oriented toward adding magic to the space. As cross-pollinators, along with the bees, they drift langourously from flower to flower, then they may relax on blades of grass. In the early morning they sip drops of dew from the leaves; at evening they kiss each blossom of the Four O'Clocks and Morning Glories good night so all may slumber peacefully.

Stroking each leaflet frond of the statuesque mimosa sheltering the deck with their turbo-charged deva wands, they bring slumber to full branches at a time!

The fairies' tasks are even more to be envied—they are not caretakers of the garden; they exist simply to flit about, enjoy and engage in fairy frolic, dancing around mushroom rings and sliding down dewdrops on tall blades of grass.

Wherever they land they leave a trail of magic, which is easy for cats and children to follow. For adults it's far more challenging.

That's why adults need a path.

The Path of Possibility

Gateways aren't absolutely necessary at a path's beginning, but a specific point of entry adds to the mystique, as do curves and bends. One is never quite sure exactly what treasures may appear next along the way.

A Moon Gate, the round stone entrance which lends so much magic throughout Bermuda, is a lovely point of embarkation. The moment I stepped through that orb shape into a lovely garden of frangipani, oleander and bougainvillea there, I knew I was collaborating with all the power in the

The Path of Possibility begins at the Spirit Gate.

One Moon Gate at the Atlanta
Botanical Garden sprouts Chihuly glass.

150

universe. Its roundness symbolizes the everlasting—the cycle that never ends. For some reason, stepping through that circle seemed to bring calm and wisdom with it.

Garden paths can be stone, or gravel, or a combination. Or even brick. Or they can be dirt paths, but preferably with stepping stones in case of rains and mud. Imagine the necessity of daintily lifting one's hem—if one were a geisha or a grand dame of the house in Victorian times—just to prevent one's garments from dragging.

Stones are practical foundations—they keep us out of the mud.

Sometimes the path can't really go anywhere, so what's to be done on a path to nowhere?

Circle around and reverse direction, of course!

One must maintain the proper perspective on this. The Path of Possibility in my own garden began as a path to nowhere, but then I was seized by the hopelessness of that notion. What's the point of going nowhere?

The very idea is rather bleak. So if this is MY PATH, let it be infinite, limitless! Now I've redefined it: the fact that it circles back on itself is a powerful symbol of the cycle of life and its infinite blessings.

It's all our choice to frame the meaning we want in our minds.

At the end of the Path of Possibility rests the circle of stones, all embedded in the ground like the others on the path, all walkable. It's a miniature power patio, this graceful yin/yang swirl to the energy vortex in the center of the stone circle.

How do I know this energy vortex exists? The stone in dead center of the power patio is one of Hillary's favorite resting spots. As Zen masters, cats follow the energy. There she'll roll and loll, lie and bask, soaking up the currents from

151

the earth, the stone, the sun and the concentration of energy flow to the vortex.

Eventually she nonchalantly washes her face, pretends not to notice that I'm observing her, flips up her tail and strolls away.

Good Juju

The power spot is irresistible to people too. At parties or spiritual gatherings, from our vantage point on the screened porch overlooking the garden, someone admires the Spirit Gate. Drawn to its subtly lighted arch, we are beckoned into its mysteries. Usually a small, intrepid group troops down the steps to explore. Sometimes it's the entire party.

When we release the constrictions of our brains that always clamor for results, production, and certainty, deeper awareness is possible. The Path opens up a little space for magic and intuition with Alfred E. Neuman's "what-me-worry" MAD approach to life!

Drawn through the Spirit Gate, we feel the atmosphere shift as we emerge on the opposite end of this ten-foot amble beneath the vine-tumbled pergola. In the hush of an evening, sometimes seeing our breath hanging in chill air, we're ready to step out gingerly, rock to rock amidst the grass; symbolically moving forward into places where we desire to invest more of our time and our essence, even without knowing exactly what that means, or what it might require of us.

Stepping "into the mystic" we leave the chatter-brain behind. What a relief!

Customarily, people who have been happily chit-chatting cease their talk when passing through the Spirit Gate, step-

The Torii spirit gate honors a continuous shifting between this world and the next. Magic is afoot! Photo: Houston D. Smith III

ping into the beyond. Even though it's "just" the back yard, it is no longer simply a place: it's now a feeling. A certainty that there is more to life than meets the eye. Magic is afoot.

Every few yards the path is illuminated by a graceful low-light lamp, two feet above ground on a curved swan neck, with coral bell-shaped smoked glass caps. I didn't have to confer with the devas and fairies regarding their tastes in this matter—I'd learned in Brownie Scouts exactly what would inspire them to cluster 'round!

White coral bells upon a slender stalk,
Lilies of the valley deck my garden walk.
O, don't you wish that you could hear them ring?
That will happen only when the fairies sing!

Often we hold hands, all of us in a row, streaming out along the Path of Possibility in the dimly lighted evening, stepping out and giggling like a group of eager kindergartners, eyes wide, hearts beating roundly, ears attuned to the night calls of birds or the soft whoosh of a bat near our faces.

This is a natural little paradise, the Enchanted Forest of Avondale, filled with decades-old giant oaks and hardwoods; a perfect environment for magic, even inside the humming perimeter of Atlanta.

Hot Toddy

At Winter Solstice, the longest, darkest night of the year (and one of my favorite nights for partying, along with Halloween) we cluster around a bonfire near the house as we all write on red streamers whatever we want to release—old losses, resentments or bad juju—so we can greet the return of lighter days unburdened, with fresh energy and renewed resolve.

Tying those streamers to the "burning branch" transforms it into a fabulous, garish, multi-antlered icon, paraded by a jovial crowd along the Path of Possibility, out to the power circle. Someone drags along the mobile fire pit with its hissing, spitting bonfire, positioning it over the power spot, while the crowd sways with anticipation and laughter.

Joining hands, we try to slap some solemnity on our faces, to no avail.

But in keeping with ceremony, I release to the Universe whatever my friends are releasing from their lives, symbolically written on the streamers.

With an absolutely regal gesture, the man holding the crazily-antlered branch aloft then thrusts it into the bonfire and we all hold our breaths. And it won't burn! The streamers are manufactured of fire retardant paper!

We all have a great laugh; eventually the thing burns; and all the old bad stuff is released—mine so effectively vanquished I can't even remember what it was. Something to do with fear. All gone. All, all gone.

Gathered around the power circle, hands clasped, we then pray for our psyches, our hearts, hopes and dreams to be healed.

How many of us have experienced our hopes and dreams dashed and shattered and scattered like so many shards of stone? How many of us, at this moment in time, are unemployed, or barely scraping by, or suffering along with our children who are on drugs or the children of our friends serving in the military in wars based on pretense? How many of us are feeling unloved and barely able to love ourselves? Welcome to the human race!

155

The power spot is a place of deep healing among a potent circle of friends. If someone feels drained when they venture out along the path, chances are they'll experience a complete energy infusion before turning around and coming full circle.

The resurgence of energy comes from a progression of steps.

First, intention. Writing down and thinking about what is to be released.

Second, a hushed and contemplative walk beneath the Spirit Gate, toting a branch, a symbol of life and death, and of reaching into the beyond.

Third, the raucous burning and release of the old bad juju.

Fourth, a prayer of restoration to lock in the good intention.

And next, high hilarity reminding ourselves that this magical night is not all solemn ceremony, but also holds promise of a strong toddy concocted of two parts happiness and one part uninhibited joy!

Hokey Pokey

What could be a more perfect addition to this toddy than the Hokey Pokey?

All the elements of this childhood dancing game speak deeply to the way we can choose to live full and happy lives. At first somewhat tentative, we put our right hand in—but then we pull it out. Still undecided as to whether we'll go for the gusto.

And then we shake it all about—just to rattle ourselves a bit more alive! To jar ourselves out of our complacent rut!

The whole sequence repeats several times—left hand, right foot, left foot—until there's nothing left to do but throw our WHOLE SELF in!

Right there we are, whole selves in the thick of the action, fully, richly in the moment, doing the hokey pokey, laughing our heads off at our goofiness. Turning ourselves around, witnessing the joy all around us right here in the moment—and realizing that's truly what it's all about! What else is there but here and now and the Ho-key Po-key?

Jumping into the circle is key to a rich, abundant, happy life. We must take the initiative. We must experience the moment. Because soon enough, we will disappear from this little circle of our earthly plane, and begin to experience the next level of what it's all about.

For all we know, the "directions for use" on the package of the next plane may be exactly the same!

Infinite amounts of good energy have been created in this sacred space while shaking our whole selves in the Hokey Pokey. Everyone sheds egos. At least by glancing around and seeing everyone else acting like complete goofballs they feel more free to drop the pretenses. Adult façades drift away, for just a little while.

There at the power spot, where we've all gravitated including the cat (who in the midst of the goofball antics has plopped herself down in the center of circle of stones—where else?), we all soak it up—the love, the happiness, the moment. That's what it's all about, Yes Sir!

The Haunted Bed

Just as the cats have their power spots in the garden, shifting and changing on the wings of cat logic one day and pure whimsy the next, we humans have our power spots in the house. And we have our power drains as well.

Like buried treasure, the power spots must be revealed, and the power drains must be closed using a system employing ancient wisdom of energy flow: Feng Shui, pronounced fung schway.

"If you don't love it, get rid of it."

Those words of the Feng Shui consultant were like a slap to my face.

There it sat—the ancestral bed—dominating an entire room.

In 1900 my grandfather had been born in it. For decades my parents had slept in it. I had inherited it—stately and over-whelming with its tall, polished mahogany headboard nearly touching the ten-foot ceiling.

A family heirloom, one of which I should be proud!

As a young girl, terrified by nightmares and bogeymen lurking beyond my parents' calming presence, I'd slunk there almost nightly to climb in next to my mother for solace. As an adolescent I'd sat with girlfriends upon it, giggling, gossiping and watching TV in the only air-conditioned room upstairs.

And as a teen I'd been lectured from it. My mother would rag on for hours, swilling Early Times and punctuating her endless harangues about the caliber of our friends with another deep drag of a cigarette.

"I raised you to be leaders, but you're acting like followers! Just listen to you! Where did you learn that gutter language?"

My sister and I and cat Purr smile from the 'Haunted Bed'—
posed by my mother for an early Christmas card.

Far below, seated on the floor, my sister and I would hack on the thick smoke and glare up at them, hating their rightness. My father, her silent henchman, sat by.

By now I was the owner of the Haunted Bed. In fact, I'd received it in a shipment to my first home, when I'd been grateful for any stick of furniture.

To all outward appearances it was a coup. Wasn't I supposed to be thrilled to own such a magnificent piece—along with its companions, a marble-topped washstand and filigreed, mirrored chest?

Outsiders could never comprehend the undercurrents of inadequacy, regret and sadness fostered by these antiques and their ghostly memories—compounded by the promise to my mother that I would never sell the family heirlooms at Charley's Bargain Barn. She always laughed when she said it, but the mantra from her final years stuck with me.

The irony was that my mother's attachment to all of her "beautiful things" was what had brought her literal downfall, and now she had handed down that sad legacy, along with many of her beautiful things, to me.

It happened when she attempted to rescue an antique rocker from their basement, which was seeping water.

In a drunken rage at my father for letting things get so out of hand (this was her projection—she could have done something about it if she'd wanted to), she slipped and fell backwards down the steps, severing her spinal cord at the fifth cervical vertebra in her neck.

In a flash she rendered herself quadriplegic at age 48 for the remainder of her life; eighteen years of paralysis from the chest down.

Some, like my hero Christopher Reeve whose injury was even worse than my mother's, are able to wrench themselves out of the depths of despair and create meaning in their lives once again.

Unfortunately, my mother was not one of those. Alcoholism had already defeated her spirit. This injury was the final insult. Negative consequences unrolled for what seemed like endless years after that.

The honest pity was that she had derived so much meaning from outward appearances. She placed so much importance on the externals that she completely ignored the meaning and being she might have sought and found within herself—the true essence of life.

All our hearts broke that day, one day before my father's birthday.

After the pitched battle that had been their marriage for more than a decade, it was as though she'd subconsciously chosen to memorialize that day with a horrible gift that he'd never forget. I suppose it was no coincidence that he'd been born on Friday the 13th, fifty-one years earlier.

Shrine to the Dead or Den for the Living?

Which was more important—maintaining the Victorian room in my home as a shrine to my dear departed mother? Or creating a comfortable den that I might actually use?

Friends teased me, calling the room with all its gaggle of eyes-rolled-back antique dolls and ancestral portraits "the Haunted Room." One man laughed that you'd have to wear a crown of thorns to sleep in that bed.

"You're too young to turn your house into a museum!" said another. Or did he mean mausoleum?

The burden of the past combined with the guilt of the present was fast becoming my millstone of the future.

"If you don't love it, get rid of it!"

The Feng Shui lecture gave me the courage to hear my heart's answer and release the dictates and the debris of the past.

Within a week I bought a comfortable love seat and ottoman, central to my new, relaxing space. A room for me— no longer a shrine to the dead.

On the morning of the furniture switch, I took a stick of burning sage in to the haunted bed, smudged the room and the bed, blessed and released the spirits and memories, and told my mother how much I love, appreciate and respect her. It felt like the right way to honor her, while honoring my own mid-life transition positively.

I stored the magnificent headboard and footboard in the laundry room as a friendly gesture to my mother, whose favorite housewife pastime had been folding fresh laundry.

After the accident, how she had longed to accomplish even such a simple activity! A task she couldn't manage with para- lyzed hands. Sadly she stared at them, mostly useless on her lap.

Years after her death, we're all reconciled to the gifts and sorrows of her life. And when I told my father about the new arrangement for the Haunted Bed he just laughed and said that when he visits, he'll sleep in the laundry room. Such a lovely, all-accepting man, with such a sense of humor!

Within a matter of weeks after shifting things in the haunted room, a spectacular whoosh of energy began flowing through my personal and professional lives—new friends, new clients, even new directions in my career.

Mary Beth in happier times.

163

All this because I found the courage to honor the needs of the living and let myself live in the day-to-day, as much as I cherish the dead.

Hidden Treasure

Once the old has been cleared away and you begin to open to the energy of the new, your vision may show up in the most amazing ways!

The creation of Treasure Maps (also called Dream or Goal Charts) and your very own Personal Crests can help make the vision appear in your outer world more quickly.

Since the mind grasps vivid images or symbols more easily than it comprehends fuzzy concepts, it's important to feed your mind in the manner it wants to be fed. Also, remember, what the mind focuses on is what it attracts, so always put pictures on your map that you want to see manifest in your life—not what you don't want to see or experience.

For example, if you're trying to become more slender, leave out the picture of the luscious chocolate cake with the OFF-LIMITS slash through it. Your mind will only see the cake and not the symbolic denial.

Treasure Maps can be created for individual areas of your life like relationships, travel or career, or for all aspects in one: family, personal, health, and all above. Some people make different maps or even picture books for a variety of aspects of their lives.

They consist of magazine photos or headline cut-outs, "play money" in large denominations or big checks made out to you for an infinite amount from the Bank of the Universe, photos of yourself and loved ones (always put yourself in the picture), and some visual form of the Infinite (a sun, moon or star, a Buddha, an Om symbol, a cross, a Star of David, the infinity symbol), and whatever you want to manifest in life.

If you love to dance and want to do a lot of it, a picture of dancing goes on the Treasure Map. If you desire a beautiful environment, fancy car, serene inner aspect, exotic vacation, financial success—all go on the Treasure Map. Your concept of the ideal mate goes on it.

Headlines about success, winning, bounty, joy, peace, love and giving back to others go on it. Affirmations of the kind of person you want to be. A goofy mock-up of your head glued onto a model's body might be just the incentive for the subconscious mind to help you morph into the body you want to become.

Plus, a sense of humor really counts! Treasure Mapping is not only a real, results-producing method of priming the universe to render up what you want; it's fun! Let yourself become childlike when you do it. The important thing is, just do it.

As a boat needs to be in the current in order for an adjustment on the rudder to affect its direction, so it is also important to take the steps offered in this book and so many others like it rather than thinking to yourself, "Oh, that won't work for me," and never attempting the methods that have worked so well for others throughout history.

What we think about is what we attract. Adjusting our minds to that simple fact and taking action on it is key.

Make it easy on yourself. Every time you flip through a magazine, be on the lookout for the kinds of things you want to attract into your life. Clip them out and put them in a file. Soon you'll have more than enough to create a very stimulating visual map for yourself. Set aside a couple hours on a weekend afternoon and slap it all on a cardboard (or, if you're very fastidious and artistic, take your time and make it a true work of art). Most of all remember, it doesn't have to be perfect. It's a work in progress, as is your life.

Shove your boat out into the stream, put your hand on the rudder, and go.

Also important: Include the affirmation that "this or something better now manifests for the greatest good of all involved." We affirm something better because we may not be aware of the greatest good that awaits us—in fact, our own vision may be self-limiting. The Divine Mind knows our greatest good; we simply must be willing to let it unfold.

I remember when I was exposed to the concept of Treasure Maps in Shakti Gawain's pivotal book *Creative Visualization*. My first thought was that this woman had a lot of chutzpah to give herself that name, and I liked it. My second thought was that I needed to give Treasure Maps a try, immediately!

At the time I was living in a brick ranch with a tiny kitchen window overlooking a small, chain-link fenced back yard that was so bleak I think I ventured into it five times during the entire ten years I lived there. And then I was swatting mosquitoes and wondering why I'd even bothered to go outside.

Rather than imprinting my consciousness by staring out over a wasteland, I put a bulletin board on the wall opposite where I ate my meals, and on it I tacked beautiful photos of the kind of environment I looked forward to enjoying, ASAP!

Luscious gardens, beautiful trees, large windows overlooking verdant landscapes—that's what I imagined for myself.

I'll confess, at the time I wasn't as skilled at manifesting as I am today. It took ten years, but ultimately I moved into a beautiful environment inside the perimeter—an Enchanted Forest—everything that I'd envisioned, and better.

Make Your Vision Vivid

Have you ever wondered how to make things happen more quickly in your life? If so, try an exercise called Make Your Vision Vivid. Its purpose is to place you smack into a fabulous 3-D experience by imagining yourself in it. By injecting it with emotion, you make it come to pass more quickly. To bring it alive, use present tense and incorporate all five senses: sight, sound, smell, taste and touch.

In the very first *Get the Life You Love* class I taught, Julia (name is changed), a very sharp woman in her mid-30s, was stumped by the exercise, which was completely out of character for her. I'd known her as a successful salesperson for years, and she always knew how to make things happen, especially in her professional life.

At the time, she had established an excellent sales situation, working from her home selling tech warranties at the peak of the high tech boom. Although the bosses had fought against her working out of the home, she'd observed how pleasant my life was after I created a home office, and she was completely disgusted with her long commute in soul-crushing Atlanta traffic.

An extremely diligent salesperson, she was able to force herself to take all necessary steps to earn in the six figures. This meant fifty to sixty cold calls every single day. She'd worked with me in the Sales Course several times, and she's simply one of those people who is capable of doing what it takes to become successful in sales. It's not for the faint of heart or for people lacking focus.

Inception of the Palazzo

As we began the Make Your Vision Vivid exercise she blurted out, "I can honestly say that the only thing that even comes to mind is a swimming pool in my backyard! I have no idea how I'll pay for it. I'm quitting my sales job and going back to grad school. In fact, it seems insane even to think about it."

"It doesn't matter how insane it seems—describe it," I encouraged her. "Describe how you feel while you're enjoying it!"

So she proceeded, writing it down in present tense, which is very important. We must put ourselves in the moment, since that's all that exists.

"I see myself reclining on a chaise lounge next to my perfect pool in Brookhaven. I hear mellow music as I sip a cold drink and chat with friends. I feel the sun's rays streaming down on my skin. The aromas of suntan lotion and honeysuckle are in the air."

As she described the divine scenario aloud, we all observed her face light up and her eyes soften. She really put herself into the picture, and the five senses clinched it for her emotionally.

I asked her what this scene meant to her, why she wanted it.

"Freedom, complete freedom! Work is inside, and I'll get to it later," she said.

Next I asked her to experience the degree of gratitude she would feel when this vision became a reality.

"But it hasn't happened yet. Why should I feel grateful for something that doesn't exist?" she asked.

Feeling gratitude before the fact sends positive energy into the universe. Movies such as "What the Bleep!" describe what physicists and spiritual leaders have been teaching for awhile—that witnesses to any experiment actually alter the nature of its outcome. In other words, by "witnessing" a positive outcome in advance we strengthen its possibility.

This phenomenon has its foundation in the Law of Attraction.

Expressing gratitude over the vision you want to manifest helps speed up the outcome. Remember always to add the thought, "This or something better." Greater things than we imagine may be in store.

These fundamental truths have brought health, happiness and prosperity to tens of millions of people, but regrettably most of the people on earth don't know about these universal laws. Even if they know them, they often choose to ignore them.

Julia chose to hold on to the vision of her swimming pool and create a new life for herself. Four years later, well on the way to her Ph.D., she celebrated her 40th birthday in her freshly renovated Brookhaven "palazzo" with a swimming pool. How did she manage to afford it?

During her graduate studies, she began writing textbooks on English for Speakers of Other Languages. Wisely she chose not to take an hourly rate for her work. Instead, she took a very small percentage of sales, which renders a substantial annual commission.

Four years after she made her vision vivid we sat by her pool sipping a glass of chilled wine, and she laughed about the fact that it had all started with that seemingly goofy vision exercise.

"Do you remember I told you I wanted to quit working but still have tons of money rolling in so I could pursue what I really wanted—and I had no clue about how any of that was going to happen but you told me to write it down anyway? All I wanted, really, was a swimming pool. That's all I knew," she reminded me.

"All because I wanted a swimming pool, Patrice, and didn't have a clue how I was going to get this lifestyle that I'd envisioned for myself. And you encouraged me to go for it with all the Treasure Maps, the Personal Crest, and visualization, and here I am!"

We toasted her fabulous success, and chills ran through my body. This exercise really works!

One of my coaching clients, an extremely success investment banker, was in the process of starting his own firm when we did the Vivid Vision exercise. I asked him to imagine six months in the future and he described an office humming on January 1st as he wrote the list of pending deals on a white board. He could smell the markers and taste his coffee, as he and his longtime, trusted assistant worked productively together.

Although at first he didn't understand the purpose of the exercise, he was willing to go along. I explained that attaching strong emotion to a vision helps it come into being faster, and within the projected timeframe it had all come to fruition.

Another very polished young woman who is a top salesperson at her financial services company confessed that the vivid vision she created to describe her first home with her husband is exactly where they now live—a comfortable home with a swimming pool where they can welcome friends and family. Our thoughts pull our reality to us like magnets.

A young man from India, now working successfully toward his goal of becoming a highly paid photographer, said that since childhood he had imagined himself in the United States. He attached great emotion to the idea of living his dream, and although he originally came here on a high-tech work visa, he eventually parlayed that into learning more photography skills until he was able to relocate to Los Angeles to pursue his dream.

My own sister passionately pursued every avenue to have a baby for more than eight years before her vision came to fruition in the form of her beautiful child Elizabeth. During that time, long before the baby's conception, she bought E's christening gown and hung it where she could see it frequently in her home. Now our entire family is blessed with the presence of this delightful child.

What fabulous success stories from several who were willing to permit themselves to dream, then throw the energy and effort into pursuing their dreams!

"As you think, you travel; and as you love, you attract," is how philosopher James Allen states it.

Faith Talks

How I dreamed about my own course for the fifteen years I taught Dale Carnegie sales training! File folders bulged with articles, anecdotes and examples I collected for my own class.

Steadily I was shaping my life with information from the articles I'd read, tapes I absorbed and workshops and classes I took or taught for years—slowly chipping away at my negative mindsets, self-destructive behaviors and defeatist attitudes.

The Sales Course was so pivotal to my understanding of what creates a beautiful life—not only the good habits essential to success such as goal setting, planning the work and working the plan, but also what underlies all the outer activity.

Precious, lively Elizabeth displays her sense of humor.

The most important lesson of all in the entire twelve-week sales course consumed only twenty minutes of the entire fifty classroom hours. The topic was "Faith Talks" and "Pep Talks"—a means to access the power of the subconscious mind and guide it to work toward our advantage.

Although the time invested on that topic in class was short, it changed my life. I began to read every book I could find on the subconscious mind and the magic of thinking and dreaming big.

I held steady with the vision of my class and envisioned a future that I wanted to create. As I watch it unfold, now the objective is to manifest it more quickly.

However, if so much good had come to me in the past, I wouldn't have been capable of receiving it.

The fact is that even if all the wisdom of the universe is available to us and we're not able to receive, it remains untapped.

All things do truly unfold in Divine Order. Unlike in the past, after years of work, my degree of self-acceptance, self-respect and self-love is high enough to accept the bounty.

People become what they think about, as Napoleon Hill, author of *Think and Grow Rich*, stated it. He researched dozens of successful people and discovered the secret workings of the subconscious mind. People become what they think about.

What are you thinking about? Does the notion scare you? If so, the antidote is simple but may not be easy: change your thinking and you change your life.

Do not be conformed to this world, but be transformed by the renewing of your minds. Romans 12:2

How Things Work

Treasure Maps and strong mental images work for several reasons. The visual images help us become more intentional about manifesting the good that we want in our lives, even if at times (even subconsciously) we don't believe we deserve it.

One woman in my class confessed that she began to recognize the level of her resistance to visual, concrete images of her unmet goals in life. She balked at the difficulty of the tasks she envisioned for herself. But she was self-aware enough to realize that this was partially a defense mechanism, an attempt to allay frustration and disappointment that she'd already experienced.

She now knows that the solution is to focus more on what she does want than what has disappointed her in the past, and therefore she is more likely to draw the positives to herself.

If she expresses gratitude for what she does have rather than resenting what she lacks, her higher vibrational level of gratitude will attract more people, more successful experiences, happiness and love for which to be grateful.

Having pictures of what we want before our eyes for long periods of time causes an internal shift and enables the subconscious mind to get proactive.

The individual mind connects with the universal mind in terms of visual images rather than words, so the more colorful your map and images, the better.

When you think of a rose, you envision a lovely bud or a blossom of red, pink, white, yellow or any of a profusion of colors in which roses manifest. You don't think of the written word r-o-s-e. Therefore, if you make your vision vivid and attach emotion to it, your subconscious mind is activated to draw it to you in some way.

Seeing the Good

By having these pictures in our view, we're also better able to RECOGNIZE the good when it comes into our lives. From birth our brains are conditioned to see only what we've been trained to see. As a result, we often stumble over everything else—or block it out completely.

Several years ago I received a lovely postcard from a Japanese friend—a pen and ink artwork of a very content orange and gray striped tabby cat. I liked the look of it so much I put it in the center of my bulletin board. Years after that, I adopted a mountain kitty (the aforementioned Hillary Rodham Kitten) with orange and gray stripes. Only later did it occur to me that I'd been staring at her picture for at least two years before our first encounter. Then when she sauntered into my life I easily recognized her and knew she was for me!

Tiny Baby Feet

Many other friends from my classes have had powerful experiences with Treasure Maps and visualization in manifesting bold new lives for themselves.

A lovely, intelligent medical doctor in her early thirties was not happy about her employment situation, working freelance in the prison system. Although equally discontented with her lack of a meaningful relationship, she hesitated to put her

175

heart's desire on her Treasure Map. Her hesitation stemmed partially from the perceived stigma of tossing off a medical career to become a wife and mother.

Although my generation of Baby Boomer females was told that we could have it all, Generation X has become a bit skeptical as they discover how truly difficult it is to juggle career, marriage and parenthood. The number of strained marriages and divorces had made Janet (name is changed) hesitate to express what her heart craved.

I encouraged her to include everything she wanted to manifest. At the end of our map-making session, she planted the cutest magazine photo of a pair of tiny baby feet in a prominent position on her map.

I can still see those baby feet! She blushed when she glued them to the map. Why is it that we so often hesitate to let ourselves express what we really want?

When we truly admit to ourselves that we are who we are, it's far easier to make a statement about what we desire in life. That's why self-awareness is key to sustained happiness. It was as though she could barely admit to herself who she was beneath the polished professional exterior—a woman who longed to nurture a family.

What a wonderful gift to share with the world! Each individual gesture of love and nurturing benefits the entire human race. Acting as the microcosm we all contribute to the whole.

Since true change occurs organically, from the grass roots upward, the more people who experience a loving environment as their foundation, the more likely the entire earth will be able to shift toward that open-heartedness and willingness to accept ourselves and others.

Less than two years later I learned the exciting news that Janet had re-connected with a man who had been her first date in high school. Not long after that they were married, and actively engaged in creating the tiny baby feet (and the rest of a precious child) that she envisioned years earlier. Now she and her husband have a darling baby girl!

She expanded her comfort zone taking some improv acting classes and established herself in a well-situated medical practice. Her life was enriched all around because she dared to believe she deserved it. She glued her vision to her treasure map and brought it to life.

One young woman's goal was to move to New York City and snag a high-powered TV position, writing financial news. On her Treasure Map she placed several images including the Manhattan skyline, the Dow Jones electronic ticker, dollar signs, and logos of several of the leading financial news organizations located there.

"Positive thinking has opened up a lot of doors, especially in my job hunt," said Dana (name is changed).

"When CNBC granted me an interview, I visualized myself already working there, and repeated affirmations about being qualified for the job and doing my best at the interviews and on the writing test. The most amazing thing is that I wasn't really nervous about how things would work out—I had a good feeling they would be fine… and they were."

Another highly creative woman who felt completely stifled in her banking position dreamed of somehow utilizing horses in a therapeutic practice for abused children. Decisively she placed a picture of a horse on her map, knowing that it symbolized far more than just pleasure riding.

Throughout her life her parents had intimidated her with the notion that she was not creative enough to do anything outside of the corporate box. She was even an English major, stifled by working with numbers and bored stiff.

Several months after the class ended, Elaine (name is changed) emailed me.

177

"I have just moved to Austin, TX and plan to attend grad school at UT to become a counselor. In the meantime, I am helping a friend start her jewelry design business and am thinking of starting my own business as a 'clutter consultant' or professional organizer to help people get rid of all the crap that is weighing them down and get organized to get more out of life. I plan to take some classes in Feng Shui.

"I have a friend here in the documentary film business that filmed a horse whisperer and hopefully will get to meet him very soon. My vision for myself was to somehow utilize horses as therapy in a counseling practice....Finally getting closer to that reality—and your class really helped me to visualize what I wanted to set me on my path."

I've got to get a Life!

Yet another woman experienced an amazing series of synchronicities leading up to her enrollment with the class, followed by a delightful revelation about her next avenue in life. She'd been stuck in a slump, and yearning for change.

The first synchronicity was our link through our shiatsu therapist. Shiatsu is the Japanese word for acupressure (refined from Chinese forms of bodywork) that stimulates the movement and balance of qi (pronounced chee) or life force energy throughout the body. Its benefits are cumulative. A naturopathic M.D. had recommended the therapy to me to lower my blood pressure, and I'd enjoyed it for several years.

More than just a body worker, Yolanda Asher, Dipl. ABT (NCCAOM), is an intuitive who helps release emotions and memories that have been blocking clients, while at the same time she gets the energy flowing with her skilled fingers, elbows, hands and feet—applying pressure in just the right ways.

I tell her what's going on in my life, my joys and sorrows, victories and defeats, dates of my upcoming classes, status of projects and such. We share a lot of laughter, and many times she has helped me release tears and arise from the shiatsu futon refreshed and ready for life again.

I rarely meet Yolanda's other clients, but one day passing through I met Robbie (name is changed), who had recently experienced the death of one of her beloved sisters to cancer. The three surviving sisters were still reeling from the devastating course of the disease and their grief over the loss.

Later I learned this: Robbie, whose children had recently grown up and moved out of the house, had moaned to Yolanda during a session, "I've GOT to get a LIFE!"

Bells went off in Yola's mind. Intuitively, she connected Robbie's plaintive remark to the title of my course, *Get the Life You Love.* "You need to take Patrice's class!" she told Robbie in a rush.

Serendipitously, Robbie had been looking at the course description in the recent Evening at Emory brochure, and this was the last little bit of urging she needed to sign up.

From here on, Robbie's life seemed to jump onto a more streamlined track toward fulfillment—but she had a long way to come after the depression following her sister's death.

It began with one of the first assignments in class: Everyone is to write down at least 100 of their own strengths.

This simple task seems formidable to a lot of people at first, and for good reason. We've spent our entire lives (most of us) with a checklist of the many ways we're inferior, unworthy, successful only because of dumb luck, or other skillful means of self-sabotage (often instilled, I regret to say, by organized religion).

179

These nasty jibes from the monkey mind serve no purpose other than keeping us down and apart from our true inner light, the universal intelligence or Christ spirit that enriches us all—if we but know how to access it.

I usually tell the class that I first received this assignment when I was 24 years old from my wonderful boss at Dale Carnegie Institute of Atlanta, Stan McQuain, whose mission was to help others grow into lives that were happy, healthy and whole.

The assignment stumped me. At that age I was so mired in self-hatred I believe I could only come up with twenty strengths, even after thinking about it for a long time.

Here's what Robbie, a very bright, loving and well-loved wife and mother in her mid-fifties had to say about the exercise:

"You will be pleased to know that I finished my list of 100 personal strengths! I am so proud of myself. A few weeks ago I could never have come up with 25, much less 100. It felt so good. There are days when I feel like I lose momentum, but other days I'm really feeling upbeat and encouraged."

As class unfolded, so did Robbie. During our session on Treasure Maps, she placed a small picture of a chef in the very center, which corresponded to her career "bagua" area based on Feng Shui, the study of energy movement.

Later that evening she logged onto email and there, unsolicited, was a roster of several culinary schools in New York. Since she'd already put the chef on her map, when another cue (look this way!) appeared in front of her face she paid attention instead of deleting it, and decided to inquire.

It dawned on her that during her sister's illness she'd experienced great pleasure in preparing holistic foods to serve her. Somehow the little chef's picture triggered something that helped her realize she could hold that vision, follow it, and change her life.

That's exactly what happened over the next six months. She and her husband, a businessman who travels just as much as he's in the Atlanta area, sublet a New York apartment that perfectly accommodated her two beloved dogs, and she entered culinary school for holistic cuisine. At school's finish she served an internship at a Florida resort during the worst months of winter, and now she's embarking upon her next life as a holistic chef!

In a summary as class ended she stated, "I had been searching for a new direction in my life for about two years. Then in March of this year I decided to take *Get the Life You Love* and my life changed. My participation in the class activities, especially creating a treasure map, set into motion a series of synchronistic and serendipitous events. I have actually changed my attitude from feeling at times hopeless that I would ever find my authentic life, to feeling optimistic that indeed I will find a purposeful and fulfilling life. My self-esteem has improved greatly. I feel lighter.

"As a result of these events I am about to move temporarily to New York City for what I believe will be one of the most exciting adventures of my life, as I study and train for a new career. I have found my direction, and I believe my life is going to change in ways I have not yet imagined. I am open to whatever the Universe has planned for me. I am so grateful for the work I did in class that started me on my way."

Personal Crest

Put the date on your Personal Crest and place it where you can look at it often. Then see what comes into being!

182

Mystic Power
in a Personal Crest

Treasure maps are posted all over my office walls—along with Personal Crests I've created from chalk and markers to reinforce the magazine images on the maps.

A Personal Crest is shaped in the form of a shield with a stripe through the middle. The shield contains four quadrants and the stripe provides space for a slogan about what you're creating.

The quadrants represent different areas of one's life where you are envisioning forward movement—changes large or small. Areas might be health, spiritual growth, relationships, community, career, finances or wealth, or whatever else you desire—all expressed with a symbol that attaches a certain meaning to the subconscious mind.

Carl Jung said it, and all the great myths throughout human history exhibit it: The subconscious thrives on symbolism.

These brightly colored symbols on the personal crests are an extremely powerful combination with the Treasure Maps and the "Valentines to ourselves," hearts that we color in class, often with loving slogans written on them.

One former class member, recently divorced and having lost her job, told me she still has her hearts from class papered on her walls as a reminder that even the most tired, broken, oppressed and distressed little heart can heal.

My office walls serve as one giant Petri dish feeding my subconscious with the soul food it needs to move to the next level. The joyous aspect is witnessing these things as they come into being!

Often these shifts do not occur on our own timetable, because the manifestations sometimes refuse to appear until we're ready to see them. I discovered this in a most uncanny way, involving a woman who considered me to be her hated rival.

non-fatal Attraction

Desperate to drive me away from my boyfriend for whom she was lusting, this woman attacked me with hate mail and nasty phone calls like a bad rerun of *Fatal Attraction*.

Unfortunately, he was leading her on and she was about to get her heart stomped. Although he and I eventually parted ways, it was not on her timetable, and that infuriated her! In the process, her mean behavior toward me exhibited what kind of person she was to him, and he told her to get lost.

Retrospectively her attacks may seem harmless, but at the time, when I left his place to discover my car had been "keyed"—(scratched all the way along its side)—and arrived home to her raving diatribes on voice mail, I was rather upset.

My customary response to such attacks in the past would have been to take the offensive, but at the time I felt so overwhelmed that I took my own best advice and just let it go.

With all the lies and hurtful words flying in every direction, there was no place to turn. In addition, she seemed so pathetic that I felt more sorry for her than vindictive. Here she was futilely striving for the seeming big prize: a man who would end up cheating on her eventually, no matter how long they were together!

Shortly after this episode, he and I parted ways for good. I was devastated, and luckily leading my class at the time (remember how we teach what we most need to learn?)

So I had all sorts of little encouragements that helped me heal, including *My Little Heart Song*.

I also created a personal crest during this time, shortly after I'd begun to practice yoga in earnest.

Despite a near nuclear meltdown feeling of devastation, I drew a little picture of myself in lotus position and next to it I wrote the words "Forgiveness, Perfect Acceptance, Peace, Yoga and Meditation."

Two years elapsed and I continued my yoga practice. Well on the way to achieving my own certification as a yoga teacher, I worked on incorporating all the yogic principles of perfect acceptance of life's twists and turns through yoga and meditation, and being in the moment.

One day I was attending a yoga class at the Decatur YMCA. We had just completed a brief closing meditation when I looked up and noticed a woman smiling at me from across the room. I didn't recognize her.

When class ended I was tying my shoes in the hallway and she came up and asked my name, then introduced herself—it was my former nemesis—the woman who had keyed my car, written hate mail and left nasty messages on my machine!

In one of the lovely, uncanny manifestations of grace, I felt that everything had been resolved between us. I felt absolutely no anger, frustration or electrochemical charge of any kind toward this woman who had done her best to torture me in so many adolescent ways. I felt nothing but perfect peace and acceptance of what had transpired between us two years earlier.

There it was, the expression of my heartfelt desire right before me, and within me: Forgiveness, Perfect Acceptance,

Peace, Yoga and Meditation. And it happened in a yoga class, just so I'd be sure to "get it!"

It was pure synchronicity that made me aware of this perfect unfolding in the outer world of my original inner desire. That evening while preparing for class, just before we created our Personal Crests, I had re-discovered that particular crest I had created two years earlier in some papers I was reviewing.

There I was staring at a drawing of myself in Samadhi (blissful) state, and that's what I'd manifested with this supposed "enemy!"

How often we can't even see what's right before our eyes! Often it takes distance to get the proper perspective. Then creative pursuits (symbols on the personal crest) in connection with the cosmic consciousness (intentionality) enable the analytical mind to go "sproing!!!" get out of the way and wake up to our own higher good.

That is all God wants for us: to wake up to our good. "Sleepers awake! Oh hear the happy noise!"

The joyous news is that the kingdom of heaven is within, and it's ours to claim—we don't have to wait until some time-after-death to experience the magnitude of the lives we were meant to live.

Such a bounteous world, with so many gifts at hand—but only if we can recognize and accept the gifts can we make them ours. Reach out your hand—seek and you shall find—knock and it shall be opened unto you.

How many people stumble through life completely blind to the gifts to which they're entitled, thinking, "Aw shucks, that must be for someone else; it's certainly too good for me." Or a variation on that theme: "I don't deserve to live, but if God lets me..."

Independence Day

Several decades ago on July 4, 1946, my father was honorably discharged from military service in the United States Army Air Corps.

The mere notion of his being that young and my being as old as I am seems so unreal that I count it on my fingers like a child learning abacus speed math.

How could all that time have passed since he was a young strapping handsome Irishman?

And now I, Daughter Number Two, join him on a holiday weekend in Buffalo, New York, to help him clear out some of the impediments of his life and fortify a safer path through the Vortex—his office.

Although his second wife swept through most of the house like a white tornado, this was the place she feared to tread in case of stepping on his feelings (or some other booby trap) and never being sighted again.

She was the irresistible force, but he was the immovable object, and resist he did. And so they parted ways and his daughters swooped in to deal with the perilous possibility of his falling, wedged among high stacks of papers, a daunting VHS tape collection, old Christmas cards, scrapbooks, cartons of trophies, half-strung suspenders, piles of folded towels and billows of dust, and not being able to get up.

Dear old thing, he can't help it. Being a packrat stems from a very basic insecurity about one's place in the world—a deficit at the very root of one's existence, in the first and second chakras, which relate to survival and creativity.

Many people who experienced childhood during the Great Depression retain that packrat mentality long after they've

187

become financially secure and successful, because they don't feel fully grounded; they don't feel quite secure. Therefore they gird themselves with stuff to anchor themselves to the ground. (Anodea Judith's *Eastern Body, Western Mind* offers many constructive exercises for balancing all the chakras, whether one experiences deficits or excesses in any of them).

He grew up in the Depression. And then he had to deal with my mother.

How he survived the emotional abuse and psychic carnage of that so-called life with my mother over those years I'll never know, but he did manage to rise above and carve out a life of service for himself which was, and is, truly admirable. Recently he trained to deliver communion to shut-ins for his church, where he serves as a deacon. Deacon Dickey, I tease him. This is a man whose arthritis leaves him barely able to walk!

For years he donned his goofy Santa Claus suit and "Ho! Ho! Ho'd!" through hospital wards to cheer up sick and injured children. He also sponsored Youth Hockey games for mentally retarded children and got involved with fundraisers of every kind for the Shriners, Kiwanis, and the Masons.

For decades he uplifted himself and others while singing a strong baritone with the Buffalo Philharmonic chorus and Shrine Chanters. Like everyone, he has his issues, but he's certainly one who gives back. What a great example for me, and all of us!

In his Walter Mitty-esque way, he always dreamed of fantastic escapes, and yet stayed steady at the rudder of our family's tossed ship during my mother's downhill slide into alcoholism and eighteen years of paralysis.

Without complaint he put two daughters through college, supported his own elderly mother for decades and his father in a nursing home, and paid hundreds of thousands for my mother's care out of his own pocket, well above and beyond what insurance covered.

Although not flashy heroism, isn't that the definition of a modern-day hero—one who quietly and calmly does his perceived duty, trudging through each day without saying, "Look at me—aren't I great?"

A mere wink of the eye ago my father was the best looking young man in his home town of Cambridge Springs in northwestern Pennsylvania—an idyll in the road.

Old Corny's Memoirs

Several hills over lies Meadville, where our daring ancestor Cornelius Van Horne (old Corny, my dad always calls him) fought the natives and was captured, escaped, traversed muddy trails on horseback to Washington D.C. with General David Meade and General George Washington himself before he became president. Married for the first time at age 65, Old Corny fathered eight children before his death in his 90s. Perhaps he had a bet going with the Father of our Country!

Quite stoked with the longevity gene, my dad is. His own mother, my dear grandmother Gee Gee, was still letting forth full steam on the church organ for her tiny Methodist congregation until she retired as organist at age 85—and was sharp as a tack until three weeks before her death at age 98.

Old Corny lived a long, rich life, especially for that hardscrabble era of not-great nutrition, harrowing escapes and no dental care. Remember, George Washington had false teeth made of wood—no wonder he never smiled in portraits.

One of Cornelius Van Horne's predecessors eventually went insane in the wilderness and eased off to hang himself

My father Joe Dickey
was the best looking young man at Allegheny College, where
my mother first invited him to a Sadie Hawkins dance.

from a tree in a cornfield. And who wouldn't be tempted to do that with loneliness and the drudgery of endless, back-breaking work? The man slipped into darkness and couldn't find his way back to the light, bless his soul.

It's all recorded in a neat, handwritten account passed down from the 1700s—hand copied as though by a friar at some later date.

A Sign

Posted on Dad's office door is a sign: Enter at Your Own Risk—The Vortex!

What a journey into the family's ancient history is this office vortex, groaning with stuff! Several funeral books, the family Bible with its carefully recorded births and deaths, the cycle of life right there in spindly handwriting next to those big color plates of a shiny blond Jesus knocking at heaven's door and holding up his lantern to light our way.

On that holiday weekend a surgical strike on The Vortex by me, his neatnik daughter number two, rendered it pass-able. As they say, the pendulum swings first in one direction and counterbalances in the other, and I'm the neat and organized type. Dad didn't have a clue where he could store these things—the house aches with treasure—another's junk, or vice versa.

The lower vortex, the basement, continually disgorges more stuff, and it's even more perilous with its sharp-edged tools, jutting corners and jars of everything stacked willy-nilly on magazines, old hatboxes, flyswatters, Halloween costumes, bicycle seats, children's toys, broken lamps, artwork of steel

191

mills and box after empty box, coffee can after empty coffee can.

With every visit, a random clue from the past will have unearthed itself to appear on the kitchen table. Such was the case with the pink tutu I wore in a Kindergarten ballet recital as a "Pretty Baby."

Sister Sue and I raise an eyebrow and laugh. Do these things crawl up the steps at night, on their own, while no one is around to monitor their docility?

Holiday Gene

I inherit the packrat gene in a vastly diminished version than the variation my sister inherited.

We tease our Philadelphia girl about being as over-the-top as my father as she spews forth cartons from her attic to enliven every holiday with is prizes: Every size of bear dressed for any occasion or celebration, and for this mid-summer holiday, July 4th, she displays tiny patriotic flags, toy-sized Statues of Liberty, Benjamin Franklin in full oration, the Liberty Bell, Betsy Ross House, Independence Hall and toy soldiers (mostly from her bear family) ready to defend our freedom. All this just for a "lesser" holiday!

Sworn into collusion with the family idiosyncrasy by our mother, Susan also collects dolls from all the world over, and shelf after shelf of children's books, for her daughter, of course!

As an elementary school teacher my mother was quite the brilliant inspiration for small children, always ready with some fresh excitement when the perennial expected complaint resounded: "Mommy, I'm bored."

Mother Mary Beth would grab our little hands and break out into a can-can in a frenetic Offenbach kick through the house, or teach us how to cut out paper dolls or make ghosties and carnations from Kleenex, or hostess a tea party for all of our dolls, and us.

But mostly she taught us a love of books and reading, which was quite generous of spirit for one who suffered dyslexia.

She had a special technique of reading books for herself by scanning the first page, then the last page, one or two pages in the middle, and making up whatever went in between.

This perfunctory glimpse at the material didn't prevent her from scoring quite well on all her college courses—well enough, certainly, to become an elementary school teacher if not a rocket scientist. But she was a genius with young children, and for her children, she read us endless stories, every single word, or so she said!

Most of all, my mother loved her "beautiful things"—fabulous antiques including the Haunted Bed were funneled to her from every direction in our shrinking family. Regrettably it was her love of her things that did her in when she fell down the steps.

And on the eve of my own 48th birthday, which I had approached with some dread because it was such a horrible year for my mother, I discovered that rather than becoming what I'd feared—a clone of my mother—I had become what I hoped for—a clone of my mother!

That joyous, intelligent, intuitive woman, the gifted teacher, the understanding listener, the creative resource who helped every child see the best aspects of themselves. She was all those things until she was no longer capable of seeing the good in herself because her vision was distorted by alcoholism and depression.

Whatever it takes to free yourself from the pain or challenges of growing up in your particular situation with your particular parent(s), grant yourself as an adult the gift of rediscovering their best aspects once again manifesting in you, as you.

Even if no redeeming times existed *with them* at all, reconnect with their eternal essence.

I am so grateful that my father has lived this long and I've discovered that underneath all the clutter, there's pure, unconditional love.

His granddaughter sees it—to her he's a great big teddy bear. Maybe that's why my sister has been so fond of collecting teddy bears. We just couldn't see we had one right there with us our entire lives.

Boxes, Feng Shui, and the Middle Ground

I learned in my study of Feng Shui that three of the places where my father's ever-expanding hoardings are stashed are among the most critical to maintain clearance and order: the hallways, under the bed, and in the basement.

If one keeps especially these areas clear, positive energy flows, opening the way for good mental and physical health.

Although the single hallway in my home is slick as a whistle, lacking even a runner along its hardwood floor, I pause to ponder the challenge that is the storage area of my lower level—a garage below my bedroom.

I confess. I am a box collector. The idea of actually going to a store and paying money for a packing carton, or simply not being able to locate the box of perfect size and heft for any mailing occasion—a Tiffany's re-use for that elegant effect, or a sturdier shipping carton complete with its layers of bubble wrap—is quite alarming to me. And how could anyone possibly think of discarding a hand-embroidered box from Asia!

But regarding these three key areas: under the beds, in the hallways and basements, Feng Shui wisdom indicates several things.

The area beneath beds should be clear because it relates to creative energy, sexuality and the unconscious. Clutter here may hamper sleep, creativity and fertility.

How long have those plastic containers filled with sweaters and mothballs, or boxes of shoes, or papers, or empty suitcases been stored beneath the bed? Or everyday debris, magazines and garbage that's shoved out of sight, affecting your ovulation, sperm count, or the progress on your work of great literature?

How can we let anything as mundane as sweaters-in-a-can crowd the psychic space where dreams are woven, the place where magic occurs, where wonders are conceived—the access point between the ego and the greatest depths of the soul? Only magic is welcome here! Even though dust bunnies also seem to propagate, well, like bunnies, they can easily be whisked away, releasing energy flow.

Next, look at your hallways, which are akin to the body's arteries. If energy (qi) cannot flow freely through the house, then life begins to stagnate.

The basement is a reflection of the subconscious mind. Have you ever seen Orson Welles' movie classic *Citizen Kane?* How my heart broke for the wealthy newspaperman who traveled the world buying beautiful things that were shipped in giant crates to his vast basement, never to be opened or admired again. The way he girded himself from the reality of his lonely existence with things, all those inanimate nothings that would eventually crumble to dust unseen. Aren't we attempting to do this to ourselves in the "civilized" world today?

Do you own your things or do they own you?

At the risk of sounding hackneyed, I'll use the phrase: If you always do what you've always done, you'll always get what you've always gotten.

If the path you're on looks like it's leading exactly where you're going and that's not where you want to go, it's time to assess your life and change course.

As in mowing the lawn and deriving the satisfaction of seeing real progress immediately—tangible proof before your eyes that something has been accomplished—a great place to begin is a Feng Shui assessment of your home.

In correcting the energy flow of your space, dying plants are especially a no-no, whether in your home or yard. Either heal it, or onto the compost pile it goes!

Big Neon Life Lessons

They occur frequently in our lives, but how often do we choose to ignore them?

As a younger person I honestly believed the problem was with the world and not with me. I wrote, "people are strange," "girls are cats" and "boys are creeps" on a psychological profile at a seminar I attended which prepared high school seniors for the college application process.

Actually, all this railing on life was a testament to the power of the word circulating at the time. When I filled in the blanks on this profile, various songs and advertising slogans were running through my head. But the message was that the problem was OUT THERE. And since I couldn't control the world and everything in it, chaos reigned within me and everywhere around me.

What I didn't recognize was that as I pointed the finger of blame out at the world, three fingers pointed back at me. I'd never heard of the concept of "projection"—the idea that what we see in others is a manifestation of something in ourselves.

"When you spot it, you got it." There's a handy phrase from the recovery movement.

Let's examine the concept using an exercise from Louise Hay's *You Can Heal Your Life.* This is a powerful journey into our shadow aspects.

Think of a person you really can't tolerate and write down three characteristics of that person.

One man in my class, Dave (names are changed) wrote down, "He's despicable; he's awful; he doesn't deserve to live. The world would be a better place without him."

Next in the exercise, the challenge is to look inside ourselves and see where those characteristics live in us. Dave balked.

"Oh, no, those aren't me—those are him."

"Well, wasn't that the same way Hitler felt about the Jews? The way Saddam felt about the Kurds?" I parried with him.

It's the same way anyone feels who points at the evil of "the other" and says that the world would be a better place without that person, that group, that ideology.

The debate raged, and I don't know whether he was ever able to acknowledge to himself that he harbored the shadow aspects of a little Hitler inside him, as we all do, since we all harbor all things, good and bad, dark and light, joy, sorrow and the kitchen sink!

Mark Twain expressed it this way: *"The last quarter of a century of my life has been pretty constantly and faithfully devoted to the study of the human race—that is to say, the study of myself, for in the individual person I am the entire human race compacted together. I have found that there is no ingredient of the race which I do not possess in either a small way or a large way."*

It's extremely difficult for us to admit that both the evil and the good that we see in others are all projections of what's going on inside ourselves.

To exemplify the complete opposite of the Hitler projection I mentioned Mother Teresa, working with the most destitute, diseased and forlorn populations in India. Every time she leaned down to bring a sip of water to the parched lips of a dying person or cleaned their filthy open sores, all she saw in that person was another manifestation of the Christ, which was the very essence of sacred self she had chosen to cultivate within herself.

All she projected was love, and that's what she experienced back.

Wake Up!

In my twenties I was extremely angry at the unfairness of life, the world and especially my parents for messing up their lives (and subsequently mine) so horribly. With my mother a paralyzed alcoholic and my father maintaining some semblance of order while supporting them, their lives were a challenging mess.

I thought it was my job and my responsibility to fix their lives for them. And I think, unfortunately, that they relied on my sister and me to pull them out of the emotional vortex. This impossible situation is codependency.

Because I was angry at the world but couldn't really destroy it, my next best opportunity for conquest was to destroy myself.

I had been taught that the solution would come from the externals—the right man, the right job, the right clothes, the right car, the right living environment.

Granted, all those benefits are wonderful, but they come second—they begin to appear when what's happening mentally, emotionally and spiritually—the inner—is adjusted, in the flow, and projecting positive thoughts outward.

One of several wake-up calls that helped me really "get it" in my thirties involved my little gold Buick Skyhawk, my starter car (which I eventually sold to a cute little Vietnamese family for $700—God bless 'em—I hope it served them well!)

One spring I'd been in a series of ridiculous, unconscious fender benders—three in a row. Of course I would have loved to blame these on the other drivers, except for the simple fact that they were all single car accidents and I was the one behind the wheel. It was as though my subconscious was shouting "Wake Up!" and I continued to choose to ignore it.

How many times has the universe tried to wake you up in the form of fender benders or other far worse "accidents?"

Eventually the car had to go to the shop for a total paint job, and I left it for the day. It was filled with my workout gear, a raincoat, other shoes and clothes, as well as all of my materials for Sales Course Instructor Training, in which I was currently involved—learning how to teach selling skills to a room full of 40 high-caliber, fast track salespeople who would tolerate no half-measures.

In this situation as a tandem instructor I was extremely nervous about how well I was doing and whether I was capable of meeting the grade at all. Throughout the world there were only a handful of female sales course instructors, and several of the men who had been in training with me had already dropped out because the material was so challenging and the time commitment so great.

The paint shop wasn't in a very good neighborhood, and the keys had been left in the ignition where it sat on the lot ready for next-up. Some local kids sauntered along, saw their joyride and drove off in it—along with all my clothes and gear.

What traumatized me most of all was that they took off with the entire accumulation of notes on how to lead the Sales Course—fifty hours of classroom over twelve weeks—notes which I had very scrupulously compiled over the preceding six years, which included nearly everything down to the timing of the breath!

I was so conscientious as an instructor-in-training, and hyper-concerned that I'd be challenged while leading this "man's game." (Generally thirty or more men and five to seven women were enrolled in the class). I figured that in order to be credible and acceptable as a leader, especially to the hotshot sales guys, I had to be better than perfect. And that was the nature of the material I'd compiled to gird myself for every situation in the classroom.

When my car and all my notes were stolen on April Fool's Day, I was devastated. However, I also felt certain that the car would be quickly recovered and I could get my crutch again.

The significance of the date the car was stolen wasn't lost on me. Of course I'd been a fool to leave materials so invaluable, so irreplaceable, in the car when it was going to be on its own at a paint shop!

I'd recorded every anecdote, every illustration, every pertinent witticism from nine different instructors over the years—scribbled in tiny print, sometimes even on cocktail napkins if there was a joke that would help make a point cracked by some salesguy over a beer.

As did my hero Mark Twain, I would prepare ten hours to do a ten minute impromptu talk. I'd devoted thousands of hours to study and preparation. Adhering to the principle that the shortest pencil is better than the longest memory, most of it was not stored in my head, but in my notes.

Days passed, and then weeks. I went to class and managed, while my very solid and thorough tandem instructor and good friend, a highly successful sales manager at one of Atlanta's top radio stations, tried to help me get beyond my dependency on notes. He recognized that the material was so thoroughly ingrained in me that it was second nature. Even when I was not able to believe, he was a believer.

Years after the spring that I endured this pain and had to face my fears over not being good enough, I finally got the point: the crutch of the notes was an illusion that I didn't need, and I had to have it removed from me before I'd recognize that it really wasn't so necessary after all.

Similar to the experience of Indiana Jones in his search for the Holy Grail—when he reaches the impassable chasm and steps out on faith, a bridge appears before him and he's able to cross, step by step. But not *until* he steps out in faith does the bridge appear.

In the case of my notes, I had to have them ripped away from me before I'd dare to step out. What a painful lesson that was, attempting to cling to a familiar crutch (the past) that no longer existed!

Each Sunday afternoon over the twelve weeks I'd sit on the deck to study for Monday evening's class. One Sunday weeks after my car disappeared I let all my grief and anguish over the loss of those six years' worth of notes come flooding out.

I sobbed. And through my sobbing I acknowledged that I'd never have them back, and that I was capable of going on without them. Painful, but finally accepted. I had completely released the notion that I'd ever be able to rely on that material for "reserve power" ever again. I'd have to rely on a different kind of reserve power.

In essence, I turned it over to God.

This is how things work. It seems that as soon as we let go of the outcome of the way we think it should be, another better outcome manifests. Just a few days after relinquishing my hold on that material forever, sobbing my guts out and feeling the fresh, purging relief, I got a call from the Atlanta Police Department. My little car had been retrieved!

Were the notes intact? I had no clue. Quickly I rounded up a friend who drove me past the dank, gloomy federal penitentiary to the crowded impoundment lot near the stadium. I didn't see how they could possibly cram one more vehicle onto that lot—even one as small as mine.

Slumped in a ditch it was, packed in with one tire blown out, limping along on that puny fake spare tire, with a bullet hole in its right side and almost out of gas. Not a notebook, note or scrap of clothing was in the car. My heart sank.

But then I opened the trunk, and there in a tangled mess on its floor were all of my sales books, notebook and notes. I was ecstatic! And it was Good Friday.

Coincidence? Or was I simply being instructed by the Higher Power to read the Big Neon Sign: BELIEVE IN YOURSELF! That would carry me a lot farther than a ream of notes I'd scribbled.

Ironically, by this time the class was nearly ended and the course had gone quite well. Imagine that!

Essentially, when I was able to surrender my willful longing to have everything a certain way—my way—I learned one of the most important lessons of my life, and I do get refreshers quite frequently. When I relinquish my will and turn outcomes over to God, a far better outcome emerges than any I could have ever constructed with my know-it-all ego. In other words,

Where there's no will, there's a way.

Smash the Mirror!

Linear thinkers and left-brained logicians often deny themselves the magic available along the path. They prohibit themselves from some of life's major joys—the moments of revelation when we suddenly know that we are part of a grand plan and our participation in its unfolding is vitally important.

It reinforces the reality that we live in a universe comprised of love and that we too are loved—if we stay open to the awareness of it. The love is always there for us, and so is the guidance. It is our choice whether to experience the love and follow the guidance—or not.

Often, because we are stubborn creatures who only tend to see what we expect to see, guidance appears in some very bizarre and unexpected forms, simply to get our attention.

Saturday evening, October 17, I was fixing my hair to go out and meet some girlfriends.

At the time my life was in a boring rut. It felt like a total slump. I was dating no one, feeling lonely, wondering whether the right person for me could even exist in the world—in other words, feeling extremely sorry for myself. I was also in the classic self-flagellation mode that made me feel nothing would ever change—I'd be without a partner and stuck in my dumpy little environment forever. After years of practice, I had

203

mastered the art of letting my imagination spiral off to the worst possible conclusion.

Suddenly, completely unexpectedly and without my touching it, the el-cheapo full-length mirror from K-Mart, which was attached with four or five nails to my linen closet door, literally wrenched itself from the door and shattered on the tile at my feet.

I was astounded. I'd witnessed this phenomenon with my own eyes and still couldn't believe it had happened. The mirror had been nailed there since I'd moved in; I rarely opened or closed the closet door, and never with enough force to loosen the nails. It had hung there undisturbed for at least five years.

So why now? Why had it suddenly flung itself to the floor and shattered into hundreds of shards?

The metaphor of a broken mirror sent thoughts careening through my mind. Oh, great! Seven years of bad luck!

Immediately I cancelled that thought—thankfully having gained an inkling about the power of our thoughts and the way they hold sway over our lives.

Luckily, "my generation" raised in the 70s has another metaphor for smashed mirrors: The Who's fabulous rock opera *Tommy*.

This deaf, dumb and blind kid, truly a special child who has been abused and scorned by his relatives, is initiated into his exciting, expansive new realm by the Acid Queen, a gypsy who conveys to him the absolute necessity of busting through his droopy, downtrodden and depressed self-image—by symbolically smashing the mirror. He must break through his own limitations—*no one else can do it for him.*

Suddenly I had met my own Acid Queen—there she was, a reflection of myself in the mirror, urging me to Bust Out! Do Something Different! Take Action! Go For It!

Although I'm an action person, this situation was requiring me to do something I rarely did: It was requiring me to shop.

The very fact that the mirror was broken meant I'd have to do something to replace it. Shopping is not one of my pastimes. At this stage of my life I was working like a slave to get my PR consulting business off the ground, so I rarely took time off for myself.

However, I had one week of vacation at my timeshare in Sapphire Valley (this was years before I bought the condo at Hummingbird Hill), and I figured I could find something attractive in the dozens of antique stores between Highlands and Cashiers.

Believe me, unlike a lot of women who love to explore clever little shops like these, I never would have taken time if I weren't on a specific mission.

On the last day of my vacation week I set out, starting in Sapphire and working my way west along Highway 64, visiting every single "Country Cottage" and furniture store—to no avail. On into Highlands. Anyone in the area knows that the wealthy visitors who flock here from winters in West Palm Beach and environs demand that their shops are exquisitely well stocked. The options were magnificent, but still no mirror that suited my linen closet door in Atlanta.

The last shop in Highlands was at the end of Main Street, upstairs and in the rear—a large custom furniture store manned by a proprietor with a gleam in his eye and several mirrors on his walls.

"Oh, but this isn't all I do," he said to me after the initial greeting. "I've just finished a novel and I'm looking for a publisher for my book."

I mentioned that there were many ways to get that ball rolling—did he remember *Love Story?* They released the film

205

first, and public demand was so great that they published the book later.

I knew a producer in Hollywood who might be able to help pull some strings and get something going.

Immediately we'd experienced that kinetic charge that indicates this person will play a pivotal role in life—whether as friend, mentor, lover, or teacher of some of the more difficult and painful lessons—the ones we really don't want to learn during the process, but are so relieved later that we'll probably never have to learn that particular lesson again.

Although we may blame "the other" for the anguish at the time, ultimately we know we've experienced a beautiful gift—a gift that we may not have been able to recognize if it had come in the form of joy instead of pain.

Sad irony isn't it? We tend to learn more from painful lessons than those filled with joy.

I was slightly amazed when he offered to help me hang the mirror that I bought—a large, stone-framed oval to set off my living room. (The bathroom mirror came later). After all, Highlands was more than two hours from my home! As it turned out, his manufacturing facility was in South Georgia, so he made frequent trips through Atlanta. We set a date.

By the time he showed up to help with the mirror placement, I'd read his hilarious draft of a southern coming-of-age story, *The Keepers of Echowah*. I suggested to him that I write a screenplay based on the novel and we pitch it to my friend the producer as a team. He agreed. Within a few months of hard work on weekends I had completed the screenplay and contacted my friend in LA.

I was told by my Hollywood contact to show it to his cohort in Atlanta, Fred Dresch, a screenwriter and teacher of screenwriting at Georgia State's film department—a man who had spent years in the trenches in LA, working every aspect of low budget films and familiar with the in's and out's of the industry.

And that's how the inimitable Fredresch and I became an item.

I walked into his big garage apartment one warm spring evening in May and was immediately transfixed by his rock collection. He loved the fact that I was fascinated by one of his main hobbies; here was a new convert to the magic realm of rocks!

After reading my screenplay he pronounced it the "best first screenplay" he'd ever read. Who knows, he was probably just flirting with me... but the way he insisted on shepherding the work through several levels of deal-making before it eventually tanked, I felt he was sincere.

The point of this tale is this: If I had not paid attention to the synchronicity, the meaningful coincidence of the smashed mirror on my bathroom floor on October 17, and taken some actions which led me on a quest to the hills, I never would have found what awaited me at the end of that rainbow.

And I was amazed to discover later that the author of the novel was born on October 17th!

Ultimately the liaison with Fred unfolded into one of the most important connections of all.

The Gospel Truth

After twenty-five years of disillusionment with the church, I was invited by Fred to experience Oakhurst Presbyterian Church in Decatur, led by Nibs Stroupe and Caroline Leach.

Here I discovered a beautifully rich, living, spirit-filled, integrated and diverse place—one which has been featured many times by local and national media for its remarkable people—a blend of blacks, whites, straights, gays, old and young, international leaders and kids from the 'hood.

For a quarter century I believed that spirit couldn't possibly stay alive within the confines of a religious organization housed in sticks and bricks, which I viewed as shelters for self-sanctified, self-congratulatory, close-minded denizens of a restrictive, restricted external "savior." At Oakhurst I completely reversed my opinion and was able to deepen my connection with God.

Both choirs welcomed me. The chancel choir of blacks and whites sang the standard hymnal and the eternal "white bread" pablum of the Presbytery's greatest hits. Our fearless leader was a very determined and dedicated woman, who may have felt as though she was towing a barge single-handedly against the current with her teeth. It was hard work and she was up to it! Occasionally she even managed to cajole some beautiful music out of us.

The sanctuary mass choir was joyously led by our black choral conductor, JoAnn Price, a squeezably soft dear-heart who oozed love from every pore. She pounded away on a barely-tuned baby grand piano while stoking those spirituals like Mahalia Jackson. We, another racially mixed choir, wailed doo-wop responses in the background.

Eventually, I stepped into a dream that had sprung from adolescent fantasies, a skinny white teenage girl's after-school imitations of the Queen of Soul, Aretha Franklin. Back then, I substituted a bottle of *Eau de London* for a microphone and a stack of my sister's 45's for a back-up band while striving hard to sing like a soul sister.

Here I was now, as a full-fledged grown-up adult belting out the lead for the gospel choir, having a total blast and swept up along with the clapping, sweating and shouting congregation by the power of the music. That was the *Spirit* living through me, loud and pure, especially when my voice cracked.

What if I had just remained complacent when the mirror was smashed, and had chosen to buy some rum-dum replacement at the mall? What if I hadn't viewed it as a signal to begin a very important quest? What if I hadn't chosen to see the magic?

My entire life would be completely different—whole sets of friends, an entire world of Atlanta where blacks and whites mingled together during the most segregated hour of the week! The wonderful, enriching friendships at Oakhurst Presbyterian brought such gifts!

Here I gained a deep appreciation for the richness and warmth that family means in black culture (far different from my pursed-lips WASP upbringing), while at the same time experiencing the collective love of dozens of open-hearted church ladies, retired missionaries, foot soldiers with street ministry and prison and jail project—all of this would have been lost on me.

How blessed I was to choose to pay attention, thus beginning my journey on such a delightful, path, so rich with friendships!

A study on happiness shows that members of the Forbes 400 richest Americans are only slightly happier than people in sub-Saharan Africa living in dung huts with no electricity or running water. Experts say that what makes people happy is sex, family ties, spiritual beliefs and nature.

Engaging with greenspace, not greenbacks, is what brings immense emotional benefits.

I bet if they'd gone into greater detail, they'd have included singing in a gospel choir as a sure path to joy!

One thing leads to another, as they say. We each have our unique gifts, and the guidance that the universe offers us is here to help us manifest it. We are sent messages from the universe all the time. Whether we choose to receive them or merely slough them off as random events is completely up to us.

The message of the smashed mirror was one I couldn't ignore—it was time to see myself in a new way.

Sometimes it's hard to tell exactly how our unique gifts will unfold, but if we pay attention to what we enjoy doing and "follow the energy" doors continue to open and real, valid choices appear.

Some of us have so many strengths it's difficult to tell which ones we should focus on. The degree of enjoyment we experience when "losing ourselves in the work" as well as subtle guidance provide the right clues.

My beautiful, talented aunt Susan Mauntel is a prime example of living in the flow and creating her life as a work of art by paying attention to guidance from the Lord. Several times throughout her life she has completely reinvented herself, conquering all the challenges entailed in complete career changes—and rising to the top of her profession each time. She's a natural at everything she undertakes—and always willing to put lots of energy and hard work behind her abilities.

From a modeling career she evolved into a talk show host, then eventually left west coast TV behind to sell high-end real estate (including islands, rancheros and estates). When her artistic talents called, she created "Furniture as Art" and "Fine Art Works," selling at galleries in San Diego, Aspen and Naples. After retiring to travel for a few years, she built a new studio at her place in Colorado and has taken up the paintbrush again, while serving as a pillar at her church.

She has provided a great example to me over the years

Susan Mauntel shows how 'Fine Art Works' with her boxes, trays and demi-benches recalling museum masterpieces.

211

that you can become whatever you put your mind to—with the focus of your heart and prayers.

An Inner Knowing

At age 24, when I participated in the Dale Carnegie Sales Course as a student for the first time, we were asked to write down our goal of who and what we intended to be in ten years. I wrote that I intended to be earning a certain amount of money using speaking, writing and sales skills. At that time, I wasn't even aware that those are the key skills in public relations.

My inner compass was set, especially because I had brought my awareness into the tangible, physical world by writing down my goal. From age 24 to 34 I followed my guiding star through several jobs. I sold training; handled communications at an athletic club; ran special events for the Atlanta Chamber of Commerce; and worked at three small ad agencies as "the suit" or account executive—the liaison between clients, creatives and agency owners.

Eventually it dawned on me that the only ones who earn any real money in small business are the owners.

Another strong bit of guidance: it only took three times losing a job, but by the third time I was downsized, fired, relieved of my income, it had become abundantly clear to me that I was not meant to be employed by someone else. My personality would no longer permit being dictated where to put my priorities and how to structure my life, especially when some of the people who were telling me how to spend my time were w-a-a-y off the deep end.

That final layoff combusted into a Scarlett O'Hara drama

surge and a major shift. Remember the scene in *Gone with the Wind?* After the Civil War is over and the South is vanquished, Scarlett stands in the dusty vegetable patch at Tara and pulls up one scrawny carrot. Nearly starved, she gnaws desperately at it and vows to the universe, "As God is my witness, I'll never go hungry again!"

In my case it sounded more like, "I'll never work for another male creative director again!"

As an early arrival on this new plateau, a place of nearly paralyzing fear and budding self-worth which came from stepping out on my own into business, I received some incredible advice at a very chic party in Virginia-Highland. The scene was an ultra-modern home with expansive windows opening out onto the forest.

Who she was I don't remember, but what she said still rings true: "Don't hold the goal too tightly in your hand. Don't squeeze it out. Just use it as a beacon—something to aim for. Hold the goal gently."

Her point resonated with me, and rang so extremely true during my first year in business as a PR consultant. What a challenging year that was!

Every morning I awoke in fear that I wouldn't make it on my own, and prayed for an hour in bed for the strength, guidance and sense of humor to do what needed to be done that day. *Feel the Fear and Do it Anyway* was my Bible. I earned only $10,000 while paying a $600 monthly mortgage.

For one long, lean year I subsisted on a peanut butter extravaganza, livened up by the occasional tomato sandwich. Tight money, tears and struggle, but it all unfolded in helping me feel comfortable and at home in the universe, and well-taken-care-of, despite my fears for survival. Somehow there was always enough for each day.

One aspect of the great good that unfolded for me, as

though to remind me that miracles are available from every direction, was the free "incubator" office at my former employer's ad agency. In exchange for some minimal PR duties, I had the use of their phone system, computer and printer, so I didn't have to spend any of those meager earnings on outfitting an office. It was as though the universe was holding his little bird in his outstretched palm and letting me know that whenever I was ready to take flight from that safety zone, that would be all right—but no great rush.

In retrospect the transition was amazingly gentle, although the pain of being so broke was quite palpable. However, I was very reluctant to go into consumer debt, which has become an alarming national pastime—and a very precarious situation for individuals and the economy as a whole.

I believe the transition was gentle on that third go-round because I did read the signs and pay attention—and I didn't try to buck the trend and fight to find another J-O-B at an ad agency, but rather knew and respected myself, accepted the inevitable and moved forward with it.

Where are you regarding your employment situation? Ready or not, sometimes losing a job is the best thing that could ever happen.

Beautiful Bouquet

Frequently during that time of transition God would toss me a big beautiful bouquet, just to keep me focused on the world of wonders he reveals when we're alert and open to guidance from beyond.

Although I don't really gravitate to the word "obedient," it really is a matter of recognizing that "where there's no will, there's a way." Stop trying to force my will on the outcome that I believe is THE WAY.

This statement is really a corollary to holding a goal gently in your hands—because if you don't grip that one specific goal so tightly, there's room in your hands for the Universe to place far greater miracles than you could ever imagine.

It's all a matter of knowing how and when to release willfulness and petty little demands, squawking for exactly what you think you want, exactly when you think you want it.

The gospel song tells us, "He's an on-time God, yes He is!" God definitely shows up on his timetable, not ours.

Two months into the business of PD Communications, in the dead of February, I was broke.

I'd just paid all my bills and was down to my last $40. Remember, my style is not to use credit cards and run up consumer debt unless absolutely necessary. I'm not a gambler and I consider paying that kind of interest to be the height of stupidity. That's just me.

Once again, as I'd done with the stolen car episode, I sat there sobbing, shattered and completely surrendered.

A major difference this time: it didn't take me five weeks to achieve the place of surrender, but merely a few moments. I was beginning to catch on!

Knowing of no other recourse, I turned it over.

Don't get me wrong. I hadn't been sitting around waiting for the world to roll up to my feet. In the first two months in business I'd contacted everyone I knew—and the list was extensive. But that was all I could do—rely on their knowledge of me, and a reputation for delivering what I said I would deliver in business.

Sitting there broke, after I sobbed and begged God for a solution, I felt "the peace that passes all understanding" and knew that somehow, some good would manifest.

But who could guess what form it would take?

Two or three days after I surrendered, friends who owned a special events decorating company contacted me. A year earlier I'd supervised brochure development for their well-known organization.

Prince Charles was coming to Charleston on a trip to promote "livable architecture" and my friends the events decorators had been hired to decorate Hibernian Hall, the Dock Street Theatre and the Gibbes Museum of Art. Did I think I could get them some publicity for it? Did I!

Immediately I contacted my good friend in Miami, also a PR consultant, and asked if she'd tag-team the project with me.

Everything unfolded so smoothly it felt like success was pre-ordained. She arrived in Charleston the day before I did and secured all the special clearances and Secret Service ID badges for us, so I had none of the logistical hassles... and could just roll right into gear with the numerous publicity opportunities for our client.

And we did nail those PR opps!

In the *Atlanta Constitution*, the client was featured in the first paragraph of the lead story about the prince's visit. Event trade publications from across the U.S. included features on their decor. Atlanta's leading society magazine ran my story verbatim and included all of my photos.

Television cameras delighted over the angle on five thousand freshly-cut flowers and their perfectly forced blooms; thousands of votives in crystal cups; and the other magical touches to beautify halls which only four months earlier had been blasted by Hurricane Hugo. Now they were venues fit for a king.... Or a prince.

Already decked out in our evening gowns (mine a Loehmann's special, as much as I could afford), my cohort and I hid out in the women's restroom with our Secret Service badges discreetly clipped to our décolletage—quite the fashion element at this gathering.

An hour before the event, police brought the bomb-sniffing dogs through the building, and soon a select group of four hundred Charleston elite began streaming into the Hibernian Hall. At the appropriate time, we glided down the carved stairway as though we'd been there the whole time. Certainly we were among the invited guests.

In the receiving line we angled to shake Prince Charles' hand—he exuded charm with his twinkly, blue-eyed smile, and we talked briefly about polo. I was walking on air. I'd actually shaken hands with a prince!

But the best was yet to come. How could I have guessed that my decorator client had gotten his start as a ballroom dancer on Broadway, and was the best dancer in the room?

Twirling me around the floor to the elegant strains of the Peter Duchin Orchestra as though I were Cinderella, he could make anyone glide gracefully—anyone who knew how to let him lead, that is.

My PR partner joked with me over the irony that something like this should unfold for me, a virtual Bolshevik, customarily unfazed by the glitz and glamour associated with "stars."

But to me, British royalty was different—I felt like I had my finger on the pulse of history. And I loved the opportunity to make my client shine and receive good money for it—enough to float me through the next month or so, and even buy a new pair of shoes!

I recognized later that if I'd not paid attention to the signs and gotten out of the ad agency business at the right time to create a business of my own, that this opportunity and this magic never would have come my way. It was a very strong reinforcement that I was on the right path.

I keep my photo of Prince Charles as a reminder that yes, magic happens, and I can manifest it.

Multi-Hued Abundance

Journeying back to the garden, creativity is the seed and love is the essence of the soil, the rain and the sunshine. These nurture the seed into a fragrant, graceful flower, or perhaps a towering sequoia.

Abundance manifests in many ways, and we come to discover that perhaps the least of these is a paycheck.

One evening, friends who gathered weekly at my home for Unity's Small Group Ministry were asked to bring examples of abundance manifesting in their lives.

Melanie, (names are changed) a counselor of families in challenging financial situations, presented a photo of herself and her father. After years of minimal communication, he was moving from Virginia to live with her. Her heart filled with joy; she had always wanted a relationship with him and now in adulthood it was manifesting. Now, almost two years into living together, she says all the old hurts are healing and she's very happy that he's here.

Kind, helpful Don said his symbol of abundance was currently in the mail—a photo of himself and a check addressed to the U.S. Passport Service—for a trip to Hong Kong with his 80-year-old mother.

Imagine the abundant feeling of letting your heart expand to reunite with parents, even if earlier times might have included strained moments or actual animosity?

Maturity tends to bring with it an acceptance of our parents as human beings who were (and perhaps still are) struggling with their own issues and demons just as we struggle with ours. From that perspective, how can we continue to expect them to have been what we thought they should be? Didn't they have a right to be themselves?

And then, once we have granted them forgiveness, when the heart is overflowing with good wishes, how can the world possibly seem a poor and paltry place?

More of our Small Group Ministry gathering shared their treasures. Valerie, who teaches art to mentally and emotionally challenged teens, brought a photo of herself in gypsy garb, primed to read cards and do palmistry. It took a girlfriend to convince her that she had the gift and could really do anything she wanted with her psychic abilities.

Peter, a mild, witty administrator at a local college, presented a postcard of a lovely beach scene in the Caribbean, outlined in red (for passion!) We cheered him for his intentional expansion beyond his cautiously circumscribed life.

A palm tree in the photo leaned sharply toward the water as though in forward motion—progressing along a life path that may continue to reveal itself in many more beautiful ways with his elevated and enlivened consciousness. The tree's angle also represented its ability to bend with the elements, to be in the flow.

Someone suggested that he take it to Kinko's and blow it up. As a musician he's more attuned to the auditory sense, so he thought the pocket-sized version would work for him. But since the subconscious mind responds to visual stimulus, attracting to it what it sees, we encouraged him to put that card where he could see it—and perhaps play some calypso music when he's visualizing the expansive future. Two years

219

later, it's still on the dashboard of his car as a reminder of *La Vida Loca!*

Thoughts are things—and very powerful things at that! The more we can assist the positive visions by using our five senses to make them vivid, the more quickly they will manifest.

My own symbol of abundance was the licorice plant with the green heart-shaped stone in it—the plant that had withered and died as dear Fred died, and then resurrected itself and leafed out again after his physical transition. Aptly, I had named it Fred. Surely he experienced the joy in the center of our prayer circle where we loved and supported each other.

These heart-opening and self-revealing exercises helped us become more vulnerable, sharing our real-ness with each other.

Here we were, a little cluster of Velveteen rabbits with our fur rubbed off and our button eyes missing from all the wear and tear of living and striving in the world—putting our love out there too—sometimes to experience love in return; and sometimes to learn other lessons.

Count it All Joy!

Here's a question—how would you respond to these events?

You forget your wallet and license in the company truck, and get a ticket while driving your own car without a license. You're involved in a car chase and then help block the escape of a hit-and-run underage driver. You change the flat tire of a man with late stage AIDS. You go home to discover that your home has been burglarized.

A mixed bag of a day, and Don, a man of many talents including professional photographer and tree-climber and cutter, chose to count it all joy.

He held up the parking ticket as another symbol of his abundance. I wondered aloud whether it was because he knew he had the money to pay the fine. Actually, his logic was that he would make an appearance in court and not have to pay at all—in fact he was counting on that.

Don said he and his tree-cutting partner were sitting by the roadside for five minutes for no particular reason when along came a sick man who needed his tire changed.

"I could call Triple A," the man commented.

"You can call me Triple A," Don jumped in. It worked out for them in perfect order. A major step for Don was his accepting the $12 the man paid him for changing the tire. In the past he said he'd done plenty of favors like that but never accepted payment for them.

Living abundantly involves energy exchange. It's a universal law, from which more plenty flows. We must know how to give as well as how to receive.

Learning to Receive

How many of us find it incredibly difficult to accept the good that comes our way? Perhaps it stems from early training or from Bible passages such as "It is more blessed to give than to receive," but under universal law, everything has an equal and opposite reaction, so when we give we must be open to receive as well.

Our friend Don had mentioned the numerous times that he would do small favors for people like changing a flat tire,

---

and when they offered him money he refused, saying that they should just do another good deed for someone else.

Later it occurred to him that by blocking the flow of good coming back to him or by trying to deflect it to someone else, that he was trying to subvert the universal law of give and take, the law of energy exchange. He may have expected the best, but he was not able to accept the bounty. Perhaps he didn't see it was meant for him when it appeared before him, even though it was his energy that had been expended on behalf of someone else's good.

Count it all joy! Powerful words, powerful reminders to ourselves, even when we're down financially, or ill, or going through a tough time in relationships, or feeling abandoned or misunderstood—count it all joy.

Underlying the seemingly negative events on the surface, lies the purpose—an opportunity for greater awareness and greater connection with God.

By synchronicity, at the very moment I was thinking about those words and our discussion of them in the Small Group Ministry, outside my window appeared something I'd never seen before on my deck in Atlanta—a hummingbird, symbol of joy!

It very busily sampled the salvia, red and lush from inches and inches of spring rain. Abundance burgeons as the Hanging Gardens of Babylon with pots and planters balancing along the deck railing, on a two tiered rattan table from the 1940s and scattered about the deck in colorful profusion of red, white, purple, yellow, orange, pink, fuschia and all degrees of bright, light and pale greens. An abundance of inner joy expressing in the outer.

The question is, if our outer circumstances reflect our inner aspects, which came first, the joy or the hummingbird?

222

Hanging Gardens of Babylon abundant on the deck.

Ruts in the Road

Habits are first cobwebs, then cables, as the Spanish proverb says. And it makes no difference whether the habits are positive or negative, once we get locked into them. So watch out which ones you're choosing for yourself!

One of the most difficult challenges for me is the renewed awareness of the power of the spoken word—and the unspoken words which drift around in my head to either support or undermine me.

It's a fact that the negative can very rapidly wear grooves in our psyches that may quickly evolve into deep, hard ruts— just like the ruts in an old country clay road.

To wrench ourselves back onto the smooth track we must first fill in the old rut of negativity, and then begin to wear in a new, more positive track.

Unity teaches us that using Denials and Affirmations helps us stay on track, and they actually do this, if repeated frequently enough, by burning new neural pathways in our brains. *The Handbook of Positive Prayer* by Hypatia Hasbrouck is a powerful guide.

First, Deny that the old tapes or thought processes have any hold whatsoever over you. "I release those old thoughts and words that have no effect on me!"

Next, Affirm that you are creating something better in your life: "I am happy, healthy, whole and free!"

Here's how they work. First, remember that negative appearances are not ultimately real and have only the power we are willing to give them. The denial states our unwilling-ness to give power to anything that threatens to take or keep our good away from us. When we think or say denials, we tell our subconscious mind that it is not to react to the negative appearances but is to act upon the affirmations, which we make next.

An example of a denial is: "This situation is powerless to take or keep my good from me."

For affirmations, use present tense throughout your prayer. Whenever possible, insert the word NOW.

To keep prayers positive, it may help to begin prayer statements with "I know that" or "I give thanks for." Additionally, instead of "God, please heal me," say "I know that God is healing me now.' For example, "What God has done for others, God can do for me, and more."

Here are some examples of my denials and affirmations.

Abundance Denial: My hesitation to expand into my true wealth is powerless to withhold me from God's incredible abundance.

Affirmation: I am the successful author of best sellers and enjoying all the benefits of that creative life.

Spiritual Growth Denial: What appear to be my human flaws are powerless to prevent my spiritual growth.

Affirmation: With each expansion, I can never shrink back to the place that I was before. God makes me whole, well and free! Thank you God!

Success Denial: My fears and hesitations to step into the spotlight have no power over me.

Affirmation: I am in the Flow, born to succeed as God's child.

Will Denial: My willfulness is powerless to keep my good from me.

Affirmation: Where there's no will (except God's) there's a way. I thrive in the Flow! Life is rich and wonderful in God's plan!

"Do not be conformed to this world, but be transformed by the renewal of your mind."

In *You Can Heal Your Life,* Louise Hay speaks of the thousands of affirmations she recited to herself before she was able to heal. Her book is an incredible testimony to the power of mind over matter, filled with hope.

This is a good place for you to think of a simple denial and affirmation for yourself. We have to retrain our brains to get back to the garden. What a beautiful place it is, once we grant ourselves access. It's all up to us.

Several doctors had told Myrtle Fillmore, co-founder of Unity with her husband Charles, that she had six months to live with her advanced tuberculosis, a disease taken for granted as a death sentence in the late 1800s when she was diagnosed.

One pivotal evening she attended a lecture in which she heard the words "we were not born to inherit illness"—words that she completely took to heart.

She went home and set up two chairs—she sat on one, and on the other she placed a picture of Jesus the Christ. For two hours every day for almost two years she sat and meditated on Christ, and her own Christ spirit within—and she was able to heal herself completely of the disease.

Despite the nay-saying of the "experts" she was able to fill in the old rut of negativity and death, and redefine her path into one of positive results and good health.

The Unity School of Christianity emerged as a result. Her friends and neighbors wanted to experience what Myrtle Fillmore had.

Negative energy can be extremely powerful once we allow ourselves into its grip. On the other hand, positive energy is even more powerful.

One very thoughtful member of our Small Group Ministry

mentioned that when she feels in the physical grip of some negativity, she visualizes the positive outcome right then, so she can harness the energy that sways her over into a lighter place.

This concept is linked to the power of reversing an objection. Often when we state why we can't do something, for example, "I can't go to the lake because I can't swim," that might be the very reason why we should do it. Step into the lake—face the fear—in the shallows of course at first, and begin to learn how to swim!

It's a way of taking ourselves by surprise—throwing us out of our old ingrained rut and into something fresh, creative and life-affirming. After all, if we're not growing, we're dying.

We must continually add new tools to the garden shed— and keep the old ones sharpened.

Consider a denial as a pick and shovel duo, hacking out the old dead ideas. Affirmations are the fresh, amended and fertilized soil. Then add the love—sunshine and rain—to the seeds of creativity and see what springs up out of that path that looked so parched and dead before. A paradise!

Here's what happens: as we expand into the flow and enact the principles of Truth, we come to believe that we truly have everything that we need in order to grow and thrive.

Going Sane

After several years of intense hard work ramping up my PR consulting business and churning out six figures for several years in a row, it began to dawn on me that I really was not enjoying the workaholic lifestyle—putting in ten hour

Sundays and 12-14 hours on virtually every other day of the week.

My self-talk became, "I'm going to have a nervous break-down," until I realized that such negativity was a self-fulfilling prophecy. I decided to snap out of it and get some balance back into my life.

In talking with my financial advisor, he informed me that I'd be quite comfortable with a certain amount of income and still have a lovely, rich and balanced life.

Around six years into the business I began to experience the fluctuations that happen with every business—clients go and come, ebb and flow, just like all the cycles of nature.

That year my largest client moved on—about a third of my income. At first I panicked a bit, but then I realized that the Great Power would fulfill my needs so that I could continue on my path. The time and financial comfort level to pursue my creative interests and express myself through the written word would be available to me.

Things continued to work out beautifully; I became accustomed to the ebb and flow of clients and income, to the point where I no longer even speculate at the beginning of the year what may happen—I simply know that God will provide.

In fact, in a meditative and symbolic gesture that has occurred several times, when I lose a large piece of business I take myself back to the garden and work with the soil, and spread the fertilizer around and dig it in a bit. With plant food a-plenty in the freshly dug holes, I place the tender little plantlings into their new spaces and croon to them that they are going to be so beautiful, and big and strong...

This exercise in the outer reflects something in the inner that then reappears in the world as a feeling of calm, or actual new growth in my other creative pursuits or business. A time

Tears are an organic fertilizer that God
really understands. The result: Pansies smile back at me.

of rumination, singing, and trust in God, especially in the perfumed air of spring!

Many times I have sat with my pots and planters all around, crying in a warm and gentle rain, planting flowers, repotting plants and letting the tears run down my arms and hands and into the soil, an organic fertilizer that God really understands.

This exercise in faith yields new growth in other areas almost immediately—in effect, it primes the spiritual pump for miracles to occur.

Here, I believe, is the true meaning of abundance—recognizing that providence and plenty come from every direction if only we are open and receptive to their many manifestations. Friendships, the surrounding beauty, opportunities that present themselves. It's our choice which ones we take.

Checks appear from out of nowhere (that long-forgotten tax refund or the money owed for a loan); calls come from unexpected benefactors. Staying attuned to the perfect ebb and flow of the universe, and stepping out in faith like The Fool in the Tarot deck, never knowing what the next day will bring, but fully expecting our daily bread.

Some called Jesus The Fool. Some thought the same of young and wealthy Siddhartha Gautama when he renounced all his worldly treasures to step onto the seeker's path, eventually to bring his understanding, compassion and wisdom to the world as Buddha, the Enlightened One.

We all have a path upon which God supports us, and it's a matter of reading the signs to know whether we are on the right one.

In Adventures on the Quest, Richard and Mary-Alice JaFolla offer their ideas as to how we can know whether or not we're in tune with God's will. Questions we should ask about the situation:

Is it for the greater good of all involved?

Are doors continuing to open?

Is energy flowing in that direction?

If our instincts make us recoil; if the still, small voice is clamoring No, should we reverse our own objection and travel on that path?

In my opinion, the best answer lies in prayer and meditation. What are we recoiling from? Is it something that will drain our energy and prevent our journey to our own calling? If that is the case, a reconnoiter is mandatory.

Delightful Dr. Susan Jeffers states in *Feel the Fear and Do It Anyway*, "Don't protect, correct!" If we recognize shortly along one leg of our journey that it's taking us in the wrong direction, we don't need to stay the course until we crash on the rocks that we spotted from the distance.

We simply turn in another direction and steer to safety, as a good sea captain would. At times that course correction is very minor, but at other times it involves turning the entire ocean liner around. As we all know that can involve monumental effort and energy—faith, patience and trust. And time.

Envision a sailboat race, with a regatta of proud boats sporting puffed sails and darting toward their destination. Sailors know that the boats most certainly do not move in a straight line to the finish; they're constantly tacking back and forth to take advantage of the breezes and currents.

Even so, they arrive at the finish line (God willing) despite having been "off course" approximately 90% of the time!

The same holds true with airline flights. The captain or pilot (our conscious mind) is at the controls to correct the course of the sailboat, aircraft, or our life when we seem to be heading in the wrong direction. There is no need for self-flagellation or shaming when we get off course. Correction and moving forward are all that's necessary.

231

Back to the Garden

On the path back to the garden of self-awareness, self-acceptance, self-respect and self-love, we need to give ourselves all the support we can get!

Additionally, there's no reason to make anyone else wrong when we decide to make a shift. It is what it is—simply a shift—and we don't need to point the finger of blame out there because of a decision that we have made that's in our best interests.

Dr. Jeffers describes the lighter feeling that we can choose to experience when shifting course: "If you take Path A, you get to taste the strawberries. If you take Path B, you get to taste the blueberries."

And the obvious corollary: If the berries you're eating are poisonous, spit them out and go find a path with berries that nourish you instead of making you sick!

Discovering one's true path sometimes requires some real sleuth work—but it usually does hearken back to remembering what we love or what we love doing.

Famous shoe designer Manolo Blahnik experienced some very limiting careers as a young man. They tapped his creativity, but only peripherally. Eventually he found himself working at *Vogue* as a clerk. Editor Diana Vreeland spied some of his doodles of handbag designs and encouraged him in that direction, until he got back to his original love, shoe design.

As a child he'd gotten a great deal of enjoyment by fashioning tiny shoes for the lizards in his garden in the Canary Islands off Spain. He configured the tiny lizard scuffs out of the foil from his mother's cigarette packs!

Now those stylin' shoes for lizards have morphed into high fashion worth several hundred dollars a pair. What tiny pair of high heels for lizards is scampering through your psyche and ready step out on the dance floor?

Two Rich Parables

In ancient times a King had a boulder placed in the center of one of the region's main roads, then hid himself to watch the passers-by. He wanted to see how people responded to this new obstacle.

As the day passed, many wealthy merchants and some of the King's own courtiers strolled past and simply walked around the boulder, while some complained loudly and blamed the King for not keeping the roads clear. Not a one did anything to clear the boulder out of the way for others.

Eventually a peasant shuffled along, straining under his burden of vegetables, which he balanced gingerly on his head. Upon approaching the boulder, the peasant laid down his load and tried to move the stone over to the ditch. After much heaving and effort, he shoved it out of the way.

Again he hoisted his load of vegetables to his head, and suddenly noticed a purse lying in the dusty road where the boulder had been. The purse contained a wealth of gold coins and a note from the King. "This gold goes to the person who removes the boulder from the road."

The gleeful peasant, rewarded for his efforts, realized what many of us never understand: Every obstacle presents an opportunity to improve our condition.

A corollary to this is the legend about the prosperous Persian farmer who deserted his fruitful lands to search for immense wealth in mythical diamond fields.

Lured by the tales of a Buddhist priest, he roamed far and wide seeking wealth beyond imagination. As for the farmer, his own youth and wealth disappeared during this fruitless quest, and he died far from home, an old and disillusioned pauper.

233

Not long after that, acres of diamonds were found on the farmer's own land.

Our riches are not in far-away mountains or distant seas, but right at hand if we know how, and where, to look.

Are we really meant to have all this good come to us? Are we mentally, emotionally and spiritually able to accept the good when our past pattern has been to expect Murphy's Law—if something can go wrong, it will?

What we expect is what we get. And if we've enlightened ourselves to the degree that we expect the best, then whose purpose are we serving when we deflect the good that appears before us?

Remembering how many years I lived in a place I couldn't even keep a plant alive, I glance out my window at tiers of flowers and plants on my deck. How I yearned for this environment that has unfolded for me!

To get here, I used the same powerful Make Your Vision Vivid exercise that I described regarding my friend with her Brookhaven palazzo and swimming pool.

First, I knew what I wanted to manifest. Second, and even more importantly, I knew why I wanted it.

What I wanted was to have my office in my home. Why I wanted it was vital to my happiness. In order for us to get what we want, we really need to understand the WHY—the emotional underpinnings of our desire. That's what pulls us toward it—the connection of the heart to the head.

To me, the idea of having an office in my own home meant I could work undistracted by office politics and unhindered by dress codes or the need to wear a certain daily corporate mask. Being true to myself this way held infinite appeal to me. In a word it spelled FREEDOM!

Third, I reminded myself that shifting into a new work environment would be less stressful and satisfy my desire for more time to invest in creative pursuits.

Finally, I envisioned the perfect situation using all my five senses, using present tense.

I saw myself sitting on a chaise lounge with my laptop computer on my lap, working on my latest creative endeavor with phones at hand in case clients needed me. My lovely surroundings were the screened porch filled with plants and a deck overflowing with flowers. I could smell the fragrance of the tall mimosa that draped itself over the porch and below, the profusion of blooming gardenias wafting on the soft air. I felt the cool vinyl of the chaise lounge on my legs and the breeze of the overhead fan keeping me cool. I could hear the tinkle of wind chimes and birds calling in the cool morning, as the leaves rustled faintly overhead. I touched the keys of my laptop, all in my mind.

I envisioned that evening, taking a sip of wine, inhaling deeply of the fragrance of salmon on the grill, as the man who cherished me came up and brushed my neck and shoulder with his lips, telling me how glad he was to see me. I envisioned the lights along the Path of Possibility blinking on simultaneously. A magical evening was at hand, a magical evening that was my co-creation.

My model for this environment included screened porches we'd enjoyed at both grandmothers' homes, as well as homes from my childhood. Meals on the porches under the batting overhead fan, enjoying garden fragrances and the clatter of crickets and birds calling—what lovely, harmonious times with my family!

The fact that during our Ohio years we did not have a

screened porch, but rather a baking hot southwestern-facing patio where we never spent any time together, makes me realize that one of the key components of family harmony was missing—a place for us to be together outdoors, to share meals or play ping pong. Environment is key to well being.

Before this work-from-home vision manifested in my present life, I talked about it; I thought about it; imagined it; breathed it and dreamed it for more than ten years until I was able to convert my vision into reality—and then how vastly better it was than what I'd even imagined!

Not only did it have one screened porch, the porch was double-decker—with the lower "Lido deck" providing space for a hot tub. Now here's a morning commute: from the bed to the hot tub!

So very often reality unfolds in a far better way than we could ever have planned or envisioned. That's why it's important to affirm, "This or something better comes to all involved in perfect order." How can we with our limited perspectives, ever foretell our greatest good?

"If one advances confidently in the direction of his dreams and lives the life he has imagined, he will meet with a success unexpected in common hours," H.D. Thoreau told us.

But remember, action is key, and it may take a lot of work to get there. If someone else hands everything to you on a platter, it doesn't mean nearly as much—in fact that "enabling" might be the very thing that holds you back.

A man found a butterfly's chrysalis and kept it on his porch for observation. After a few days, a small opening appeared. He sat and watched the butterfly for several hours as it struggled to force its body through the hole. Then it appeared to stop making any progress.

As it seemed the butterfly could go no further, the man

decided to help it emerge, and he snipped off the remaining bit of the chrysalis with a nail scissors.

The butterfly then emerged easily. But it had a swollen body and small, shriveled wings, certainly inadequate to heave its lumpy body into the air. The man expected that at any moment the wings would enlarge and expand to support its body, which would contract in time. Neither happened!

In fact, the butterfly spent the rest of its short life crawling around with a swollen body and shriveled wings. It never was able to fly.

What the man failed to understand in his kindness and haste was that the restrictive cocoon and the struggle required for the butterfly to get through the tiny opening were nature's way of forcing fluid from the butterfly's body into its wings. That way it would be ready for flight once it achieved its freedom from its developmental time within the protective covering.

Sometimes struggles are exactly what we need in our lives. If we were to experience life without any obstacles, it would cripple us.

I still appreciate one of my father's favorite expressions: "You'll always find a helping hand....right at the end of your arm."

At one point in our lives we may have dreamed of the handsome prince or the fairy godmother appearing to rescue us from our tower, kissing us out of our slumber and carrying us forth in glory to our destiny. Now it's time to create a rope ladder out of our own sheets and climb down out of that tower—holding God's will in our mind at all times—and discover what needs to be done!

237

The Red Carpet Treatment

One of my own intentions took twenty-five years to manifest, but I was determined when I set it that I was willing to wait. God does not always operate on our timetable, after all.

Although we may think our plan is the best, we can't petition the Lord with prayer. That is true. Any amount of pleading, bargaining or cajoling God to deliver what we want on our timetable simply does not work.

The objective of prayer is to experience attunement and alignment with God, conscious contact by becoming one with the presence of God—not whining and pleading like a spoiled brat for what you want when you want it.

"For everything there is a season, and a time to every purpose under heaven." Patience is sometimes the best solution—and the only solution.

My long-held intention, which took a quarter of a century to come into being, began when I was a twenty-year-old college student, and it was also an example of the Law of Reciprocity.

A group of English majors from UNC-Chapel Hill was living in London for a month to study theater. After thirty days of fabulous adventures and fourteen outstanding theater experiences, four of us took off across Europe on a two-week backpacking trek.

Being students, our cash was limited and we spent more than one night sleeping on stone benches in rail stations or grungy couches in airports—only to be ousted by the *gendarmes* every time they passed on patrol.

One night on a crowded train from Barcelona to Paris, I slept with filthy feet in my face in a cabin jammed with the three of us students, a Bulgarian flamenco dancer, a grandmother tending her little girl covered with measles, a Parisian businessman and an American on fellowship in Paris—our translator. A colorful experience, but not one I'd necessarily be willing to repeat.

At the time, I made a vow to myself that I'd not come back to Europe until I could do everything first class. And although I didn't realize that would take 25 years to manifest, it appeared in even brighter ways than I'd imagined.

Out of the blue, my PR cohort and friend who had tag-teamed the Prince Charles adventure a decade earlier introduced me to a fabulous new client. Of course I am eternally grateful to her, as well as to the Law of Reciprocity for this cause and effect.

On media trips representing British Airways, both the airline and our destinations rolled out the red carpet for us.

London—such a captivating city with its bright baskets of flowers and human-sized architecture, graced by lush squares and formal gardens on the upscale West End where we were lodged. Five star hotels Claridge's hosted us on one visit; The Dorchester on another and 51 Buckingham Gate, steps away from Buckingham Palace, hosted a third. God's incredible bounty manifested in such an amazing manner—it was the perfect example of "this or something better" appearing in my life.

As consciousness expands, opportunities do too. The really wonderful part is that once your consciousness has expanded, you can never shrink back to the smaller person you were earlier.

Floral majesty at The Dorchester in London.

Love Yourself

"This above all, to thine own self be true. Therefore thou can be false to no man."

Shakespeare said it. Sages, seers and saints from all the ages say it. Be your own best friend. Get acquainted with the best friend you'll ever have, and fall in love with yourself!

If you have some lingering doubt that this must not be right—that it is vain or arrogant to love yourself, take into account that if we cannot love ourselves, how can we possibly love anything else?

Since our outer reality is a reflection of what's happening inwardly, the more acceptance and love we feel toward ourselves, the more love and acceptance we will experience in the world. Sages encourage us to look at ourselves with eyes of love.

"Once we accept a bad thought it is difficult to remove it, for it enters very deeply. So be yourself, and then see yourself. This is the first step in creating amity toward yourself, and when you have amity for yourself, naturally you have amity for all. A person who does not harm himself or herself is not going to harm anybody else, for in order to harm somebody, one has to harm himself first. Think of a matchstick. When the matchstick tries to ignite something, first it must burn its own face; it is not going to burn others if it does not first burn itself," says Munishree Chitrabhanu in *Inner Paths.*

It may seem obvious that learning how to take care of yourself is one very important and major aspect of being true to yourself, but some people go through their entire lifetimes without the most basic clues of self-care.

Perhaps they've gone at a young age directly from the home of their parents into the arms of a spouse who handled all the finances and made all the major life decisions, and so they never learned how to balance a checking account.

Perhaps they never learned for themselves the degree of energy it takes to earn enough money to buy a Prada purse (or even a knockoff). Have you ever heard of the person who knows the price of everything, but the value of nothing?

One hears of delicate little old ladies whose husbands managed everything in the household. Suddenly they divorce or the spouse dies, they're on their own and they discover to their horror that everything was completely leveraged and the house of cards is tumbling down around them.

Whoever buys into the myth any longer that it's a good thing to be taken care of? What could be less empowering than having everything done for you—ultimately a sickening process, and I do mean in terms of physical health.

Think of our mothers' and grandmothers' generation, the World War II generation, stifling themselves in the sterile suburbs of the fifties and sixties, the Donna Reed world where boredom was the demon to hold at bay. A whole generation was trained to believe that they had to be taken care of, and many paid far too dear a price for that "care."

The truth came to me from a good friend's mother: When you marry for money you earn every penny of it.

Now many have succumbed to the lure of easy consumer credit—unimaginable hordes who choose to deceive themselves about the extent of their credit card debt. That submerged iceberg daily undermines their peace of mind, looming just ahead on their course—and potentially leading to the extreme pain of bankruptcy if they don't steer clear.

It amazes me that by pushing the day of reckoning further and further back, individuals who really aren't doing anything to reverse the trend financially convince themselves that some day, somehow, it will all solve itself, as if landing in personal bankruptcy can be called a solution.

Living by appearance alone, precariously overextended on loans and creative financing is a dangerous game, which lends itself to dire consequences: loss of the nice home; the new leather couch and recliner removed by the loan company; the car whisked away in the dead of night by the dreaded "repo man."

Shady business, all because people are not willing to accept responsibility for their spiritual cravings, which will never be fulfilled by a fancy new car or the faux chateau in the glamorous swim and tennis community. What good is the big new home if you can't afford furniture?

But wait—you can furnish a house on zero interest with nothing down and no payments until next year—so who cares what happens until the piper calls up for his money?

It's a supreme example of how well advertising works. People have bought into the notion that in order to "be" someone that they must have all the accessories to make them look the part.

Recently I was at Lake Lanier near Atlanta, at Bald Ridge Marina. As I strolled past slip after slip filled with gigantic half-million dollar yachts and cabin cruisers on that gorgeous day, approximately only ten of 300 boats were out on the lake providing an enjoyable experience for their owners. Those actually using their boats appeared to be having a wonderful time.

But let's weigh the cost of having your property floating, unattended and unused for forty-eight out of fifty-two weekends a year or more—just collecting barnacles and payments for the dock slip. What is really the point of owning more and more things when we don't even have time or make time to enjoy what we already have?

Commercialism and me-ism are destroying our culture. The commercials tell us we won't be a thing without Baywatch breast sizes and teeth so white they're translucent. Oh, and better not forget the shoes and designer outfits!

Is this being true to our real selves—going on another shopping binge for entertainment when we haven't ever worn a third of the items in the closet?

It's a classic joke to me the suits and designer duds I find on consignment with tags still on them! A $280 silk blazer for $28. A $600 woven leather shirt for five dollars!

What has happened to our priorities in life? Or as Susan Powter says, "Stop the madness!" How is it that we've come to believe that buying the trendiest outdoor grill will make us more virile—or that driving an SUV gives us the right to barrel down the expressway, nudging the "little people" from behind as though we're the Queen of Sheba? What the heck exactly is going on?

My guess is that people are angry with themselves for being duped by the commercial culture, and so they're inflicting their feelings on anyone who is in their way.

Nothing about all these things has any connection with our essence, who we truly are, and yet we continue to swarm to them like flies to honey, convinced that they'll be our salvation—or perhaps keep other people from "finding us out."

Is it being true to ourselves to overextend until the plank we're walking snaps off and we're splashing in shark-infested waters? And why must we keep up with the Johansons in order to save face, or put on some act that makes people think we're better off than we actually are? A recent study shows that endless consumerism is the sure route not to happiness, but its opposite!

In *The Millionaire Next Door*, authors Thomas J. Stanley and William D. Danko point out that the truly wealthy rarely drive ostentatious cars or live in McMansions. In fact "old money" often lives quite modestly. "Bling-bling" is a joke.

Picture Ted Turner, one of the world's wealthiest men, driving around Atlanta in his Ford Taurus—or Wal-Mart founder Sam Walton tooling around Bentonville, Arkansas in his pick-'em-up truck. These men know that the measure of a human being is what's within and has little to do with externals, beyond a neat and acceptable appearance.

But now even men are falling into the traps women have been sucked into for decades—with the need for lasered-smooth bodies and $450 shirts.

These freshly dubbed metrosexuals may have a slick exterior, but if they don't have the inner glow of self-love, just like any of us they are but "clanging cymbals" as the Bible would say.

Escape from the Big Trap

I worked with one of my coaching clients on this harmful habit of overspending, which sprang from a great deal of pain.

Her belief that appearance was everything had gotten her overextended to an extreme. This beautiful, successful young sales professional, who from all outward appearances was on top of the world, was actually suffering deeply and using compulsive shopping and other self-destructive behaviors in an attempt to fill up the void in her life.

One phrase in class had gotten her attention: I said I didn't believe in consumer debt simply because of what it does to my peace of mind. Everyone has different levels of tolerance and I admit mine is rather low, but a friend who came from "old money" taught me that paying interest on credit cards is the most stupid waste of all.

Luckily for Kelly (name is changed), she was able to see what she was doing to herself and reverse the trend before it ate her up.

Since she was a very focused and high-powered sales producer, she was able to use large commissions to pay down debt rapidly and establish a better balance in her life.

So what's my point? My point is that, for some people, the fancier the car and the more stylin' the clothes, the less they may have their financial act together or why would they be putting on such a big show? And for whom?

Perhaps it's just to attract the attention of others who, if they are true to themselves, will rapidly disappear as soon as they learn what kind of mess this person has created just in order to "look the part." It's a rather self-defeating cycle. Except, of course, for those who prefer to hitch their wagons to an illusion.

One aspect of being true to yourself means taking care of yourself financially. That includes attracting abundance and sustaining it.

Focus on Wealth and Success

The Bible tells us that abundance and success (however we define them personally) are our birthright. As Dr. Joseph Murphy teaches in *The Power of Your Subconscious Mind*, focusing on the powerful words of wealth and success, especially just before falling asleep or just after awakening, will activate your subconscious to draw those to you.

If, however, you suffer from deservability issues and you experience a mental conflict or argument, and feel that you are lying to yourself with your affirmations for wealth or success, then your conscious mind will reject what you are saying and you will manifest the opposite result. The subconscious mind always accepts your most dominant belief.

Even if outward appearances do not immediately respond to your affirmations for wealth and success, remember the metaphor of preparing the soil, planting seeds in your garden, fertilizing and watering them, and watching them grow. You don't dig up seeds ten minutes after planting them while still expecting to harvest a beautiful garden.

By the same token, don't replace affirmations of wealth and success with fearful thoughts of poverty a few minutes later and expect to expand into your birthright of abundance. Hold the vision of what you want and let it grow.

"According to your belief it is done to you," says the Bible.

Your Health is Your True Wealth

Taking care of yourself obviously includes caring for your health—not easy in a world dominated by TV and fast food. Add to the mix vast areas with no sidewalks, few opportunities and no real necessity to walk, and there's the recipe for out-of-shape America.

With the dominance of this unholy three, we can easily rot our brains as well as our bodies.

Studies have shown that people who let their brains atrophy by watching television all the time are more likely to develop problems like Alzheimer's later in life. On top of that, by eating the zillion calorie "supersized meals" and chugging down 26 oz Big Gulp sugar water, you can morph into the one-third of the U.S. population considered obese, and throw in diabetes, heart disease, arthritis and other health problems associated with lugging around what is essentially another whole person on your body frame.

In the documentary "Supersize Me" filmmaker Morgan Spurlock ate three meals a day at McDonald's for one month. In that short period of time, he gained 24 pounds, his liver turned to "pâté" according to a medical exam; his blood pressure shot up and his blood sugar got dangerously close to diabetic levels. It took him fourteen months to lose the weight he had gained.

Thankfully, American planners are waking up to the need for sidewalks in cities and suburbs, and McDonald's has eliminated the super-sized meal.

Making the personal choices that are right for your own health is extremely empowering, and it is a key step to getting back to the garden. Program your subconscious mind to "gain health" rather than telling yourself you want to "lose weight."

Nobody wants to be a loser, and the subconscious doesn't absorb negatives.

Tell yourself, "I am healthy and at my best weight. I eat energy foods and I feel great!" (Make it into a little song—the rhymes work).

Learning how to take care of yourself feels good. I know because I only really began to learn when I absolutely had to—when I had no other choice, health wise—my blood pressure was sky high; I had parted ways with a man who had been a wonderful chef; and I didn't even know how to cook for myself at age 43!

Many of you may be thinking, "That's pretty lame, not

knowing how to cook at that age," and you're right, it was! Basically all I could "cook" was canned soup, frozen dinners, and eggs.

Friends would tease me about the "pressed rat" shaved meat I kept for sandwiches—loaded with salt, certainly bad for high blood pressure. Those bad-for-me processed meats, a six-pack of beer and a few colors of nail polish were about the only things in my refrigerator for twenty years—literally! (Keeping the nail polish refrigerated makes it last longer—no, I wasn't drinking it.)

Although it was extremely painful to recognize and admit to myself that it was time to learn how to take care of ME and my own health with proper nutrition, it was also one of the most liberating advances I've ever made.

Now I have at least three or four gourmet meals in my repertoire, and can easily invite friends over for dinner on the screened porch. When it's a potluck and everyone brings a dish, it's simple and fun because we all contribute, and people usually like to share their signature dish.

Even more than that, having learned how to cook I feel so adult. I don't need mommy to make me a peanut butter sandwich anymore—I can fix my own, thank you.

Remember that rush when you were a little kid and you were finally tall enough to reach the top of the counter? At age 43 that feeling paid an unexpected revisit when I learned to cook.

I continue to enjoy having a man in my life who cooks, but one of the reasons we're attracted to people is because we want to develop those characteristics in ourselves. This is part of the path to wholeness.

It's the alchemical union of masculine and feminine within, expressed outwardly—sometimes through people we draw into our lives to counterbalance our own characteristics.

Self-nurturing

I remember when even the mention of the word "nurture" made me feel nauseated. Deep down I didn't feel that I deserved to be nurtured. I didn't feel I had earned the right. What a pathetic and painful stretch of years that was. Thank God I got beyond it with inner work and learning to turn things over to the Higher Power.

The fact is, we all have earned the right for nurturance from others, along with self-nurturance and self-love. And we demonstrate that by taking care of ourselves.

Remember, the key components of good health are proper nutrition, the right amounts of exercise and sleep, and peace of mind, which comes from forgiveness and the inner life.

During Yoga Teacher Training at Peachtree Yoga Center in Atlanta, among many of his gems, our teacher Graham Fowler said, "I'm not going to tell you how to eat, but as you're walking down the grocery store aisle and picking things up, ask yourself, 'Is this really food?'"

A purist, he is vegan. I'm not, but I have considerably cut back on red meat and hard-to-digest items. I take supplements and drink a protein shake of soymilk, whey protein, seaweed/algae powder, flax oil and a banana almost every morning, which keeps me revved up, sometimes until four pm.

But I didn't shift to this healthy food format until a visit to a naturopath in my early forties. My chief complaint at the time was hot flashes and inability to sleep due to perimenopause. I already found hormone replacement therapy suspect, years before studies revealed that it increases risks of heart attack, stroke and other negative side effects, and so I've never used HRT.

It was so refreshing to me that the naturopath chose to help me improve my health through a better diet instead of drug therapy.

If you're reading this book, odds are you're already interested in natural alternatives for an overall happier, healthier life. If you haven't consulted with a naturopath or dietitian yet, it's something to consider. Regrettably, most medical doctors receive no training whatsoever in nutrition, so they're clueless to help us help ourselves in the most natural ways possible—through what we put in our mouths.

I remember in my twenties being astounded at the notion that eating red meat makes us more aggressive or "bloodthirsty." When you think about it, isn't that logical?

Cultural leaders like Oprah have clued people into the dire effects of "the whites:" White flour, sugar, dairy products.

Despite what advertising tells us, most dairy products are not the best source of calcium, and most people shouldn't drink milk at all. Actually, almonds have almost double the amount of milligrams of calcium than milk does. But here I am doing what I said I wouldn't do—telling you how to eat.

Fresh fruit and vegetables, olive oil, the "Mediterranean" diet lends itself to improved health and longevity, especially compared to our fat-laden foods in America. Now the food mega-manufacturers are seeing the writing on the wall regarding the lawsuits that hit the tobacco industry in the late nineties. People are suing fast food places for making them obese.

Of course it's up to us, always. Can't we choose to take responsibility for ourselves and our health? Why do we feel compelled to run to Big Mama Litigator when the consequences of our own actions are not to our liking?

Cigarettes, Bleah!

On to the next burning issue. If you smoke, do whatever it takes, *whatever it takes*, to stop. Think of it as gaining your freedom.

If it takes Nicorette, acupuncture, hypnotherapy, smoking cessation support groups or even switching your addiction to something else that's slightly less harmful (and which you can tackle later), exert yourself to release cigarettes from your life.

Can you tell I'm a reformed smoker? In fact I was a heavy smoker for more than twenty years—at least a pack a day, especially at college in North Carolina. It was cheaper to smoke than to eat!

I didn't realize how disgusting the habit was when so many others around me smoked as well.

In our twenties my sister broke a revelation over me when she gave me *Compassion and Self-Hate* by psychiatrist Theodore Isaac Rubin, and for that I am forever grateful. In the book he outlines dozens of ways that we demonstrate self-hatred. As I recall, smoking cigarettes was number one on the list. Others included drug abuse, over-drinking, dwelling on the negative and—the clincher—obsessing about nuclear holocaust. In my younger years I obsessed about nuclear oblivion for weeks at a time. What a great way to wreck a sunny day—or month!

Recognizing a problem is fifty percent of its solution. I didn't even know smoking cigarettes was an example of self-hatred until Rubin's book pointed it out.

In what ways are you undermining yourself and your universal right to happiness?

When the universe does begin to honor us with guidance,

it is our responsibility to honor it by paying attention and following it.

What if your intuition tells you to slow down for something just around the corner? Do you speed up? No! Just around the bend may be a dog—or worse, a big truck in your lane. Pay attention. That's why the messages exist.

When we operate in a state of openness and receptivity toward what is being revealed, the universe begins to bless us with more and more information and energy that we can put to use—for our personal benefit and ultimately the benefit of the world. Since we are all connected, when one person begins to get healthier it gives everyone else a lift. God knows with all the bad habits we've developed to stuff down emotions, we need that lift NOW.

Get Yo' Mojo Workin'

The next key area in good health is exercise. How much do you get, and how much do you need to make you feel good and energized so that you can enjoy your life?

For everyone it's an individual decision, and studies now indicate that moderate exercise like walking for at least thirty minutes, four or five days a week, is sufficient for good health. Sitting with the TV remote and a can of beer or soda doing 12-ounce curls is not the ticket. It's a sad travesty that so many people choose to let their lives get sucked into the vortex of too much television and no exercise. You feel so good after getting up and moving!

My exercise has shifted with my age. In my twenties it was running after a Frisbee and dancing until all hours of the night; next came athletic club aerobics like a banshee; then to bring more balance to my life I added Tai Chi, Qi Gong and walking through the neighborhood.

Now that we're in the new millennium, I practice yoga and work out with weights. A few years ago I read that regular weight bearing exercise lifts twenty biological years from your age. Talk about an incentive! Lots of walking and meditation also help keep me balanced.

As a yoga teacher, I'm convinced that every yoga practice benefits the world in a subtle yet profound manner. So many of the poses channel energy from the sky down through the heart center and into the earth. Surely the earth must be slowly healing through this concentrated focus of heart-filtered intention. We can feel our hearts opening during the practice, letting our own inner radiance stream forth as our gift to the world. It's gentle and powerful at the same time. Healing for ourselves and for the planet.

Whatever type of exercise floats your boat—figure it out and go for it. And after exercise, make sure you get the proper amount of rest and sleep. Recent studies indicate that even adults need at least seven hours of sleep a night.

Peace of Mind

Volumes have been written on attaining peace of mind, and the wisdom of the ages always leads back to seeking the stillness within.

As YogaGraham mysteriously said, "If there's anything you take away from Yoga Teacher Training and make it a habit, let it be meditation. It will change your life."

Earning his living as a professional musician in the 1970s, Graham learned to meditate from a well-known Indian guru shortly after the Beatles learned the technique to "slip through the gap" into the magnitude within themselves.

Graham is so centered and grounded, few things seem to rock his world. "Doing the poses on the yoga mat translates positively into your life situations. Meditation smoothes out the rough spots," he says.

Another longtime meditator and one of my teachers at Unity states this every time he leads a class: "I can have a lot happening in my life, but if I meditate, life operates more smoothly and I feel very centered and even keel. When my life begins to get chaotic and things are flying out of control, I look around and notice that I'm not meditating. That's when I get back on track with meditation, and life begins to smooth out again."

Tapping into God energy through meditation creates the subtle shifts on an individual level, which will ultimately percolate up through the masses of people and eventually shift the world.

My Unity teacher describes meditation as a means of projecting out into the super-conscious all the needs that must be attended by the conscious mind. In that receptive state, the answers flow. He sometimes even jots a note or two to ensure that he takes action on the information so generously offered by the powers far more developed than his little ego.

At times the concept of meditation appears so overpowering to people—as though they must do it perfectly (as they must keep a perfect journal!) or it will be a complete waste.

Not so! In trying to make it less intimidating to people, I mention that I've started out with ten minutes—but even for those who can only tolerate sitting still for three minutes, that's okay too.

Or take a slow walk, breathing deeply all the way into your abdomen. Or sit and stare at a candle for awhile.

Everything has a beginning. Even the giant sequoias began from tiny seeds only three thousandths of an inch in diameter.

Don't beat yourself up because you aren't the perfect meditator! Just do it. Find some quiet time every day; sit erect on the front of a chair with hands on your lap and feet squarely on the floor. This creates a connection from the sky through your body and into the earth, and you become a channel for universal energy.

I so very much wanted to change my life, but had no idea until I incorporated this practice what a profound impact it would have. My mantra is simple: I breathe in Divine, and breathe out Love. Divine Love. It becomes a very relaxing cadence. "God Mind" or "Divine Order" are other favorites.

Being Still for Cotton Carnival

A successful Memphis businessman who has been spiritually focused throughout his life told me meditation helped him stay on an even keel during the months-long party of Cotton Carnival, especially the season he served as King, with the endless social engagements and all their chit-chat and small talk.

At our thirtieth high school reunion, he shared his mantra with me. He'd begun with the Biblical phrase, "Be still, and know that I am God," and used that phrase for quite awhile.

Then he shortened it to "Be still and know that I am." Eventually he whittled that down to "Be still and know."

Ultimately his phrase for entering the deep silence within himself is simply, "Be still."

A mantra is a signal to your conscious mind that it is time

to relax, let go, and let God. Stop the frantic struggle to figure everything out. God knows, honestly.

Some people focus on the breath to get into that place. Remember, it is virtually impossible to chain the monkey mind, so just let it subside into the background. Pick a mantra that works for you—it doesn't have to be something that is ceremoniously bestowed upon you after you've paid hundreds of dollars for it. Simply choose one that resonates for you. Then begin.

It will change your life. Enjoy that calm place within, and if it seems that your thoughts roll annoyingly and endlessly, just remember the little observer/guide on your shoulder, watching everything flow past. It's all for a reason.

The Tiny Oxen

The combination of proper nutrition, exercise, sleep and meditation has powerful beneficial effects. The differences between those who practice these habits and those who don't are glaring. Do an experiment. Just observe what happens to people who aren't getting what they need.

One July Fourth was truly a nerve-wracking day. As customary, my sister and I had converged on Buffalo, New York, to enjoy the holiday with my father and to lend a hand on some of the things he can't tackle on his own.

A looming task was the transfer of a pile of wood from the back yard to the front curb where it could be hauled away. It had been rotting for a year out back after the construction of a tool shed. Grubs, slugs and worms were propagating beneath it—an ugh-ly sight!

I'd already adjusted my mind to the job ahead. At the time

Back to the Garden

I felt rather centered and grounded through daily meditation and frequent yoga practice. So I felt very connected to the flow as I began the task of hauling long boards, one or two at a time, the 150 yards or so to the street.

My sister, however, was not in the flow with the task, nor with much else in her frenzied life as a nursing professor, intensified by her precious and lively six-year-old daughter (Susan was 50 at the time) and all the challenges that come with running a family, commuting up to four hours a day, an unsupportive spouse, and not enough sleep or rest—without a meditation program or regular exercise.

Rather than accepting the "what is" of the woodpile situation and going about the task with a peaceful mind, she chose to moan about my father's choice to let the wood rot in the back yard instead of hiring someone to haul it away.

We all know (as all of us should know about our parents), he is who he is, he does what he does, and nothing—no amount of bitching and moaning especially—is going to change that. He's in his seventies and women have tried to tell him what to do for his entire life, not that anyone's the better for it. Every single one of the irresistible forces (the women in his life) failed to budge the immovable object (which is my father), and my sister wasn't going to change him now. What we resist, persists.

Instead, she wrecked her own peace of mind by thinking something would be changed by her complaining. But when she shifted and faced the situation at hand, what had begun as a "woodpile kind of July Fourth" evolved into a productive bit of teamwork.

Hauling the wood, we got in rhythm together while singing the theme of "The Tiny Oxen," which caused us to burst out laughing and forget the load. This favorite childhood cartoon had taught us the results of a steady work ethic as the tiny

Dr. Susan Dickey and Patrice Dickey;
and Susie Beth and Patty Jane 35 years earlier.

oxen, undaunted by every setback, eventually reaped the rich rewards of their labors.

Granted, I'm no saint and my sister could share plenty of less-than-saintly gems about me. My point is this: By shifting and accepting the "what is" of the situation, we accomplished the task at hand, had fun and deepened that sisterly mystery in the process.

Reading the Signs

Sometimes all the fizz goes out of your champagne. The car breaks down. Then the loaner car gets a flat. You trip on the steps while carrying in groceries and land on your face amid a pile of broken eggs, broken celery and a broken nose.

You get word that you have to make a presentation before the board to justify your life. You create a fabulous life justification document and just before heading to the meeting you spill coffee on it—all twelve copies. Checks bounce. People stiff you on the money you're owed. Your favorite plant drops all its leaves. The diagnosis comes back positive, which is really a big giant negative. Life sucks.

But aren't these important signs too? Where was it you needed to rush, needing the car so badly? Was there a message in staying right where you were? Did you need to be stuck in order to see something? Was it the little black cloud over your head that seems to have been following you around all day?

Perhaps you've been told that a major client is going to disappear—the client that affords your salary, or the lifestyle to which you want to become accustomed. You have a couple of options: scramble to get some evidence together supporting the client's decision to stay. After all, a threat to leave is really an objection—a request for more input, more information, more attention.

Or you can skulk off to your cube and emit the kind of "don't talk to me" vibes that make even your friendly co-workers wonder what you're doing there.

Isn't the ebb and flow of business simply the nature of life? Clients come and go—and when enough of them disappear isn't that a sign that you're really no longer interested in that business anyway? Why shouldn't they disappear if your energy is elsewhere?

It's the same with anything in life. Our energy drifts; we aren't paying attention to the signs and suddenly it seems like a big shock when we're given the opportunity to go new places, meet new people and learn new things.

In fact we may even be amazed that we're no longer employed at a place for which we'd built up an active resentment. What's that all about? Whatever is happening, this too shall pass.

How astute of one class participant who stated that one of the things he gained from class was dealing with setbacks and adversity better. "Specifically, I understand that not every day is supposed to be wonderful, and that each bad day is not the end of the world." He'd learned to silence that negative internal voice.

His perspective shifted in a very important way—how he viewed setbacks. When setbacks begin piling up into mountains of molehills, perhaps that is the message—it's time to reassess.

Perspective and prayer give us the wisdom to know when to make a change, or a change will be made for us.

What the
Doctor Doesn't Tell You

Success in life is so often about shifting one's perspective or energy.

Like most Americans, I was raised to believe that doctors know best, but I was also reminded that "An apple a day keeps the doctor away." It's the classic conundrum. We don't necessarily want to have to go to the doctor, but when we do we're conditioned to turn our power over completely to the Medical Deity.

When I was trying to get my business off the ground and didn't have enough money to spend on doctors, my hands began to get stiff, especially in the mornings when I first awoke.

I knew how most MD's work—at the time the charge would have been about $75 to go in and hear one say, "You have a pre-arthritic condition; here's a prescription." That was not a palatable game plan for me, because at age 35, a. I didn't want to be told I had a chronic condition that could only be treated by drugs, and b. I didn't want to be on expensive medications for the rest of my life.

Coincidentally (or was it), at the time I was representing a holistic health expo whose keynote speaker was a renowned hypnotherapist with his own college of hypnotherapy in Louisiana.

Immersing myself in Dr. Arthur Winkler's books and advance materials so I could effectively promote him and the Expo, I discovered that his hypnotherapy sessions had been instrumental in helping people heal from diseases ranging from arthritis to AIDS. Surely he could help me!

Already experimenting with changing my life through altering the programming of my subconscious mind, I'd used subliminal tapes, visioning, and putting pictures of what I wanted to experience in life in front of me at my dreary little kitchen table.

At an earlier lecture, I'd learned about hypnotherapy and its effectiveness with certain types of people. Those who walked or talked in their sleep were "hyper-suggestible," meaning that they had a more permeable "filter" between their conscious, which occupies about ten percent of the mind, and the other ninety percent—the subconscious mind.

As a child I'd both walked and talked in my sleep—and had also experienced extremely vivid dreams, which is true even today—so I knew I was a prime candidate for benefiting from healing suggestions to my subconscious mind.

In order to prepare myself even more deeply for the natural unfolding of this subconscious healing, I read every bit of material I could find before our keynote speaker's arrival.

As Jesus pointed out, *"It is his faith that has made him whole."* Jesus was also quite adamant about healings and the other miracles that he performed, that, *"All these things you shall do, and greater."* I was ready!

Nothing Woo-Woo

The appointment with Dr. Winkler was about as straight-forward as one could be. Nothing far out, creepy, woo-woo or cosmic about it, and above all, no relinquishment of control, being made to cluck like a chicken or do any of the other ridiculous things that people associate with "floor show hypnosis," which is often a turn-off, frightening people away from what can be an extremely effective means of improving their lives.

For years hypnotherapy has been successful in aiding people with challenges like weight loss, smoking cessation, pain management, phobias and other seemingly intractable problems that can't be fixed through sheer "willpower." Great strides have been made with autoimmune diseases where the body attacks itself, as well as others.

However, many still hesitate to try it because they misperceive that they will be unconscious during the session and anything could happen while they aren't in control. On the contrary, during hypnotherapy the subject is deeply relaxed and extremely alert at the same time.

The hypnotherapist was a gentle, white-haired older gentleman, somewhat reminiscent of the Wizard of Oz (the man behind the curtain). He sported bushy, quizzical eyebrows and a calm, confident demeanor.

I lay down comfortably on a couch. He sat next to me and gave me the suggestion that I would go deeper and deeper into a relaxed state as he counted. He also told me that I would remember everything; that my senses would be operating more clearly and sharply during and after the hypnotherapy session, and that I would awake feeling delightfully refreshed.

As I began to go under, he reminded me of some very sensible truths. When our body experiences a cut or a scrape, it knows how to heal itself, and we don't have to do much to make that happen except, at times, step out of our own way. Re-open the channels of healing and let it naturally occur.

This gentle reminder had a profound effect on my level of belief—and we all know the power of the placebo effect.

A case documented by Richard JaFolla in *Soul Surgery*—

the Ultimate Self-Healing, involves a man who had advanced cancer and shows the power of intellectual faith. The man was on oxygen, confined to his bed, and having fluid removed from his chest regularly. His body was covered with huge tumor masses.

Having heard about a new "miracle drug," he asked to be included in clinical trials. Ten days after receiving the drug, he was symptom free and remained so for two months.

Later when he read some negative publicity about the drug, within days he was back in the hospital with the massive tumors, the excess fluid and the need for oxygen.

At this point his physician told him he wanted to test an improved batch of the drug—but what he injected was actually just sterile water. However, the man improved remarkably anyway, and returned to work with no trace of cancer in his body.

Later the man read an article that the drug was "worthless in treatment of cancer," and two days later he was dead.

Obviously, thoughts are powerful in making ourselves sick, or well.

Primed by my own belief in the power of suggestion, I left the session with Dr. Winkler completely refreshed, after paying him $75 and taking a tape of the session with me.

The stiffness in my hands disappeared—and the few times it returned I listened to the tape again and gave myself a refresher. It was one of the best investments I ever made in taking charge of my health.

One thing I didn't know at the time was the profound effect that diet has on energy level, flexibility and overall wellbeing, but shortly after this experience I began experimenting with my diet.

First I eliminated dairy, which cleared up the annoying phlegm in my throat. Eventually I stopped eating wheat products, which I discovered were the true culprit of this stiff hands mystery. The naturopath told me that a huge percentage of people are allergic to wheat gluten, causing problems that manifest as symptoms ranging from arthritis to attention deficit disorder—and yet medicine's answer is far too often just that: medicine.

What an eye-opener for me to experience the power of proper diet combined with reinforcement from the subconscious mind almost immediately—while benefiting doubly by saving huge amounts of money in doctor and pharmacy bills!

My initial experiment with the subconscious could be called faith healing—recognizing that my body had the power to heal itself if I believed it could.

The difference was so profound that my journey became more focused, simply as my degree of interest increased. Where thought goes, energy flows, and I was hooked.

Emmanuel

In my early thirties I attended a weekend workshop at Seven Oaks Pathwork Center in the stunning high plateau of Virginia's Blue Ridge Mountains—my introduction to the presence Emmanuel, a channeled spirit. At the time my issues centered on the deep sorrow surrounding my mother's lengthy and painful deterioration—by then she had been paralyzed for eleven years.

She was about three quarters through her journey and drugged to the max, with no spiritual succor that I knew of beyond watching the linden tree flourish in her back yard. She also delighted in the migrating Canada geese with their daily visits for cracked corn.

A blaring television was her constant companion, along with a crew of helper girls who took shifts beginning at 8 am and ending at 11 pm, at which time my father took over for night duty.

At the channeling I was informed by Emmanuel that my mother was already in close contact with the spirits of those loved ones who had gone before her; especially her own mother. The veil becomes thinner at those magical times on the verge of the beyond, if only we know how to respond to it. The ideal response is openness to the mystery as it reveals itself—and acceptance of the insights it offers.

The departed loved ones certainly seemed to enjoy communicating with my mother. Sitting in her room, we'd see lights switch on and off, and hear the occasional chime ringing from the corner. We always figured it was Mary Beth's own dear mother, grandmother Gammie, and MB's pair of doting aunts throwing in their two cents.

One friend surmised that my mother was casting her own energy around the room and causing the phenomena, but by then she had begun to ebb so much that I believe the kindred were appearing to buoy my mother's spirits instead.

They were dear, sparkly old ladies, and we welcomed their appearance as flashing lights and tinkling chimes, which seemed perfectly appropriate. It was as though they'd included us in their tea party from the beyond.

More Than Our Physical Bodies

At the Seven Oaks Emmanual weekend the flow pushed me toward an even more pivotal experience, and the messenger was a brilliant ophthalmologist whom I met there.

267

During breaks he would sit down at the grand piano in the common area and play some astounding concert pieces. Naturally I gravitated toward him.

"If you're interested in what goes on here, you should check out the Monroe Institute down the road," he said and proceeded to describe to me how his life had improved by about 5000 percent after tapping into his subconscious with Monroe's technique.

"I was partners with five other doctors in Connecticut and our practice was thriving. I came to the Gateway week at Monroe after reading one of Bob Monroe's books, *Far Journeys*," he told me.

At the Monroe Institute, meditations are conducted using a sound technology called Hemi-Sync®, which taps into both sides of the brain. The technology strengthens the flow across the corpus callosum, in effect opening up the channels of communication in the brain.

One analogy is that you're inviting all the members of the board of directors to the meeting for better decision-making, enhanced creativity and functioning from the depths of being rather than from the mind, or ego.

By diving into the vastness within, whether using meditation, hypnotherapy or Hemi-Sync, one is able to access all the wisdom in the universe because it's all connected. As quantum physicists are teaching us, if time is simply a construct and everything is happening all at once, with these methods we are able to send our intentions out through time and space. We send out our energy and alter the planet, while at the same time answers and responses appear as if by magic.

We block them with our insistence on "cognition" and rational mind when we can tap them by simply "being," intentionally.

What happened after the Monroe visit astounded the doctor's physician partners.

During his Monroe experience he had a "knowing" of tiny discs flying over the high meadows there. Although he didn't understand exactly what that meant, he was so compelled by the vision that he went back to Connecticut, sold his share of the practice to his partners and moved to western Virginia.

"Up here my life completely shifted. I began selling soft lens contacts, which turned out to be the tiny discs I'd envisioned. I'm working about one day a week, earning more money with less hassles than I've ever experienced, and spending the rest of my time with my wife, who's also extremely happy here. I also play concerts around the region and in Charlottesville," he said enthusiastically.

The man's demeanor was happy and free, which was so refreshing to see in an older person. So many let themselves get beaten down in their later years. He appeared to have truly found himself!

His story really got my attention.

Ironically, only a couple months earlier I'd heard about the Monroe Institute from a girlfriend I'd known in junior high school. We'd not seen or spoken to each other for years. More than two decades since we'd last been in contact, from opposite sides of the country we converged at a friend's wedding.

By then she and her then-husband, an osteopath, had opened a holistic healthcare center in Albuquerque, New Mexico.

They'd attended the Monroe Gateway Voyage® together—a solid week of deep immersion in the CHEC (Controlled Holistic Environmental Chamber) units.

In the meditations, attendees go deeper and deeper into the nether realms bridging the physical and spiritual experience. Many tap into the essence and creativity that may have been buried beneath a lifetime's sludge of day-to-day grind.

They journey back to the glittering, shimmering soul, assisted by the technology Bob Monroe developed to tackle his own fears of the unknown.

As a young man, Monroe began having rather terrifying and inexplicable out of body experiences (OBEs), where he found himself "flying about" and viewing his own physical body as it lay in bed.

Unnerved by his own inability to control the OBEs, he had himself examined by a cadre of medical doctors and psychiatrists. They could offer no explanation for his eye-opening journeys, but told him he was most decidedly healthy and quite sane.

So engineer Bob Monroe decided to replicate the experiences using technology.

As the owner of radio stations, Monroe eventually settled on sound technology. He discovered that by slightly varying the hertz input into each ear, he was able to establish the cross-current in the brain, which he patented as Hemi-Sync. Essentially, it sends people into altered states without drugs, and it is similar to the meditators' sublime experience of "slipping through the gap" as Deepak Chopra describes it.

My friend and her (now ex-) husband stepped right into the river of consciousness with this technology. A major lesson she took back to the health center was a renewed trust and belief in the flow. One week as payroll time drew near she realized they would be $3000 short for their employees, but she simply continued to step out in faith, operating the clinic. The money appeared at exactly the right time.

Within a very short period, two completely different sources had led me to Monroe.

This was synchronicity I couldn't refuse! I put it on my list of "must-do's" and even though I didn't have the money and the time together for a few years, soon I experienced the Gateway Voyage.

The truly amazing thing to me, beyond my own life altering experience, was observing its profound effects on others gathered from throughout the world.

A very buttoned-down, stern faced Japanese woman who had written for scientific journals for thirty years showed up from Chicago. A skeptic, she called it "McMeditation," practically spitting out the word with her scorn.

But why was she here? She'd been sitting Zen meditation for twenty years and had never experienced the breakthrough that many seekers crave. Perhaps she hadn't grasped the essence of that universal law that if you hold a bird too tightly in your hand, the air is crushed out of it.

On the third day (the irony does not escape me here) after a meditation, she came to our group meeting beaming a radiance and wonder that filled the room. Her face had dropped twenty years of age. Her tough carapace had dissolved; her worries slipped away.

"When I finally got it," she said, "it was an explosion of light!"

McMeditation or not, she was finally ready to absorb the experience that awaited her. The entire campus shone with our merged joy—appreciating the renewed awareness that we are more than our physical bodies.

We are soul, and we are all part of the oversoul. We are all joined; we are all one. Separation is simply an illusion.

a Meeting in the Beyond

My experience at Monroe had been based on an intention that I'd set before journeying the ten hours to the Blue Ridge Mountains.

My intention was to discover the theme and direction of my first book. A novel was inside, itching to be hatched.

To repeat the Gospel of Thomas, Jesus said, *"If you bring forth what is within you, what you have will save you. If you do not have that within you, what you do not have within you [will] kill you."*

Why did the early editors of the New Testament choose to leave that truth out? My guess is that they didn't want the "little people" to recognize that we have everything we need within ourselves to redeem us—or to kill us. This made it easier for the church (a political structure) to manipulate its followers throughout the centuries with fright sermons of "sinners in the hands of an angry God" dangling like hapless spiders above a fiery hell.

Either way, I knew that based on the ophthalmologist's expansive, exciting, fulfilling new life and my friend's description of the flow in her life, that I was ready for my life to shift in some enriching and profound ways—so why not embark fully on the inner adventure?

Some people vacation in Greece (which may also create some profound shifts). Some take the perilous and rewarding journey inward.

During the meditations at the Monroe Institute, I began the trek into my innermost reaches. Around mid-week I became aware of the presence of a dear friend, my teenage soul mate, great buddy and true confessor Pat Hudson. The one who tragically drowned, while working as a bargeman on the Mississippi River more than a decade earlier than my Monroe visit, when he was 24 and I was 22.

I had been devastated. At that age, I understood very little about the thin gap between life and death and the means to bridge it. I didn't recognize the many methods of communication available to us—or how close we actually are at all times.

When Pat died, his physical remains were lost in the river—the vast expanse where he loved to work and play. His death, shortly before Memorial Day, was followed by a grand and tearful farewell service in Memphis.

How could we lose a friend so young?

Everyone knew he lived dangerously, but at that age you're supposed to live forever. Throughout our adolescent relationship, I'd sensed his reckless hold on life and had written more than one precognitive poem and short story about his drowning.

Some people are destined to die young, and those around them can read it loud and clear:

"Love me hard now because I won't be around to feel your love forever, you know!"

That's what Pat demanded of us, and although he aggravated the hell out of us with his stubborn, bull-headed ways, we loved him hard, but not enough to keep him alive.

About two months after his death, I had a dream. In it, Patrick appeared to me. He seemed proud and relaxed, happy to show me around the place he had created, his very own cocktail lounge. This beautiful sunken grotto was decorated with statuary and fountains. In the dream we were both in our mid-thirties. With a happy gleam in his eye he gestured around his lounge and conveyed his satisfaction to me in a "thought-ball" (what Monroe describes as a complete knowing, without the need for words to be exchanged). I read it loud and clear: Pat was finally at peace.

I wrote this dream in a letter to his mother, who called me as soon as she received it.

"Just last week they discovered Pat's remains—they identified his belt buckle—and we buried him on a place called The Grotto at Memphis Memorial Park. It's just like you described it in your dream!" she said.

The news resonated through my body as a chill. Immediately I began to wonder whether our being "thirty-something" in the dream meant that I'd truly be with him by that time—in the realm beyond the living. This was not a transition that I particularly relished!

As it turned out, we learned at the Monroe Institute while journeying deeper and deeper beyond the physical, that there is a place of no time, where all entities and thought forms (no matter what dimension they exist in) can meet.

After gaining access this place called Focus 15, Pat met me there. How did I recognize him? A flash of his red hair. A sensation of the physical mass that once was his body. A tingling sensation as he "pulled my leg"—the left leg, governed by the creative right brain.

Why was he trying to get my attention in so many ways? Eventually the understanding exploded over me—my first novel was to be about Pat and our modern day Tom Sawyer/Huck Finn/Becky Thatcher adventures on the Mississippi!

My heart swelled with gratitude for the revelation.

When I got home I dug into the old poems and diaries I'd written during our teenage years. We were inseparable best friends in sleepy Memphis, a time of rambling in nature and the reckonings of turbulent teenage romance.

Flipping through my notebooks, I came across one of the

Red haired, wild Pat Hudson, our own modern day
Tom Sawyer, shows off a catfish from the Mississippi River.

precognitive poems I'd written about him. It was all spelled out in the last line: "I looked again; the golden fishes drowned." Pat was the golden fish with his reddish-gold hair, his golden freckles and great love for the water—whether his own backyard swimming pool, the Wolf River behind our neighborhood, or the mighty river running past the bluff of downtown Memphis.

Just below the poem I'd written, "First novel dedicated to Pat" and dated my pledge.

It had taken me twenty-three years to rediscover what I'd always known; to unearth it again in the place of no time; to begin to bring forth what was in me.

So *Ain't No Elvis Story* was born.

The important part of my taking action on that creative endeavor, which would have eventually choked off my expression if I hadn't acknowledged it, was that I did take action.

I didn't allow it to fester inside but rather paid attention to the call and got proactive, bringing it forth.

Wrapped Up in Pride

On the other end of the spectrum, my mother killed herself by not manifesting her great gift, which was aching to burst forth and be legitimized.

A brilliant teacher devoted to young children, she began the training to become a Montessori teacher at University of Cincinnati when my sister and I were adolescents and our family lived in southwestern Ohio.

In 1969 we were transferred to Memphis, which saved my life but cost my mother hers—at least her intellectual life. She deemed the Montessori program in that area to be inferior and decided not to continue with the training. In essence, rather than going with the flow, she "wrapped herself in her pride." Even though she laughed about it when imitating her starchy great aunt's use of this phrase, this was her rather customary and classically rigid Germanic attitude toward life, which ultimately does not serve well.

As a result, she had no legitimate means of channeling her incredible gift with children and giving herself a new reason for being, a refreshed purpose in life. As her own children grew older and slipped away she turned more and more to alcohol. A ten-year slide into alcoholism led to her tragic fall and physical paralysis. But really, she'd been emotionally paralyzed for years and had no idea how to get unstuck.

I remember the day we brought her back to their home from Strong Memorial Hospital in Rochester, New York, after five months of rehab following her accident. At that time, rehab lasted months, not weeks as it is today.

A fresh college graduate, I was at their home in Buffalo where they'd moved while I was in college, trying to be helpful until I could figure out my next step in life.

Although I loved my mother from the depths of my heart, nothing I could do would save her from her plight—she had fixed it so that physically, there was no way out. And the alcohol had destroyed her spirit years before it destroyed her body.

Magnanimously, she did not expect me to stay in Buffalo and be her nursemaid, although perhaps she secretly longed for me to volunteer for that duty. I was so fearful of the request that she never made, bless her beautiful soul. As much as it may have hurt her, she knew she had to free me to become myself.

We brought her home from rehab in an ugly steel gray converted van with an undignified, screeching automatic lift.

Depression hung in the house, mingling with the smoke from my mother's cigarette, strapped with a universal cuff to her hand. My father rolled her into the living room in her wheelchair for the first time, and as gently as possible, he lifted her out of the chair and laid her broken body on the couch for a rest.

She didn't cry, but as she turned her head and looked across the room, her eyes conveyed a depth of sorrow that shattered me.

Stumbling and fumbling, I sat at the piano with trembling fingers and tears rolling down my face while making a muddled mess of "You'll Never Walk Alone." My shell-shocked father, seeing her in the house for the first time since her injury and just beginning to grasp what it would mean to their lives together, knelt by her side on the floor and wept.

I don't think I've ever seen him cry, before or since.

By denying her gift, she had denied herself—and the world. Our gifts are not ours for keeping. They exist to be given away.

Into the Void

American culture does not equip us for dealing effectively with the void, especially a void stemming from deep sorrow and loss. In fact we're conditioned throughout our lives to stuff it full of whatever is handy.

From babyhood, if the child cries we pop a pacifier into its mouth—or worse, juice or food. This unconscious reaction creates the habit of "stuffing emotions" with food or oral gratification and may lead later to habits like smoking cigarettes or overeating.

As children today, we're not granted the time to lapse into our own dream worlds and reveries—everything is scheduled and booked: soccer practice, swim team, play dates, dance lessons, computer school, horseback, piano—until each moment is slated. The pressure to perform to a certain level and to have a certain appearance is intense.

Time spent alone in the world of imagination is rarely squeezed in edgewise. Don't forget the brain-sucking scourge of television, and video games with their violence and over-stimulus to young minds.

I consider this a major red flag. Where can imagination live without a moment to itself? What about attention spans? If every moment must be filled by Game Boys or MP3s, when does the still small voice have a moment to chime in? And what happens when it's not heard?

"Nature-deficit disorder" is a term coined by Richard Louv in his book *Last Child in the Woods*. He argues that children are suffering from attention problems and higher rates of mental and physical illness because they aren't exposed to direct nature.

I agree! No wonder more children are developing chronic medical conditions like high blood pressure and diabetes, and the rate of teen suicide is going up. Our children, the leaders of the next generation, are under assault from every direction!

In the larger context, because we are conditioned to fill in every moment from dawn to dark with the blather of TV or talk radio, when do we as adults have time to think and develop notions of our own? Does all this "avoidance of the void" ultimately cultivate vast, bleating herds of very nervous and overexcited sheep, willing to blindly follow the next diatribe-spouting demagogue who pops up?

The conditioning not only prevents people from thinking, but even more frightening, it prevents us from feeling. If we are constantly popping food into our mouths, other peoples' ideas into our brains, music or talk-talk into our ears, how can we possibly experience and observe our feelings and let them roll through us—and out?

Spiritual teacher Eknath Easwaran stated it this way: *"Just as the body is made of food, the mind is made of the sense impressions it takes in. And just as there is junk food, there are junk experiences and junk thoughts—attractively packaged, but most debilitating for the mind. Training the senses means that we need to be discriminating about which shows we watch, what music we listen to, what kinds of books and magazines we read, what kind of conversation we listen to. Every day the senses give the mind a ten course dinner, and we can add to our prana, our health and vitality, but not serving it junk thoughts."*

I remember when as a young teen, I was playing Led Zeppelin's "Dazed and Confused" full blast for probably the thirtieth time in a row. Without warning my mother stormed into my bedroom, whipped it off the record player and cracked the album over her knee (with great effort—that LP plastic-ware didn't break easily!)

Later she apologized and offered to replace the album for me, but I declined. I had gotten her message, loud and clear.

What kind of messages are your children absorbing—and yourself?

Does it give you pause to think about the junked-up mental diet that most Americans feed their heads every single day?

Let's start with television news. Barry Glassner, a professor of sociology at the University of Southern California, says we have been sucked in by the "Fear-Industrial-Complex," a loose collection of political leaders, big business and media, which erroneously portrays America as a place more dangerous than ever.

In his book *The Culture of Fear*, Glassner revealed information unearthed during five years of research. Between 1990 and 1998, the nation's murder rate declined by 20 percent. This is wonderful news, right?

Actually, at the same time, the number of murder stories on network newscasts increased by 600 percent! People have the impression that rapists, burglars and muggers lurk behind every lamppost—contributing to levels of fear in a society already stressed to the max and ignoring or forgetting ways to cope.

Michael Moore also exposed the whole sick trend in his film *Bowling for Columbine*. No wonder people feel like they need to own an arsenal, the way our minds are manipulated by powerful images of disaster. What many do not seem to grasp is that the more guns that are available, the more people get killed with guns!

One question we should ask ourselves, who is making money or winning elections with this glut of doom and gloom?

Our personal peace of mind and wellbeing depend upon our ability to make mature choices for ourselves that will enrich rather than diminish us.

Have you seen the bumper sticker that says KILL YOUR TV? During the college years, that's essentially what happened for me. I lost interest and never really got back in the habit. It just seemed like such a soul-destroyer. The blank eyes, the slack jaws, the lack of engagement, the canned laughter. And that's just what was emanating from the squawk box—not what's sitting in front of it!

Marshall McLuhan called television a cool medium—one which doesn't involve its viewers, doesn't engage them.

If I were a hungry alien looking for ways to fatten up and

domesticate the earthlings so I'd have an easy food supply on hand, I'd invent TV—if it hadn't already permeated and poisoned our culture. Now with shows like Jerry Springer and reality TV bringing us to new lows, what nadir comes next?

The inimitable British have come up with their own take on reality TV—literally, a show where we can watch the paint dry. Its creator quipped that with reality TV featuring so many boring drips, they figured they'd do that themselves and have a smash hit on their hands!

I admit that plenty of educational and inspirational television exists, but when it's all about sex, violence and the lows of moral and emotional stupidity to which our culture is sinking, that diet is totally counterproductive to the nurturing of the soul and our personal growth.

Take the bumper sticker's advice. Begin to wean yourself from the Boob Tube. If you're watching more than five or ten hours a week, that's too much. You're cheating your brain.

Avoiding the Void

So you don't like the void. It's too painful to be sitting doing nothing, because then all those anxieties about the bills, the family, your sex life and dead end job start to pile up and overwhelm.

What happens if you sit back, take a deep breath, and simply observe these thoughts drift past? As the observer, we are able to step outside ourselves and recognize that all these anxieties are simply thoughts. They are not really what is happening right now, and now is all we have.

What happens if we continually attempt to not feel, not

think, by cramming ourselves (and our homes) with more and more external stuff that will never, ever fill the void?

By then we have created a huge success of not living. Going through life unconsciously, not feeling and not thinking, how can we claim to be living? Only by engaging in each rich moment, even plunging into the void, are we truly experiencing life.

In our culture we're taught that when we experience an ending, the next thing on deck is a new beginning. That is simply not so, and nature demonstrates this in the simplest ways.

Nature's cycle of life DEPENDS upon the void—the vast silence and deepness that fosters a slow unfolding of seeds of new growth. The seeds must lie dormant for a time, or they simply will not germinate. They need the silence and darkness in order to come into their true essence, their full flowering.

Our fear of experiencing that fallow time between the ending and the new beginning has contributed mightily to the schizophrenic culture that is America today. We feel compelled to rush from one pleasure to the next, from the movie theater to the amusement park to the raceway to the game arcade, piling up fun upon fun until it all seems hollow and meaningless. Cramming our brains with junk thoughts and junk pleasures and no time to assimilate the stimulus.

Consider the caterpillar crawling across an oriental carpet. At times we may feel like that caterpillar as we crawl across a large dark area of the rug, and mistakenly assume that our life is destined to be bleak forever.

Imagine how much more scary for us if we put ourselves in the caterpillar's place: When we enter the chrysalis we must go into a time of complete isolation and total darkness, away from all the distractions of the world. It's only when we emerge from the chrysalis and are able to spread our gauzy wings that we can fly over that oriental carpet and see the amazing pattern of the big picture.

Observing the whole design of our life, we see that what appeared to be a hopeless and endless black space was very small compared with the rest of the scenery. Robert Brumet describes it beautifully in *Finding Yourself in Transition, Using Life's Changes for Spiritual Awakening.*

We must die to the old in order to be born to the new.

When Jesus needed self-rejuvenation, he retreated to the desert or the garden to contemplate, meditate and pray.

We can be well served by following his example and stepping into the void—if not willingly, at least not dominated by fear of the fallow time. In that time of seeming stillness with its inactive appearance, the deep wellsprings of creativity are tapped and our next new beginning germinates.

Seeds of Endings

Change begins with endings, and sometimes endings can last an extremely long time.

Endings come when we determine that a situation is no longer right for us—either because we've read the signs or run into them.

One woman, pregnant as a young girl, realized as soon as she got married that the relationship with her husband was already ending in her own mind. However, she also decided that she'd make the best of the situation until her child was out of the nest. Her ending lasted eighteen years.

In the midst of that experience, the void, she was adrift in a state of frustration, dissatisfaction and confusion, as Susan

Jeffers defines the transitional state in *Feel the Fear and Do It Anyway.*

But because of the choice she'd made, this lengthy time period was not wasted for her. Instead she used it very productively to raise her child, finish her degree in library science, and establish herself as a university librarian, a profession she loved. Then when the time was right, she and her husband orchestrated an amicable parting of ways and she was able to move into her new beginning, a more satisfying way of life.

Although she recognized that her marriage had been a mistake practically from the outset, she still chose not to waste energy and emotion in resentment of her husband, which would have been, basically, a projection of her own negative feelings toward herself (for making a stupid mistake) onto him.

What good does it do to make other people wrong? It doesn't make the situation any more right by blaming and dumping toxic emotions. She made her choice to live in an emotional void with her husband to provide stability for her daughter.

Since a child was what she'd wanted most in the first place, she chose to joyfully experience her daughter's childhood and teen years, knowing that she was doing what felt right for her daughter's wellbeing.

Just Like Romeo and Juliet

When I was a child I believed that nothing would ever change.

Every summer the family converged upon a few rented

cottages in Ocean City, New Jersey, for fun and relaxation with the great aunts and uncles, the grandparents and the many funny cousins. En route we'd always sing a rollicking chorus: "By the sea, by the sea, by the beautiful sea—you and me, you and me, oh how happy we'll be!"

After our one or two week frolic together, it was back to Park Ridge. Dad drove off to his sales job in Chicago every day. We played Barbie or elves or fairy castles with our little friends. Mom made us peanut butter sandwiches, or bologna—we'd bite the centers and create little poodle skirts that we danced on our fingers.

The Lambrecht's man appeared at the door with his weekly cache of baked goods and the very royal sounding Chicken á la King on his foldout display basket. Occasionally we went to the Art Institute and other museums in the Loop, or the Brookfield Zoo with its polar bears, or the mysterious aquarium. Iceskating and snow forts in winter; bicycles and popsicles in summer. And school of course. Life was predictable, pleasant and suburban.

One night when I was five years old and not yet asleep, I heard my mother crying in the living room of our split-level house. Creeping to the top of the steps, I observed this scary and unusual phenomenon—had I heard her that upset over anything before that moment, ever?

She tossed potato chips at my father and begged him to take her on a trip, without the kids, and I felt fear. Was it her tears? The chips? The notion that something was shifting?

All I know is that things began changing rapidly after that. The next summer, instead of heading off to Ocean City as a family singing "By the Sea," my sister and I were sent to our grandmothers' homes for extended visits while my parents went to Europe.

This spelled a dreadfully long time away from my mother

My family at Ocean City, New Jersey:
'By the sea, by the sea... oh how happy we'll be!'

while attempting to sleep beneath the stern portraits of a menagerie of dead ancestors. Their stony-eyed demeanors made it obvious that they had not lived lives of ease!

At my dear, Dutch grandmother Gee Gee's creaky old Victorian home in Cambridge Springs, Pennsylvania, my most striking memory involved the night of too much cake and ice cream.

Sister Sue and I slept in a big brass bed at one end of a long, spooky hall. At dead center between the bedroom and the bathroom ticked an ominous clock—surely it was haunted!

With every ounce of self-restraint a child could command after such a rich dessert, I tossed about in bed and felt more and more nauseated. Finally, physiology trumped fear. In a mad dash for the bathroom I made it just to the clock, where I let loose.

Despite her midnight clean-up duty with mop and bucket, dear Gee Gee was remarkably understanding. However, when I later told my mother about the stomach upset she condemned her mother-in-law for feeding me garbage.

Of course I believed my own mother knew everything, and I worshipped the ground where she danced. Regrettably, my mother's attitude toward Gee Gee poisoned me for a long time, until I reached the age of reason and saw her for the lovely woman of faith that she was. Thank God for shifts in perspective!

With the parents still away, we were picked up by my German grandfather Monty to stay with him and my lilting and lovely German grandmother Gammie in Philadelphia. It was here that the revelation struck. With the intensity that only a five-year-old can muster, I realized that nothing would ever change.

What gave me the clue? The radio. My sister, three years

older, had just begun tuning into Top 40. For hours I stood at the casement windows looking out on damp streets, hearing the exact same play list over and over. Time crawls when you're missing your mommy, and it seemed to last forever.

The same songs kept repeating themselves. "Just like Romeo and Juliet" seemed to crank endlessly. It must have been number one. Hearing that song play incessantly during the longest week of my life, the second week of my parents' two week trip to Europe, convinced me that time had stopped and I'd be trapped at that casement window under the watchful eye of my creepy dead great-grandmother forever. It was not a heartening feeling.

Things did change, of course. My stern German ancestors stayed in their frames, but soon enough my parents returned home. My mother had a "Miss Jean Brodie" glow of exuberance about her.

Even though things seemed back to normal on the home front, the bedrock had shifted and I realized that I didn't have much say in how things were run. As a budding control freak, I didn't enjoy this feeling at all, but had no tools to deal with it.

However, not long after that, maybe a year or two, I read an experiment in *Wee Wisdom* children's magazine which gave me firsthand experience of how to affect change in my young life. It was so simple, and that was its beauty—especially for a child who felt that virtually nothing was within her control.

The experiment was to alter my handwriting. Just take one letter and change the way I wrote it. Mine was the letter a. I'd always printed it the way they taught you in elementary school, like a big round blob with a stick down its right side.

At that moment of action I decided how refined it would look if I changed it to the typography version of 'a.' Even though it took longer for me to print, it had that certain authoritative stamp to it, and made me somehow feel more in charge, more elegant, and certainly in more control of my own life.

If nothing seems to be happening in your life right now; if the rut seems so deep you can barely peer above its edge, try altering some aspect of your handwriting and see what unfolds next. If it worked for a little child, it may work for you.

Choosing The Right Path

One big question is how to know if you're on the right path.

The class discussed this question in relation to intuition and how it shows up. One woman stated that she often had "gut feelings." Although she sometimes paid attention to them, she wasn't sure if she was choosing the right ones to follow.

Gut feelings—the neural impulses in the "feeling brain" of the stomach—churn away although the thinking brain may have been distracted by the business of living, and ignoring what the feeling brain is trying to tell it!

As a personal example, I felt a really sick rumbling in my stomach when a former client emailed to discuss my potentially getting back on board to handle public relations for a new, expanded marketing campaign.

Even though my feeling brain protested quite noticeably, my thinking brain whispered, "You could really use the cash right now; your client base needs some beefing up; it was a fun account—all except for that part where they unceremoniously dumped you in a two minute phone call after you'd delivered exceptional results for four years!"

In essence my gut was screaming out, "You fool! Don't go

back to those users who know the price of everything and the value of nothing! Look at how they treat all their fulltime employees!"

Although intellectually I wanted the account, luckily for me I was not rehired. Whenever something like this occurs I chalk it up to Divine Order, which it most certainly is. To prove it, one of my favorite previous accounts came back on the scene that very month, thus filling the financial gap.

My gut message told me not to compromise, and I should have taken the satisfaction to tell them I wasn't interested. However, the universe was conspiring in my favor and things turned out perfectly, even though I actually tried to get in my own way!

Intuition also appears in the form of dreams, many of which cause major life shifts. Dreams that warn of impending health situations are most certainly not to be ignored.

One woman confided that after the session on intuition and synchronicity, she dreamed about a dark spot on her colon and was so alarmed by the possibilities that she scheduled a colonoscopy. Not a moment too soon, her doctor informed her. The black spot in her dream was a cluster of precancerous polyps removed at the time of diagnosis.

Dreams have been pivotal to my health and well being over the years. Several months after my mother's death I dreamed about a screaming skull—(a childhood nightmare stemming from a really bad, schlocky horror movie with the same title).

In essence, it was my own shadow looming up in the form of my mother's face. It screamed at me to take care of little children in the afternoon. This was quite odd, because taking care of little children was the last thing that interested me.

The dream was so alarming that I switched out of my group therapy, which seemed to be headed nowhere, and found a Jungian dream analyst and body/mind therapist who helped me do some deep, cleansing grief work—practically an exorcism—purging the grief and guilt over not being able to save my mother that I'd been carrying with me for twenty-five years.

I myself was the little child that my subconscious was telling me to nurture.

What a load to carry for such a long time. Why don't we feel that we deserve to unburden ourselves sooner? Why must we carry these ridiculous weights? Why do we not give ourselves permission to lighten up?

Breakthroughs

When synchronicity swims into view, sometimes it's impossible any longer to ignore the signs to lighten up and make the changes.

Carl Jung, who coined the term synchronicity to describe meaningful coincidence, occasionally struggled with his patients who were locked into linear thinking and boxed logic.

One afternoon he was stymied in his attempts to break through the ego constructs that an extremely bright young woman used to shut herself off from any possible alternatives to her stifling situation.

She related to Jung a dream she'd had about having received a fabulous golden scarab brooch and pinning it to her dress. In the midst of listening to her dream, Jung heard a distinct, steady tapping on the windowpane. There he spied an insect attempting to get into the darkened room from the bright day outside, which he found extremely odd. He opened the window and plucked the insect off the glass, noting that it was a lustrous greenish/gold scarab beetle, and quite large.

Handing it to the young woman he said, "Here's your scarab." From then on they were able to proceed quite productively.

What is the scarab beetle that has been tapping on your window, attempting to attract your attention? Is it some image from a dream, or some aspect of your health? Perhaps it's a gut feeling, or possibly something even more obvious, which you choose to ignore until you can no longer continue ignoring it without going over the edge. It's all a choice of which path.

For three years I worked for a client and stored every single email I received from them under the file heading "Recurring Nightmares." Looking back, it amazes me how long I stayed in that burdensome situation. This lasted until they requested me to expand my responsibilities without an increase in pay. Only then was I able to see that it was time to step aside—and quickly!

Intuition is calling out to be heard, and it's our choice whether we'll pay attention. When we do pay attention, doors seem to swing open for us, good outcomes are abundant and life begins to flow. We know we are on God's path when everything unfolds for the greater good of all involved.

Synchronicities often show us when we're on the right path. A beautiful example occurred with a woman who was grieving the recent death of her father. She'd moved back to Atlanta from New York City after 9/11 to be closer to her mother.

She had entered the void so often precipitated by a parent's death, and I had re-connected with her at an art gallery the week before my class started. "Come join us—it's perfect for people in transition," I urged her.

At the end of the first session, she shared her amazement

that she knew it was the right place to be and the right thing to do.

In her closing comments as the class ended six weeks later, she reiterated her amazement at the synchronicity of being there—what she'd mentioned at the first session.

"This class brought me back to where I started. I attended nursery school in this very building (the Glenn Memorial Church School). My dad was an Emory man, and unfortunately died here last August. And I've just felt a pull back to Emory."

One of the insights she gained from the class: "If you're not sure what to do, don't force things; more will be revealed."

This is a very important lesson for those who have lived as hard-charging go-getters through long, successful careers. She was "learning to let go of why/what I was, and starting to move toward a new, happier me."

Intuition, synchronicity and letting go of outcomes serve as our handmaidens on the journey.

Mother Ocean

In a sense, going to the ocean is going into the void—an immersion in the great mystery, which spawns all living creatures. We cast our nets for what glides in its shadowy depths, but only when we extend ourselves does the ocean reveal its secrets. Then, what buckets full of wonders may bubble up!

A large seine net, grasped on each end by two strong men and extended a couple hundred feet from shore, is looped back to the beach brimming with edibles—crabs, baby rays, fish, a junior shark or two—or inedibles like the bone-filled and flesh-deprived mullet, a skinny and difficult fish.

To each his own, the ocean teaches us! Some stalwart seafood lovers eat even mullet, hard as it is to retrieve any meat from its bony structure.

After a loss, moving into the void inside me, being at the sea provides a place of contemplation and retreat, repose and reflection, a place to repair, rejuvenate and recharge the drained and aching heart. The ocean is a stopping place, a zone of healing to contemplate the life of a loved one no longer with us.

The waves wash rhythmically over the perplexed and saddened mind and leave it rinsed and pure.

Journeying into the sacred inner place requires an annual visit to Tybee Island off the coast of Savannah—a respite in the big, rambling nineteenth century marsh side home of Ed and Maureen, purchased decades ago before Tybee caught the cachet of movie stars and moguls that may kill the island's funky charm. If the highrise condo developers get their way, that's a given.

One summer, my annual visit coincided with the one-month anniversary of the transition of Fred, and his best friends and I celebrated him in all his grungy glory. And missed him dearly.

In his honor I wore the pair of baggy South African cotton shorts we'd bought together at least eight years earlier—his own pair long since worn to a rag and tossed out.

This oddly celebratory journey took me into the place of no time, where life on the marsh slows to Pleistocene, drenched in thunderstorms to match. Who can surmise what ancient reptile or rough beast of eras past might loom out of the marshland deluge?

Toothin'

Ventures into the void with Fred as a guide always yielded up the most exciting treasures.

Off we'd trek on a hunt for shark teeth and other fossils, heads burqua'd in hats which we swathed in mosquito netting. All exposed skin slathered in sun block and mosquito repellent; ever on the alert for poisonous snakes as we hiked across the sandy expanse of deserted Jones Island in the Savannah River, searching for the perfect spot for shark teeth.

The river floor dredge from the Intercoastal Waterway is forever kicked up onto this patch, its sandy spume replenishing the treasure hunts of the intrepid.

Certain indicators signaled us: a perfect tooth lying on top of the sand "in the float" is always the strongest hint that here we should drop our gear and start digging.

Fred and Ed hauled the heavy stuff—the big box screen they'd fashioned into which we dumped shovels full of sand and gravel. As a trio we scrabbled through it wearing our heavy leather gloves, pulling out Carcharadon teeth as big as five inches across at the root. A 65-foot-long behemoth from 65 million years ago, one that could snack on human size critters as though they were mere candy bars!

The big sieve/screen also yielded the tiniest of perfect little specimens, pristine miniature dragon's teeth, long ago lining the insides of ancient monsters' mouths.

At times a Mastadon tooth would appear in the mix, or bone shards of other ancient mammals. Petrified wood, trilobites—and although we knew it couldn't be his, one fossil strongly resembled Mick Jagger's lips!

Digging as though we'd get to China, or at least find that

incredible specimen to end all specimens, when it really didn't matter at all whether something spectacular appeared or not. How many fossils does it take to make one happy, really? The thrill was always in the quest, and what we found there in that friendship of three adventurers was so much more valuable than any ancient fragment yielded up by the sand.

Hauls of 400 or more stone-infused treasures at a time, lugged across the sand in heavy canvas bags after wearing out our rough gloves while scraping through the gravel. Working ourselves to exhaustion and loving it—just that one last shovel full—until the light in the western sky had dropped so low we could hardly see our way off the island.

Back to the skiff and across the marsh to safety—sometimes pursued by a thunderstorm with its welcome, cool raindrops splatting our dusty skin as it rolled in off the ocean and into the marsh channels. Back to safety and a shower and a cold glass of wine at the rambling Tybee house.

The largest ones we counted and sorted on newspaper spread on the floor of Ed's living room after a long day sweating, swatting and swinging the shovels.

"Look at this one again Eddie and PeeDee! It's a real chunker!" Fred declared in delight so many times. How his enthusiasm lighted up the world.

A trip to Tybee always yields up triple treasures—those of earth, sea and spirit—if one knows where to dig and cast the net. Finding one's daily food and sustenance for the soul.

Even walking in the shallows, experiencing the healing warmth of ocean waters in the South, the surge of waves breaking against the legs, the cries of the gulls overhead and the odor of damp salt air clinging to the skin...

Every year the soul cries for a bath in Mother Ocean once again. Whether it's a solitary journey, camping alone on the beach and easing into the slower rhythm that permits contem-

Ed Myers and Maureen O'Leary smile welcome to Tybee Island.

plation, meditation and appreciation of Nature—or whether it's a visit with friends and family who surround us with love and laughter, a retreat enables us to reconnect with the original protoplasm which comprises us. Feel the embrace of the cosmos surrounding us—sea, sky and sand—thank you, God!

No Limits

It's refreshing to be coached by self-actualization experts like Dr. Wayne Dyer in *The Sky's the Limit*. According to him, in order to become a no-limit person, one who lives full out in the now, we really need to get back to childlike behavior and childish things.

What better place to do that than at the beach, where everything slows to the pace of right now, bicycle speed, and the day unfolds naturally rather than on a hyped-out schedule of MUST BE AT THE BEACH AT 6AM TO BEAT THE OTHER SHELL-SEEKERS (few shells to seek these days anyway) and then MUST get that job finished and MUST do this and MUST do that.

When I'm away, back in the city, I tend to forget about Tybee Time, where the day naturally unfolds after I've had quite enough hours of sleep to feel refreshed.

At Tybee I guarantee this for myself by wearing an airline eye mask. Experience has taught me how early the sun streams through the windows to awaken light sleepers. As a result, I feel completely refreshed after eight hours' sleep. In my case if I don't get it, my brain goes wonky and I morph into either a sleepwalker or a bitch!

Rather than staying in lockstep city mode, I fully succumb to the siren song of Tybee.

On this trip, a beach stroll and some yoga poses and Tai Chi facing the morning sun perfectly ratcheted me down into a deeper place of self-acceptance. I was pondering a comment by my hostess as we enjoyed the customarily late dinner at 10pm, under the batting fan on the screened porch. A delightful sea breeze kept the draining July heat and any mosquitoes at bay.

Maureen, one of the hardest-working women I know (a mother of two teenagers and a professional costumer), had called me a workaholic!

The whole notion threw me off so much that I absolutely couldn't prove her to be correct. The beach and the ocean were a powerful enough lure to draw me away from automaton work-mode and into the moment of the childlike spirit.

It's as though I'd come to the beach ready to shoulder the burdens of the world. In a sense I came here to support and mirror their sorrow over the loss of a best friend. But usually the beach is where people go to let go of their burdens, and I knew I deserved that kindness to myself as well.

By granting myself the freedom to indulge in a nice morning bike ride around the quaint, beach bum streets of Tybee with its offbeat charm, I did exactly what Wayne Dyer recommends for people in self-actualization mode—do what they love, in the moment.

But it wasn't until later in the afternoon when I had indulged some hodad slacker urges that I found validation and justification for that very appropriate behavior in Dyer's book.

Why is it that we don't allow ourselves the freedom to move smoothly from delight to delight, stopping to look in the Marine Center's seine net to see what creatures they've revealed on a cub scouts' nature walk; or tossing the frisbee a few times with a couple of grizzled beach boys; or just sitting down in the shallow surf and allowing it to wash up, splashing hat and glasses?

What is it about living in a world so pressurized that we don't even have ten minutes to conk back for the cat nap and creative process which are extremely good for our health?

It's insanity! I'm doing what I love to do, letting the words flow out onto a smooth white page, tumbling from my pen, a movement so natural that I began as an eight year old keeping a journal, but even before that would ask my mommy to jot down little notes from the day, before I could handle a pencil well enough to express myself on the blank page.

I have no doubt that both Wayne Dyer and Oprah would say, "You go, girl!"

One Month From Transition

Evidence of Fred is everywhere in the Tybee house—his photos, shark's teeth, seine net, cast net, cowboy hat. But I'm not talking about him when my heart aches to do so, one month from his departure.

Ed and Maureen have either accepted what is and are successfully moving on, or their hearts are so broken over the loss of this incredible, dynamic friend that they can't bear to talk about him either.

He's in his sailboat that they named The Freddy, which he willed to their son Devin. The artworks that he painted scattered about the house, hung on the wood paneling in the camper room. One painting of Fred and Ed hauling the skiff onto the shore of disappearing Cockspur Island—a photo I shot ten years earlier, which Fred used as a model for his artwork. The acrylic painting of the old rambling house that he created during our 17-day kitty-sitting adventure here.

Ed, his best friend in life, tacked the big blown-up photographs of Fred from his memorial services onto the kitchen walls. There he will forever be poised with his cast net, fishing for dinner, reminding us all of the reality of our daily bread—our daily crab catch—for that was the way he lived his life.

Oh yes, there were "thoughts for the morrow," but how grateful he must have been when he first received his dire cancer prognosis at age 52 that he had not cancelled a fabulous solo trip around the world to celebrate his 50th year.

Fred was scheduled to direct a movie and that fell through just before his departure, meaning he'd be coming home (as was the norm) to no income. And he traveled anyway.

He'd already bought his plane ticket; and friends in France, South Africa, Korea, Japan, Hawaii and elsewhere were poised to enjoy his rich, earthy spirit, his interest in everything. He absolutely had to go.

The world called to him to step out in faith, and that's how he lived every single day. A man with passion, devoted to pursuing life's intensity in every moment.

When someone picks up Fred's baton, does that make him or her a workaholic, or simply a passionate shepherd of one's allotted minutes?

Tybee Morning

The house is quiet as the teenagers begin to unfurl their petals, stoked last night by a late evening screening of "Zoolander" and some frozen peach yogurt. The delights of a summer's eve.

Getting From Shadow to Joy

A bunny rabbit bounds through the yard, one hundred feet distant near the altar of Buddha and bowling balls, the line of demarcation between the yard's grassy expanse and the wild marsh beyond.

A mourning dove or two peck for treasures in the center beneath palm trees rescued with props and ropes from a hurricane in the mid-eighties. This house itself has already withstood one "hundred year storm" when Tybee wasn't nearly such a trendy spot with houses on stilts walking down every narrow alleyway.

Being in the presence of four teens is an exercise in willfulness. Watching daughter Laura pit her will against her mother's will, longer honed of finer steel. Amazingly, the test of wills stays rather calm as Laura tells Maureen that she's going back to Atlanta unsupervised with her boyfriend for the next few days and Maureen quietly tells her she'll have no money or credit cards.

"This is a girl who reminded me to bring her security and happiness huggy toy down with me when I came," said Mo. "She thinks I'm going to let her be by herself in Atlanta?"

More amazement: these kids apparently don't drink OR do drugs. It's encouraging to think how many healthy, creative young ones are evolving into their rightful places on the leader ship. To me, they spell hope for the world.

Laura and Devin were raised the Wayne Dyer way— moving naturally from one creative pursuit to the next, following an artistic path, giving themselves time, space and inner permission to expose what's calling out to be revealed from inside.

Everywhere I look is evidence of the family's creative natures: the little alien man shaped from bits of buoys and Styrofoam collected in the marsh—its crooked eyeglasses formed of a bent wire. Creeping towards the Buddha, a flotilla of giant horseshoe crabs treks across the back yard where the ants and critters perform nature's cleansing—nibbling off any tiny bits of flesh remaining on these ancient creatures washed ashore on a distant island. The bowling ball altar itself—multi-colored balls snatched up at yard sales and flea markets, stacked on top of each other or positioned on a row of unmatched pedestals of varying heights, with a smiling Buddha perched in the center.

Who needs any more "religion" than this?

Necklaces fashioned of shells and beads dangle from light switches; wire masks peer from button eyes and a plastic swatch of a smile; driftwood covered in barnacles is positioned as sculpture; row upon row of bleached, dried conch shells line the porch railings.

A large seawater aquarium whose prize is a plug-ugly toadfish—growling with a prehistoric scowl that makes the shrimp, minnows and polefish clear the way.

Next to that a smaller terrarium houses tiny green lizards, one almost translucent in its delicate goblin form. Nautical gear hangs from hooks surrounding the porch—a pyramid-shaped crab trap; box turtle shells, driftwood, fishnets. The seine net leans against the palm tree to which a clothesline is strung; bright blue, yellow, orange and aqua towels and bathing suits well-rinsed in last evening's drenching, cooling downpour.

A weathered surfboard leans against another tree, near the birdbath. The big cooling-off above ground swimming pool welcomes all, just near the Buddha/bowling ball altar at marsh edge. A large right whale skeleton enjoys the ant treatment in its neat replication on the rough grass out back.

What creative spirit would not thrive in this childlike paradise, this Eden of spontaneous creative production?

Just beyond the porch dangles a gigantic wire frame, ball-shaped, to which soon 5000 Presbyterian church CDs will be hot-glued to form a giant disco ball, twenty feet in diameter. (I can think of fewer better uses than this for 5000 Presbyterian CDs!)

Hoisted a few feet above the grass by a pulley, this glittering globe will shine out over the marsh in every direction—what a wonderful manifestation of Ed's busting loose to the world!

Ed modestly labels himself an almost-artist. Surrounded by artists and always actively in the process of creation, he still draws humble comparisons to himself that deny his own artistry among the mélange of his wife, sister, mother and best friend Fred, all of whom are (or were) professed artists, and a very talented lot they are! And now his son and daughter dance into their birthright as creators.

But since Fred has stepped aside, the message to Ed is to step into his own light and let his own creative genius reveal itself.

And if that begins to manifest as a giant disco ball fashioned of Presbyterian CDs and looking like a UFO or perhaps Sputnik (for those of us who remember), so be it.

The important thing about creativity is to remain non-judgmental and let the glory flow out. In this unstructured environment at Tybee where the eye is greeted by new natural treasures at every turn, the atmosphere almost forces one's light to shine and reflect in every direction—bouncing off that giant disco ball as far as the eye can see.

Communion with the Departed

The Tibetan Book of the Dead states that the spirit of the deceased lingers on the earthly plane for 45 days after transition. During that time, friends and loved ones are to tell stories about the departed one; to talk to him; to express their love and well-wishes for him so that he might gain "merits" to send him higher into Shambhala.

One way to communicate is through tears—just letting them come when they will; tasting their salty furrows down the cheeks. Experiencing tears of remembrance is equally as important as absorbing laughter about some great tale of derring-do. Recognizing the widespread impact of one soul on so many who loved him.

Another way to communicate is through Tarot cards, an intuitive portal to the beyond.

The reading we did on Fred rang so true, so "dead on" that it reinforced my feelings of its validity. Whether a simple reading of only three cards or the full reading, I always invoke the Lord's name because I want to summon up only the forces of good.

"Dear Lord, help us communicate with our friend. Fred, how are you?"

It really didn't surprise me that the card I drew for "recent past" was the Death card, straight up. There he was, having shed his mortal coil, having made it through the eye of the needle as depicted on the card, a snake that had slithered through the crook of two birch trees and left its worldly baggage behind. It had moulted its old skin, so very *déclassé* (not to mention bulky!) in the spirit world.

The Death card always means a time of great transition,

but does not always mean physical death. When Fred's earthly work was done, his soul created a disease that enabled his body to free itself up, fast. In just two and a half months he was free, as hard as his ego struggled to hold on and hang in.

We human beings still shuffling around in our mortal coils are left with the great mystery of the soul's journey. Surely Fred's life had meaning and impact, but what was the meaning and purpose of his death, so young?

Was it partly a reminder to us that if you abuse your body, you lose your body? Knowing full well that the Self is not the body and the soul operates in ways the ego can never comprehend.

When we read the Tarot cards at Tybee, Fred had "used up" more than 30 of his allotted 45 days to malinger on this plane. The fact that he was physically gone still hadn't struck many of us yet.

Especially Ed. Whenever something exciting happened he immediately wanted to chew it over in detail with Fred. Then Ed remembered, "Oh, he's not exactly available for discussion anymore. Not like before."

Our hearts were breaking but we hardly know how to express it—how to honor and acknowledge the incredible void in our lives. I just continued to let the tears roll—and to look for signs.

The first sign came when I relaxed into deep meditation upon my arrival at Tybee, in the midst of which I smelled Fred's burning cigarette. Nobody at the Tybee house smoked.

The second sign blew in as Maureen, Ed and I sat on the porch discussing him, and his Pharr House Productions flyer appeared out of nowhere on a gust of a breeze. Ed hadn't even realized one was at the Tybee house.

The third sign came as I walked back into the air-conditioned "camper room" he and I had always shared. On the floor at my feet, just inside the door lay the poster-sized photo of him casting a perfect circle with his cast net. How had it drifted in there? It had been in the kitchen. So I knew he was present with us.

Continuing the reading, I drew his second Tarot card, signifying "the present." The Strength card was reversed (perfectly upside down, which is not all that normal with the round cards of the Motherpeace tarot deck).

Obviously he was not in his physical strength any longer. Was he still struggling with that issue somehow? A man who formerly muscled through every challenge, attempting with sheer will to force the outcomes that he preferred. Probably part of what killed him—he was always so determined, so rigid, so right.

The third card, signifying "the future," showed him in his soul element—the place we all seek our entire lives—the Lovers, with a slight tilt toward the masculine energies—his reunion with God the Father, the Christ spirit within, the place of solace, succor, release. It probably also signaled his reunion with his own dear father, his namesake Fred, who had departed this earth only a couple of years earlier.

Based on the wisdom of the *Tibetan Book of the Dead* and the cards, I believed he was still on that journey to solace. In the meantime, to aid him on his journey we offered our prayers and paeans to his beautiful life; holding his memory dear; sending our love.

As the *Book of Five Rings* states, *"Believe in those things which cannot be seen."*

It was absolutely appropriate that I appeared at Tybee on the one-month anniversary of Fred's passage, so I could assist his best friends in acknowledging and releasing him as well. I sensed a stuckness like a fishbone caught in the craws of our hearts; the sobs that wouldn't come.

Getting From Shadow to Joy

Ed played Ken Burns' mournful tunes from "The West"—music that he'd played for Fred at the hospice, mere days before his transition. Still caught in anger and denial, Fred didn't want to hear the Native Americans chanting dolefully for dying chiefs, the songs about death on the trail. "Turn it down, Eddie!"

And later, so weak, barely able to talk, holding Ed's hand. "Am I going home Eddie? Am I going home?"

"Yes, you're going home."

Above the Tybee marsh,
proof of the very existence of silver linings.

All Things Pass

A prominent Atlanta family lost twelve members from three generations when their charter plane crashed into Mount Kenya on what was hoped to be a fabulous family vacation in Africa. Eventually even this overwhelming pain will be absorbed into the sands of time, hard as it is to imagine at the time of tragedy.

The heart aches to imagine the degree of suffering in the world. And likewise, the heart expands to the endless bounds of the universe when immersed in a baby's laughter or the ecstatic welcome home of a dog for its people.

So what are we going to focus on? At times it appears that all that exists is the negative, the absence, the void, as with the death of a friend or family member.

But if we look closely enough, nature offers other answers.

At the Tybee Island house, part of Ed's ritual at sundown is to set up a Bolex camera with a stop-action photography mechanism and shoot stills of the setting sun.

Way in the back yard beyond the palm trees, where the expanse of mown grass merges into the timeless marsh, the sun sets. Beyond the altar of Buddha and bowling balls, clouds pass through the frames and the sun glints around their puffed edges, proving the very existence of silver linings. After all, they're captured on film!

Even in the process of letting Fred go, Ed captured the silver lining as the dark cloud of Fred's passing overshadowed our souls.

The body is so tenacious—it tries to make us believe that it is all there is! The everlasting joke is on us when we ultimately discover that all these silly trappings were just that—a silly trap, keeping us from experiencing our true essence, our unity of souls.

What hardship we place on ourselves with this false belief! All praise to those who can stay focused on the soul when the body cries out in agony and demands to be assuaged. Read the body's signals. Honor the process of change. What transition could be more momentous than that from life to death?

The hospice nurses feel a holy awe; privileged to assist the dear souls' passing from one plane of existence to the next.

I want to be packed up and ready to go, just like in the gospel song.

Packing Up

Packing for a long weekend in the mountains brings a great degree of happiness—organizing some of the entertainments that give me so much joy. Photos prepped and orderly to go into albums; a stack of magazines to read in leisurely sloth without nattering myself over the work I could be doing; a selection of rental videos. Then just imagining the seamless time to do exactly what I want—read and write and sit listening to music while observing the hummingbirds buzz around the feeders and dive bomb each other in their little Star Wars ballet.

When I am dying, will I experience the same degree of joy over packing my things and getting ready to go?

Healing Power in the Blue Ridge

Regular escapes to the mountains transport me back to the garden in my core. At a certain spot while driving up from the piedmont, my heart lifts at first glimpse of the wispy clouds adrift over the distant Blue Ridge.

The wisps of clouds add a depth to the rounded hills, limning their shapes against a misted gray-blue sky. Deep lush green, endless pines and hardwoods and sentry rows of planted crops in the fields alongside the highway point north to my solace. Thank you God! Thank you!

The hills grew in so lushly at long last, after a long, dreary drought of five years. It hurts to watch green things turn brown and lose their leaves prematurely.

My heart still hurt over Fred's dropping his metaphorical leaves so young, and disappearing back into the earth before our eyes. Even if it is the way we all end up, reconciling the reminders of death amidst burgeoning life feels like an intolerable oxymoron.

That particular weekend trip to the Blue Ridge brought to a close the proscribed timetable of the *Tibetan Book of the Dead* for Fred's spirit, which limits the period the spirit lingers on earth to 45 days.

I headed to Burnsville, North Carolina to visit cousins Deana and Chuck at their Selena studio. Deana's mother, my aunt Martha, then a tiny old woman with a still-huge belly laugh, was also visiting.

Part of my mission at the close of Fred's 45-day window was to transport his "muscle shirt" with me to the renowned Spruce Pine Gem & Mineral Show, one of Fred's favorite buying junkets. I figured if he were alive he'd probably have made the trek in person, and might have even been wearing that T-shirt in the hot summer weather.

On our amble through the big high school auditorium, Aunt Martha and I made a jolly pair. She sported through the hall on her four-pronged cane like a tiny crab darting across the sand.

Walking around the high-drafted Pinebridge Gym, I encountered a young jewelry maker from Lenoir who showed me a bikini of beads in hopes that I would purchase her hand-crafted masterpiece. Her eyes practically begged me to buy something, anything, after such a slow sales day.

"What else could you wear with it?" I asked.

"A toe ring, I suppose," she flirted with the notion, and we laughed together at her creative response. I bought a handful of items I didn't need, but not the bikini.

On the lookout for a hostess gift for her daughter, Aunt Martha showed me a palm-sized fairy tree of twisted wire and stones. I told her Deana wasn't much on tchotchkes—one more thing to dust—and recommended a pyrite sun, which I knew her creative daughter would enjoy more because it was nature's beauty.

This dear little 88-year-old elf was also determined to find something I'd like, so we settled on a piece of serpentine for each of us—99 cents apiece—because of its connection with the Appalachians.

This particular range flows all the way up from Georgia through Pennsylvania, and then Nova Scotia and across Iceland and Greenland, then back down through the Celtic lands, where serpentine is also plentiful and called Connemara marble. One more reason the Scots and Irish felt so at home in these hills, simply an extension of the mother-land. Amazing lore, and the kind of thing Fred knew and shared, bringing enrichment to the gem show experience.

His undershirt was stowed in my purse.

Surreptitiously, I pulled it out and wiped the entrance hand stamp (a big diamond shape) onto it, so he could truly feel as though he'd attended. He was always one for the earthy contact.

In his honor I bought a bear totem necklace and earrings of highly polished malachite—the same shape he carved endlessly in his cave, and sometimes cast in silver.

On my bookshelf I still harbor two of his bear totems carved of soapstone and granite. They butt noses with each other—symbolizing us—always butting heads, never quite seeing eye to eye.

Back at the house, Martha and I shared our Gem Show treasures, to the delighted "oohs and ahhs" of my cousins. Then, to assimilate the day and get some exercise, Deana and I hiked up the steep hill to the swing overlooking their peaceful valley on Sweet Hollow Road. Far below, Chuck's smoke signals curled upward as he stoked a campfire for a weenie roast.

On our peaceful amble, Deana and I compared notes as we often do regarding family idiosyncrasies. We concurred that several of us in the family had inherited the enthusiasm gene from our grandmother Gee Gee, exhibited so tangibly with the frequent use of exclamation points in our letters.

I laughed that Gee Gee ended practically every sentence with an exclamation point, and that reading her letters almost drove me nuts with their exuberance! Deana said she'd been trying to limit herself to only one per letter but it was tough! Must be a genetic trait—excessive overuse of the exclamatory!

Really, I'm glad it's part of my gene pool to have that enthusiastic, optimistic approach to life. Dad certainly has it too. How else would he have survived all the slings and arrows in his lifetime and still be able to muster up a smile?

Getting From Shadow to Joy

Back down the hill at the campfire area, we hauled out four big plastic chairs to sit around the fire, roaring by this time under Chuck's skillful coaxing.

Aunt Martha quipped that she felt like a character from the Ya-Ya sisters, with her glass of single malt scotch and her walker.

A couple more wooden folding chairs for the weenies, s'more fixins, tortilla chips and condiments created a cozy, civilized setup.

Chuck had retrieved the roasting sticks from the reeds where they'd been tossed after the grandchildren's recent visit. Deana said they'd discovered how much the big kids enjoy a weenie roast too, and that they'd eaten more hot dogs that summer than in their entire years together. With that she made a funny face, acknowledging the downside of hot dogs.

So we roasted our weenies, and circled our chairs around the fire and gazed out over Sweet Hollow, the misty mountains in the distance and an expansive fully leafed oak a couple hundred yards away, shading the dirt road to civilization.

Fireflies blinked their magic, and we all agreed that it just doesn't get any better than this, although we missed my father, Martha's brother, and wished he could have been there to enjoy it too. He'd called because he was lonely, going through a divorce, and we were sending him our love across the miles.

A phone call is not a complete panacea for our odd familial longings for connection and our herky-jerky relationship over the years. But it's better than no contact at all, or pretending the need for connection doesn't exist.

Tentatively we extend our feelers toward each other and recount the day's activities, signing off with a perfunctory "love you" and wishing that phrase could convey all the forgiveness in our hearts.

Only after my mother died did our family even begin to

315

share our love verbally—she probably thought it rang hollow, and why bother saying it anyway when we all knew it was true, at least on some level.

Even if we wanted to kill each other, we were bound by our love and loyalty and it was as simple as that. Now it's the standard sign-off, and I think it's a good way to close. You never know when you'll meet again.

Somewhere into her scotch Martha announced that she must be drunk. We asked how she knew and she said, "'Cause I feel like singing!"

So we launched into some of the old favorites, in harmony. "You Are My Sunshine," "White Coral Bells," "By the Sea" and one multi-verse tune the moral of which was "Never tell a lie" but Chuck and I altered the chorus to, "Never up and die" because it was about a man who went to hell for telling a lie. "Amazing Grace," "Down to the River to Pray" and some of the other old favorites that were part of our family's musical heritage.

I'd hung Fred's T-shirt over a chair to include in our merry little gathering, and as the sun began to set we staged a rather abrupt send-off. I couldn't help but think that the meal and the setting were absolutely perfect for him—a campfire, weenies and s'mores, the dream meal of an adolescent boy, which was where Fred lived as our eternally young Peter Pan.

As much of an adventurer as he fancied himself, he probably appreciated the brevity and non-sentimentality of this farewell.

"Tally ho, Fred! On to the next realm," I said, lifting my wineglass and looking at the Blue Ridge.

That was the culmination of his forty-five days on earth after his physical death. I threw his shirt on the fire. It burned slowly.

Unpacking and Attracting

After leaving Deana and Chuck's Sweet Hollow, when I got to Sapphire Valley I shook off thoughts of death and engaged in the customary process of settling in—hauling food and libations down from the car, unpacking and arranging my toiletries on the bathroom counter, inspecting the two bedroom condo to discover what the cleaning service forgot and what needed to be put back in its proper position—a pillow here, a lamp there; Gee Gee's mohair throw nowhere to be found until I checked on the porch.

A quick start on the ritual of cleaning out the hummingbird feeders with a bottlebrush is essential to immediately attract these precious creatures, always so infinitely entertaining.

If tiny, delicate hummingbirds still exist, and still somehow manage to make their trek from the Appalachians across the Gulf of Mexico to the tropics every single autumn and back again in spring, the world can't quite be going to hell, can it?

Like anyone, at times I need a big dose of optimism even though I've created a life around teaching and sharing it. The precious denizens of the cool highlands, the hummingbirds, transport that optimism on their indomitable tiny wings. A combination of everything—the cool air, fragrance of the pines, the patter of rainfall on the forest floor, the delicious solitude—all cast the magic spell found in these higher climes.

How would I feel if I were a young person in the military and had some cockeyed belief that I'd have easy service in the reserves for a few weekends a year, and believed my chances of getting called up were really slim—and then suddenly I

317

found myself in downtown Baghdad, in full gear in 120 degree weather, being shot at by guerrillas, bombed by insurgents and scorned by the locals I'd come to rescue from Saddam Hussein. What degree of equanimity would I be able to muster then?

Questions like these reverberated in my mind as I strolled down Juju Lane, so named for its rows of giant evergreen trees, thanking them for their blessed presence and healing energy. The trees are my friends—so filled with life force, their crooked limbs reaching out to greet and occasionally caress me as I amble down to the placid lake.

Thinking about those poor soldiers and civilians caught in the crosshairs of war; it matters not their nationality or creed. Humans turned into killers—a vicious waste of minds and lives! A sad statement about the lack of consciousness that still plagues us. We are worse than animals, who only kill what they need for survival. We kill for oil. And power. And money. Senseless doings of the ego.

Back to this life and this space: I am so lucky; so deeply blessed. Bald Rock looms into view over the lake; its massive energy sings through me!

The power of the Sapphire Energy Vortex pours up from the earth into the soles of my feet. The giant, lone longleaf pine at the lakeshore is my graceful partner in the dance of Tai Chi.

I, all alone but not at all alone, surrounded by my friends the trees. The Trues, I called them. What a perfect Freudian slip!

Yes, when others are driven by their own secret motivations, secret perhaps even to themselves, the trees remain true, truly friends. I'll never walk alone, even though at times I may have loneliness in my heart. I know that I am following the path God has chosen for me because it continues to unfold.

Getting From Shadow to Joy

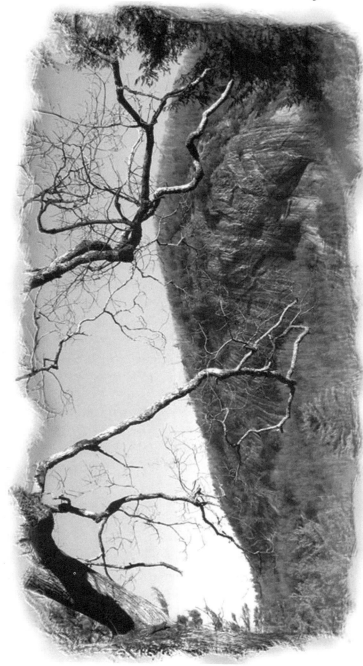

"I will lift up mine eyes unto the hills where resides my strength."

319

*The lone, giant longleaf pine is
my graceful partner in the dance of Tai Chi.*

What gratitude I feel standing on the shore, late afternoon sun slanting across the still waters, rippled by one lone canoe on the far side. Tai Chi in the great bliss of open air.

Hiking back up the hill from Tai Chi at the lake I let out a sigh of such deep gratitude that the fisherman who was walking away with his wife heard me, turned and looked for a moment. What did he detect in my tone? Sadness, satisfaction, solace?

Study War no More

I am so grateful to be in this beautiful mountain place in complete freedom and not in some God-awful hellhole fighting on behalf of people who want to slaughter me for my efforts.

Of course my government would have me believe that soldiers are fighting over there to grant me safety and freedom over here but I'm one of those "no blood for oil" people who believes the battle has always been over control of the Middle East oilfields. And that our attacks have just encouraged the recruitment of more suicide bombers around the world.

It's time for us to rally in a truly productive way. If we were able to put a man on the moon in less than a decade with the limited technology of the 1960s, surely we can develop alternate fuels, stop polluting the planet and end the savaging over oil supplies!

Has there ever been a time in history without war? Even when a war-free window existed, such as the Pax Romanis, it only occurred because of the enforcement of externally imposed troops, which meant subjugating some of the people and therefore war a-brewing as they plotted revenge.

When will we begin to recognize that the challenge we need

to conquer is within—and that all our projections outward are just our own manifestations of self-hate?

Peace Like a River

"The committee"—the nattering voices in my head—often tells me that I'm not a patient person. However, this has begun to shift as I've concentrated more on it. The amazing thing is that I'm perceived by others to be patient.

My prayer partner pointed out that she saw me as extremely patient in working with people in Small Group Ministry.

Don had come into our meeting speaking about having to euthanize his beloved dog that day. What could be more important, more real, and therefore more spiritual than expressing his grief about the passage of his beloved pet?

It simply felt human, the natural thing, to veer off the lesson and let a man express his sorrow, albeit in a very measured and contained manner as most men have been socialized to do—never to let on the true depth of their emotions for fear of being perceived as weak or even worse, a sissy. A weak sister.

Ironic, isn't it, that it is through our vulnerability that we experience our greatest connection with God—and hence our strength. When we become real, we manifest God essence.

To my astonishment, my prayer partner said I projected patience when a woman posed this conundrum: "Do you think God has a God?"

That is one of the most profound questions I've ever heard!

This perception of me as a patient person is evidence of

an unfolding miracle. Perhaps this budding equanimity springs from my staring at my own mandala of a wide-open eye—around which I've written "I commit to seeing through other peoples' eyes. Humility. Peace. Calm."

Perhaps I am growing patiently into patience.

According to external appearances I am evolving from the hair-trigger hothead with a flashing temper to a person in whom peace flows like a river. This is a lovely and long-desired transition and I embrace it. Peace like a river in my soul.

If I can do it, others can shift too, and it can build to the long-awaited tipping point in the world. The proposed U.S. Department of Peace sounds like a wonderful step in the right direction.

Integrity to purpose

Here's a potent fear: That we might not live our lives with integrity to our own purpose and then, in dying, discover that we have not truly lived. (All gratitude to my hero, Thoreau).

One of our class exercises involves thinking of the many people we respect and admire from any time in our life—whether family or friend; mentor or myth; historical or current; characters from movies or books—anyone counts. Next to their names we write words to describe them. From all those descriptive words we then choose the adjectives which most resonate for us, personally.

These descriptive words are the traits which we see in ourselves, that form our standards of integrity. If we're able to see them in others, that means they exist in us.

One young woman, a recovering alcoholic, was surprised to note that the words she picked were not descriptive of how she'd lived her life so far, but were more focused on how she wanted to live from now on. Her "impetus toward integrity" will elicit those budding traits from within herself. Rather than picking "determined" she said she was now focused on being more relaxed and open hearted as a new mother.

I pointed out that in order to be a successful salesperson, which she had been, that she had to exhibit daily determination to force herself to do the things that must be done, like it or not. Now that she was stepping off that external treadmill, she was finding a healing path into her own heart—absolutely mandatory for one in recovery from addiction of any kind.

After all, why do addicts abuse? Mainly because they are not being true to their selves, their souls. They just keep trying to pile on the externals, and nothing satisfies.

Another young woman, Tonya, (name is changed) age 29, sported a great track record to her credit: scholarships all through college; bought her first home at age 25 "to beat all my friends," she said. Now with masters degree in tow, she wondered whether she'd ever be able to cease this obsessive striving.

How to achieve the next great milestone in her life: contentment.

How can we find contentment when from every direction we are bombarded with must-haves that in many cases are tempting—but which have nothing to do with who we really are?

How many pairs of shoes can any one person wear at one time?

At one point I counted at least sixteen pairs of black shoes in my closet. If I got rid of one I had to buy another to fill the void! Insanity, ultimately, and one of the reasons we suffer without the means of finding inner peace.

Although the class agreed that many people in their twenties strive for the material things, they also concurred that simply checking those things off the list and zooming on to the next one will never satisfy the soul.

In order to appreciate life, Tonya and all of us need to view it as a process and enjoy it along the way. The BMW may make her feel good for a minute, but then what?

Whenever we do something in order to "prove it" to family, friends or associates—to go back to the old home place and flaunt what big stuff we've become, it's a hollow victory which may plunge us into deep depression, once we see how meaningless all our strivings were.

Having set her priorities straight, Karen the pediatrician mentioned that as part of her "one year to live" experiment she'd decided to work on detaching from any fears about money. Within a day, her car engine died and she suddenly faced a $7000 expenditure.

"I had the money, but this wasn't exactly how I'd planned to spend it," she said. "And as I was thinking about it and wondering how detached I could be, I got a call from my fourteen-year-old daughter, who had just witnessed her dog being hit and killed by a car. She was sobbing and my heart was going out to her. Immediately I knew what was more important in life."

Such a poignant example of how meaningless it is to stoke ourselves with things! Family, friendships and love—pets, trees, nature's beauty are what supply the meaning—not some fancy shiny car that loses thousands in value the moment it's driven off the lot!

The Beacon of Integrity

A key question in getting back to the garden is to determine our own standards of integrity to serve as a beacon—and as a reminder when we feel we're veering off-course.

In the past I was always attracted to artists and musicians because of the Imago Process described by Harville Hendrix in *Getting the Love You Want*.

We always seek someone with the attributes we desire to cultivate within ourselves. The only problem with my artists was that they were generally of the starving artist tribe—lacking prosperity consciousness and suffering from deservability issues, which prevented them from doing anything but struggle all their lives.

By focusing all my energy on them and their problems, I took the focus off myself and my own issues of growth and wellbeing.

To society this often appears to be "the way things should be"—the woman selflessly devoting herself to her man and his success. What it actually does is dilute the strength of society considerably by diverting such a huge proportion of the population from growing into themselves.

What I discovered was that in cultivating the union of the masculine and feminine within myself, I have created an artwork of my own life and I no longer have to look outward for an artist to "complete me."

I can enter into my next relationship as a whole human being—and attract a whole person to me. What a gift to myself, and to the other, no longer basing a relationship on the false expectation that someone else can make me whole!

What a cheat that we are led into this myth from such

early ages—waiting for the handsome prince to come along and kiss us awake from our slumbers, or the fairy godmother to wave her wand and make our lives beautiful. It's time to set the alarm and wake up our own selves!

The successful pediatrician mentioned that after marrying her husband, a doctor, she realized that she wanted to be a doctor herself. But her husband wanted a doctor's wife, one to take care of him and support him and his growth and the growth of his practice. When she wanted to go to medical school, he didn't necessarily want another doctor in the family, and so eventually they parted ways.

No one (on the outside) could understand this. He was a good provider for her and their three children. He wasn't abusive or an alcoholic.

But she had found in herself what she saw reflected in him—a healer. She cultivated it within herself and nurtured it into a successful practice, which was far more satisfying to her than staying in a supporting role. She desired to be on the main stage in her own life, and she achieved it.

We can all do this; in fact, it is what we are called to do. Discover your role and take your place on the stage.

Perfection is All Around

One lovely woman in the class mentioned how excited she was to have found the perfect volunteer opportunity—to mentor teenage girls in a running club. She's a runner and that all seemed quite logical.

Only later did she explain why this group had its particular appeal. She'd lost her own eighteen-year-old daughter one year earlier.

As she revealed this, our group, which was spread out on the floor creating Treasure Maps, stopped chatting and the mood became rather subdued.

This was an opportunity for us all to become very real with each other. I acknowledged how hard it must be to live through the death of a child, and asked how she'd lost her daughter. She had taken her own life.

Her daughter was bipolar, and during the good times she'd excelled in everything—as a cheerleader, in student government, surrounded by friends. But the lows, which continued to come even with medication, were so devastating that she could no longer tolerate the notion of enduring another one.

The group instinctively wanted to shy away from a darker topic—the great shadow of Death—and yet it is so important to acknowledge the cycles of life in everything.

It all comes so naturally in a garden—the seasons change, the snows or rains come, leaves fall, flowers blossom and wither. Birds build their nests and the little hatchlings appear. Some fall out of the nest; a cat comes along; the cycle of life continues.

Someone mentioned that on a farm death is not sanitized and people witness it constantly, so it loses some of its fearful power.

The group provided this grieving mother a space to tell her story of love for her daughter. She expressed her amazement at the strength of Kati's faith and the knowledge that she was in a better place than the living hell from which she couldn't escape.

Hearts opened, leading to a deeper understanding and vulnerability among all of us. A flush of humanity and bonding filled the room. This brave, grieving mother experienced an opportunity to express rather than stifle her emotions.

We witnessed the miracle of a woman envisioning her shattered heart grow whole once again. And now she is in the process of re-establishing a vision for herself.

On the first anniversary of Kati's late spring transition, family and friends gathered at her grandparents' home to contribute bulbs, plants, sweat, elbow grease and love to the creation of a perennial garden in honor of this delightful, troubled child who touched so many lives.

Their efforts yielded a beautiful, magical place with at least twenty varieties of flowers and plants, benches, birdbaths and butterflies.

Three years after Kati's "Angel Date" (a beautiful name for the date of her transition), the family continues to heal. They gather in Kati's garden spot to release balloons of her favorite color, purple, filled with wildflower seeds. An enclosure card states that the balloons and seeds, which are literally scattered to the winds by the magical purple balloons, are to honor this complex girl who was loved by so many.

After the balloons have popped or sunk to the ground, others find the cards and contact Kati's family to extend their love and well wishes. Kati's essence and influence continue to spread, even though she is no longer of the earthly plane, while her mother and family continue to heal through this meaningful magic.

Part of the cycle of life is the re-emergence of the individual after a time of being sequestered, just as trees and flowers bud out in spring after living in the shadow of winter's void for months. We all emerge and spread into light.

Opening to the Dream

A profound wonder occurred in the class where several gave themselves permission to dream for the first time.

Their yearnings had all been stifled down into hard little knots, clogging their systems and their souls—knots that looked like jobs they hated, or extra layers of fat, or life without meaningful relationships—whether they'd cut themselves off from family, depth with friends, significant partners, God or any combination thereof.

Most of all, when they shifted, they gave themselves permission to accept themselves right where they were.

How to describe what it means when people who have gravitated to abusive relationships all their lives, and found themselves in jobs they hate, begin to grant themselves permission to expand into the roles that will help them become happy, healthy and whole?

What does it look like when a person begins to free herself?

It's like witnessing someone who's been living in a sewer beginning to push up that heavy manhole cover and peer out into the light. At last, after perhaps a lifetime in darkness, she senses that it really is safe to emerge, then carefully pulls herself up and out into the sunshine and fresh air. Although tentatively at first, she then stretches arms up wide to the sky!

People live under mental siege, constantly telling themselves that they're too fat, not good enough, not rich enough, don't have the right clothes, car, personality, bust size, lack of cellulite, white enough teeth, *ad nauseum*. So many beautiful spirits in my class are just beginning to emerge from the sewer of their self-doubt.

330

All these years after my own emergence, I can barely remember what that felt like—to be so pickled in my own lack of self-love that I didn't even dare to dream—but it hasn't been so many years ago.

And what if I hadn't carried that burden of shame and self-doubt? For one I wouldn't have the background necessary to help others like myself, and for that I am grateful.

Sure, I could have done without all those years of pain and self-hatred—and so can all of us. But the percentage of people who never try to pull themselves out of the ditch is so, so huge.

In class I witness people beginning to unfurl their wings, finally able to journey back in time and discover the childhood beliefs that triggered them to accept abusive jobs and relationships.

To be able to physically follow their bliss, people begin exercising and work on correcting their health problems so they can reshape their lives and contribute to the benefit of the world. What breakthroughs—all from permitting themselves to dream!

If we were to write letters to ourselves at our current age from our perspective as eighty-year-olds, here's what I'd say to myself and to others who have joined me on this journey:

"Steady on the Path. Stay on course. You've found your way Back to the Garden; and whether you've realized it or not, you've been cultivating that lovely place for your entire life. Your choices are good ones; you've come to know yourself, and you're treating yourself with love and respect, as though you were your own dearest friend. By accepting God's grace yourself, you're sharing it with others. Carry on, and know that you are blessed."

About the Author

Even while active in other careers, much of Patrice Dickey's "real" life has revolved around helping people lift themselves up to lead happier, more self-aware and fulfilled lives, in essence, as a Guide to the Life You Love™.

In writing and launching *Back to the Garden*, she leapt out from a highly successful 20-year public relations career to share her stories in workshops and classes that enrich people's understanding of why they are here and what they can give back.

In 1999 she created 'Art of Positive Change' for Emory University's Center for Lifelong Learning. A few years into leading this popular course she recognized that no one really wants to change, but *everyone* wants to live a life they love, so the class evolved into Get the Life You Love™. Self-awareness, self-acceptance, self-respect and self-love are its foundation principles.

When class participants asked, "What's next?" she tapped into her 15-year background as an award-winning instructor of the demanding Dale Carnegie Sales Training. She earned Registered Corporate Coach (WABC), Qualified Myers Briggs Type Indicator (CAPT) and Registered Yoga Teacher designations to help clients deepen their understanding of who they are and how they can make simple, positive life shifts. Coaching clients, workshop and class participants consistently rate her highly for workable solutions and a dynamic, engaging style.

A journalism/English honors graduate of the University of North Carolina at Chapel Hill, she regularly writes articles on health and well being, and is invited to review some of the world's top spas for the leading skincare and spa trade publication in the U.S.

Lighten Up with

Your Guide to the Life You Love™
Complimentary Newsletter/E-zine

At the Right Time. . . On a Regular Basis,

Patrice shares tips, tools and insights on how to enrich your life, expand your horizons and experience *Your Personal Definition* of success. Plus she feeds you cool mind candy to sweeten your day. Try some—it has that hopeful flavor.

Sign Up

It's Free! Your Guide to the Life You Love™ newsletter/ezine awaits at **www.artofchange.org**, along with other complimentary eBooks and articles including: **101 Simple Ways to Kick the Depression Habit & Get Happier Without Prozac**. Her inspirational articles previously published in major magazines may be just the quick pick-me-up you need right now.

Speaking Engagements & Workshops

Patrice Dickey's enthusiastic presentations about getting the life you love and living more passionately through creativity will get your group fired up!

To contact her about enlivening your next event, visit Contact Information at **www.artofchange.org**, or blog at **www.PatriceDickey.com**.

Acknowledgements:

Kind acknowledgement is made for permission to quote or reprint the following:

Passages reprinted from *Adventures on the Quest* by Richard and Mary-Alice JaFolla with permission of Unity and the authors. For information go to www.unityonline.org.

Passages reprinted from *Handbook of Positive Prayer* by Hypatia Hasbrouck with permission of Unity. For more information go to www.unityonline.org.

Passages paraphrased from *Feel the Fear and Do It Anyway* by Dr. Susan Jeffers, copyright 1987, Ballantine Books, with author's permission.

Quote of Munishree Chitrabanu, reprinted from *Inner Paths*, Honesdale, PA, Himalayan International Institute of Yoga Science & Philosophy, copyright 1969, with publisher's permission.

Passages reprinted from *Soul Surgery—the Ultimate Self-Healing* by Richard JaFolla, DeVorss & Co, copyright 1987, with the author's permission. Book is out of print.

Quote reprinted by permission of Nilgiri Press, PO Box 256, Tomales, CA, 94971, www.easwaran.org, from *Thousand Names of Vishnu* by Eknath Easwaran, founder of Blue Mountain Center of Meditation, copyright 1987.

Passages paraphrased from *Finding Yourself in Transition, Using Life's Changes for Spiritual Awakening* by Robert Brumet, with permission of Unity and the author. For more information go to www.unityonline.org.

Beautiful heart art by Claire Vohman used with artist's permission. Visit wwwClaireWasHere.com for more fun, wit and whimsy from magnets to murals.

Information from *You Can Heal Your Life* by Louise Hay, Hay House, copyright 1974, included with author's permission.